Terra-Cotta Skyline

Terra-Cotta

Skyline

New York's Architectural Ornament

Susan Tunick

contemporary photographs by *PETER MAUSS*

PRINCETON ARCHITECTURAL PRESS

PUBLISHED BY

Princeton Architectural Press

37 East 7th Street

New York, New York   10003

(212) 995.9620

00 99 98 97   5 4 3 2 1

FIRST EDITION

LIBRARY OF CONGRESS CATALOGING-IN-PUBLICATION DATA

Tunick, Susan

    Terra-cotta skyline: New York's architectural ornament / Susan Tunick; contemporary photographs by
    Peter Mauss. — 1st ed.

        p. cm.

      Includes bibliographical references and index.

      ISBN 1-56898-105-8

    1. Architectural terra-cotta—New York (State)—New York.

    2. Decoration and ornament, Architectural—New York (State)—New York. 3. New York (N. Y.)—
    Buildings, structures, etc. I. Mauss, Peter. II. Title.

    NA3511.N48T86 1997

    729'.5—DC21   96-52343

Editing and design: Sara E. Stemen

Special thanks to Caroline Green, Clare Jacobson, Therese Kelly, Mark Lamster,
and Annie Nitschke of Princeton Architectural Press —KEVIN C. LIPPERT, PUBLISHER

For a free catalog of other Princeton Architectural Press titles, call (800) 722.6657.
Visit Princeton Architectural Press on the World Wide Web at http:/www.papress.com.

Contents

Dedicated to our grandfather

MORRIS ABRAMS

1890–1990

A lifelong New Yorker whose enthusiasm for the city was contagious

THIS PUBLICATION WOULD NOT HAVE BEEN POSSIBLE WITH-
out the financial, intellectual, and moral support and assistance of many
individuals and organizations. I am especially grateful for the generous
financial support of the New York State Council on the Arts (Architecture, Planning and Design Division), as well as to Furthermore, the
publication program of the J. M. Kaplan Fund. The grant that helped me first start
research in 1981 came from the Educational Facilities Laboratory, a division of the
Academy for Educational Development.

Many individuals aided in the research and writing of this work. I owe the
greatest debt to my husband, Paul Tunick, for his continuous encouragement, ideas,
and patience. In addition, Jane Stanicki, Andrew Scott Dolkart, Lenore Newman,
Jay Shockley, and Diana S. Waite carefully reviewed the manuscript in its various
stages and contributed invaluable advice.

Colleagues who contributed ideas that assisted in the research include Janice
Carapellucci, Susan McDaniel Ceccacci, Philip Copp, Sharon Darling, Ellen
Denker, Riley Doty, Gail Fenske, Virginia Ferriday, Alice Frelinghuysen, Christo-
pher Gray, Elizabeth Gulacsy, Laura Hansen, Helen Henderson, Chris and Joel
Huber, Gary F. Kurutz, Sarah Bradford Landau, John Margolies, Nancy McCros-
key, Barbara Millstein, Dorothy Miner, Susan Montgomery, William D. Moore,
Susan Myers, Jeffrey Saunders, Vincent Seyfried, Sandy Scofield, Jewel Stern,
Michael Stratton, Edgar Tafel, Anne Van Ingen, Richard Veit, Carol Willis, and
Anthony C. Wood.

Special thanks to those who have a personal connection with architectural terra
cotta and shared their insight or archival materials with me: Clem Baldwin, Daniel
Barton, George A. Berry III, Rhodes and Karla Copithorn, Alice Eskesen Ganzel,
Walter H. Kilham, Gretchen and John Krouse, Ken McGee, Janice Moore, Catha
and Viggo Rambusch, Peg Rase, Bruce Richmond, Tom Saywer, Mr. and Mrs.
Viktor Schreckengost, David Taylor, David Wilkenson, and Roger Yepsen. The staff
at various research institutions aided my endeavors, most especially Avery Library at
Columbia University, the New York Public Library, the New-York Historical Society,
the New York City Municipal Archives, the Architectural League of New York, the
National Building Museum, the Athenaeum of Philadelphia, the Northwest Architectural Archives, and the New York City Landmarks Preservation Commission.

I am indebted to many people who allowed their possessions to be photographed or lent photographic works of their own: Charles Blitman, John Burns, Alastair Gordon, Stephen Hoffman, O. Aldon James, Emily L. Moore, Cleota Reed, Lenny Schechter and Gil Shapiro of Urban Archaeology, and Mary Swisher.

Of course, the uniquely fine quality of the contemporary photographs is due to the vision and skill of my brother, Peter Mauss, who has helped me with the photographic documentation of terra-cotta buildings for the last fifteen years.

Finally, Paul and Anna Tunick; my parents, Evelyn and Irv Mauss; my brother Steven; his wife Edith Thompson; my sister-in-law, Phyllis Odessey; my mother-in-law, Elinore Tunick; and Maybelline, our very own terra cat-ta, deserve the greatest thanks for tolerating (generally cheerfully) my obsession with architectural terra cotta.

A RCHITECTURAL TERRA COTTA BECAME AN INTEGRAL PART OF the buildings in New York City well over one hundred years ago. During much of the last century, however, this exceptional material has received little attention, escaping the notice of most city dwellers. It was not until 1980, when my husband and I moved into our fifth Manhattan residence, The Gramercy, that I discovered terra cotta. I found myself drawn to the ornamental brick walls of the building's light court, which were as clearly visible from our windows as Gramercy Park's beautiful trees and flower beds. Bands of simple geometric patterns were inset into the lower and upper floors, while vigorously sculpted Indian heads, eagles, and figures enlivened the middle of the facade. It seemed logical that this decoration, deep red in color and used in combination with red clay bricks, might also be clay. My long-standing love of clay (I received a graduate degree in ceramics) and a desire to know more about The Gramercy (New York's oldest surviving cooperative apartment house) piqued my curiosity.

I began by attempting to locate publications in the field of architectural ceramics, tiles, and terra cotta. Unfortunately, it soon became clear that there was a paucity of material on the subject. *The Decorative Tradition* by Julian Barnard and *Architectural Ceramics* by David Hamilton were two of the most useful books in print, but both focused on English architecture and manufacturers. After considerable investigation, I realized that with the exception of Sharon Darling's *Chicago Ceramics & Glass*, rare books and old journals were the primary sources of information, along with several graduate theses that concentrated on specific areas of this large subject.[1] The more time I spent consulting this literature in libraries, the greater became my desire to explore the streets and to study the city's wealth of historic buildings firsthand.

Late in 1981, I began to conduct a systematic survey with the help of a grant from the Educational Facilities Laboratory, a division of the Academy for Educational Development. This funding supported preliminary research and photo documentation of significant terra-cotta buildings in New York. Many images in this book date to that first adventure. My brother Peter Mauss, an architectural photographer, worked diligently with me in documenting a select group of buildings.

My efforts began with bicycle trips, frequently with my toddler strapped into her safety helmet and bike seat. A neighborhood-by-neighborhood review made it obvious that hundreds of structures using terra cotta could be found in the city.

Many of these dated back to the early twentieth century, confirming a startling statistic reported in a 1911 *New York Times* article titled "Architectural Terra Cotta a Big Factor in New Building." It stated that "the New York skyline—which, without exaggeration, is the most wonderful building district in the world—is more than half architectural terra cotta.... And yet—not more than one lay mind in a thousand appreciates the fact, and even to some architects and builders, this truth will come as a surprise."[2]

Following each bicycle ride, I would return on foot for a closer examination. The details discovered through binoculars (as well as the sometimes deteriorated conditions) were a revelation. Besides the unexpected wealth of color and pattern, much of the ornament possessed great whimsy and humor. The rich imagery on the upper reaches of New York's tall buildings is aptly described by Anatole Broyard in a 1981 article in the *New York Times*: "So many of its architectural idiosyncrasies are high up in the air, where the pedestrian cannot see them. Statues, towers, miniature temples, spires, gargoyles, masks, Mayan-like shapes and colors, Art Nouveau sinuosities, Gothic extravaganzas and cubistic jumbles all perched 40 or 50 stories above the streets, instead of being within easy reach of the eye, as their original models were. It's like a secret city existing on an ethereal plane."[3]

Like Broyard, I frequently wondered why a great deal of ornament had been placed so high up that it could not be readily appreciated by pedestrians. Surely it was not the result of generous speculative builders, willing to incur expense for the pleasure of those in neighboring towers. More likely, architects with their beautiful renderings successfully persuaded owners of the potential financial benefits of elaborate ornamentation. Architectural display became part of the owners' marketing strategies, and the visual showmanship of many commercial buildings intentionally expressed the underlying competitiveness of the city's business community.[4] There has been little aesthetic analysis of this particular decorative practice, but one pragmatic turn-of-the-century ceramist, Charles Fergus Binns, did express his disdain for it: "I would like to enter a plea for broader and less ornate work at the tops of high buildings. The mass of detail is absolutely unintelligible to a passerby."[5] He thought that inconspicuous waste was as bad as conspicuous consumption.

The idea that New York was a "clay jungle" rather than the more familiar image of a "concrete jungle" tantalized me. Throughout my training in the arts, there was a pervasive attitude that the fine arts of painting and sculpture were really paramount, while the decorative arts, including the crafts of ceramics and pottery, were considered to be less significant.[6] It therefore amazed me to discover that a monumental clay legacy existed. This heritage of vast ceramic skyscrapers stood in stark contrast to the belittling treatment that the crafts received from the world of fine arts. Clay had never entered into the picture when artists described the personal impact of New York's buildings. Even Peter Voulkos, one of America's most important ceramic artists, was unaware of the role terra cotta played in shaping these structures. His vivid description of the city's architecture lacks any reference to clay: "My scale comes out of what I see. I always liked large things. Take New York skyscrapers. Those are more awesome to me than mountains. You take a mountain for granted, but a skyscraper just blows my mind.... Manmade is a different trip—like even those spaces between buildings in New York—they're fantastic."[7]

As I became skilled at recognizing terra cotta and distinguishing it from brownstone, granite, and limestone, I began to realize how frequently terra cotta appeared in building facades. It soon became obvious that only a tiny percentage of the existing terra-cotta buildings could be represented in any list that was to be compiled. (A selective directory of two hundred unusual buildings in the five boroughs, representing a wide range of styles, terra-cotta manufacturers, and architectural firms can be found in Appendix D.)

While investigating the widespread use of clay in architecture, I learned about the Friends of Terra Cotta. The original members of this preservation organization were inspired by a tour of Gladding, McBean & Company, the manufacturer of clay pipe and architectural terra cotta in Lincoln, California. Founded in 1875, it is the oldest surviving terra-cotta company in the United States. From all accounts, that visit to the factory was a remarkable experience, revealing the versatility and early popularity of this material. Original company photographs and archives (since donated to the California State Library), along with many early plaster molds and ornamental glazed pieces, provided evidence of the powerful impact that terra cotta had on American architecture.

Following the tour, which took place in April 1981, the Friends of Terra Cotta was founded as an organization that would help preserve architectural terra cotta. Its goals included raising awareness of the use of architectural terra cotta among the general public as well as building professionals; providing information and resources for those seeking to learn about terra-cotta buildings and the history of the material; and sharing information concerning maintenance, restoration, and replacement techniques. Through advocacy activities, seminars, workshops, walking tours, exhibitions, publications, and lectures, the Friends of Terra Cotta has been able to reach a very wide audience. In the fifteen years it has been active, a new respect for the craft of ceramics and an increased awareness of the impact of terra cotta—still visible on Main Streets across America—have grown steadily.

An example of the progress that has been made can be found in a paragraph from Paul Goldberger's *The City Observed: New York* (1979). He offers an engaging description of the Hotel Lucerne, one of the terra-cotta treasures of the Upper West Side: "This one stands out, in part because of the wonderful richness of its brownstone. It could almost be wet mud, so alive and sharp is the color, or child's clay, molded carefully and then baked. The detailing is heavy and thick, making the building seem all the more like clay, but it is skillful enough so that it never feels

FIG. I. *Hotel Lucerne, 201 West 79th Street, New York City, 1903–4, Harry B. Mulliken. The glass negative for this photograph was found in the office of the New York Architectural Terra Cotta Company.*

overbearing"[8] (*Figure 1*). Today, without a doubt, Goldberger and other architectural critics would know that this superb landmark *is* baked and modeled clay.

A renewed interest in terra cotta can be attributed to several factors. One major development has been the recognition of our architectural heritage through the field of historic preservation. This has led to a great increase in the carefully executed restoration and maintenance of older buildings. A focus on preservation has resulted in the founding of many local and worldwide preservation organizations, each with a range of specific concerns (see Appendix E). Continuing maturation of the preservation movement at city, state, and national levels is encouraging; however, its growth cannot match the march of new, large-scale construction projects across the country.

New York City's preservation efforts have been impressive, although an ongoing struggle with developers continues. Through the unrelenting work of the city's preservation community and the New York City Landmarks Preservation Commission, New York has been successful in protecting important buildings and neighborhoods. Since its founding in 1965, the Landmarks Commission has designated over nineteen thousand buildings; more than one thousand are individual landmarks, and the balance are located within sixty-nine historic districts. Many of these landmarks (the Flatiron, the Woolworth, Carnegie Hall, the Plaza Hotel) are ornamented or entirely clad with terra cotta.

The reintroduction of ornament, color, and surface pattern into contemporary architecture has also been a contributing factor to the increased interest in terra cotta. After many years of steel-and-glass structures, architects are now using a wider range of materials and incorporating more rich and varied elements into their buildings. The architectural firm of Venturi, Scott Brown and Associates, for example, has taken a bold stand in favor of ceramic ornament in both the Medical Research Laboratories at UCLA in Los Angeles and the Seattle Art Museum. Other large projects of note are Hardy Holzman Pfeiffer's addition to the Los Angeles County Museum and John Burgee's cream-colored terra-cotta skyscraper at 343 Sansome Street in San Francisco.

Contemporary terra-cotta manufacturers have been receptive to developing original designs, thereby reestablishing the collaborative relationships once commonplace in the industry among craftsmen, artists, and architects. These positive signs suggest that the prophecy published in an article nearly ninety years ago may still come true: "We predict that terra cotta will rear its head once again as an artistic ornament and rightly take its place as an interpreter of the architect's pencil."[9]

SUSAN TUNICK
PRESIDENT, FRIENDS OF TERRA COTTA

Note: Throughout the text, the term "terra cotta" has been hyphenated when used as an adjective, but not when used as a noun.

Part One

America's Early Terra-Cotta Industry: A Struggle for Acceptance

The St. Denis Hotel is visible on the left side of this photograph, which provides a view west on 11th Street from Broadway.

TERRA COTTA IS A CLAY PRODUCT FREQUENTLY USED TO FACE or ornament building surfaces. The term can be translated literally as "burnt earth," and has been used loosely since Roman times to refer to a glazed or unglazed ceramic ware intended primarily for architectural elements and large statuary. Its manufacture was abandoned for many centuries after the fall of the Roman Empire, until the fourteenth and fifteenth centuries, when interest in terra cotta was revived in Western Europe, especially in northern Italy. The terra-cotta industry began to flourish in England during the early nineteenth century, when brick buildings were often embellished with blocks of molded clay ornament. Architectural terra cotta manufactured by European companies was incorporated into building facades throughout Europe in much the same way as it was used in England.

The popularity of terra cotta in Europe, especially in England, had a direct influence on its use in the United States in the last quarter of the nineteenth century. Prior to this, pioneering efforts to successfully market architectural terra cotta in this country were carried out by Henry Tolman of Worcester, Massachusetts. His small company, which was established in 1848–49, has been identified as the earliest American terra-cotta manufacturer.[10] Tolman produced ready-made terra-cotta ornament, which was sold by a Worcester architect, Elbridge Boyden. In 1889, Boyden described this joint effort in a brief presentation to the Worcester Society of Antiquity:

> I conceived the idea of using burnt clay for ornaments. I interested a potter in the notion, started some potteries, and had some ornaments made which proved a success. The man [Tolman] who started up the manufactory built up a large business;…it was afterwards made in New York and Boston, and the manufacture of Terra-cotta is now an important branch of industry. The use of this burnt clay enabled me to make many changes in the style of finish, and a taste was excited for a better class of work.[11]

An account book from Tolman's firm lists the variety of architectural elements that were available, including column capitals, consoles, bracket drops, moldings, and cornices (*Figure 2*). They were intended to imitate carved brownstone and were purchased most frequently by builders from central Massachusetts. In 1851, Tolman joined with Jonathan Luther to establish Tolman, Luther & Company, which had

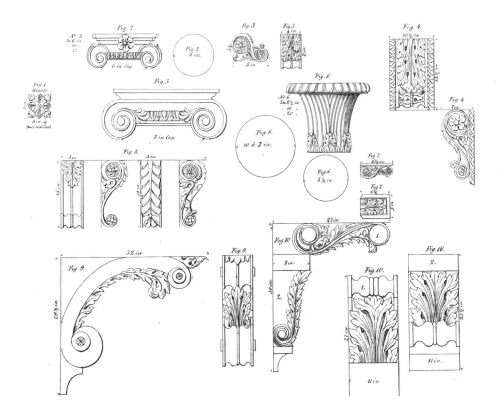

ABOVE: FIG. 2. *A page from the Tolman, Luther & Company 1852 catalogue.*

LEFT: FIG. 3. *The Trinity Building, 1851–53, used terra-cotta lintels and lion's-head keystones executed by the Hudson River Pottery and Terra Cotta Works.*

[3]

FIG. 4. *The St. Denis Hotel, 1853, can be seen in this postcard view of 11th Street and Broadway, New York City. The terra-cotta ornament for this building was produced in Alexander Young's drainpipe factory.*

been set up exclusively for the manufacture of architectural terra cotta. They exhibited in the Crystal Palace Exhibition of the Industry of All Nations, held in New York in 1853.[12] Tolman's company, which went through three more name changes, remained active until 1860.[13] It provided architectural ornament for buildings in Boston, Massachusetts; Bangor, Maine; Charleston, South Carolina; and Portsmouth, New Hampshire.

Other pioneers in the use of terra cotta were active in New York, notably, architects Richard Upjohn and James Renwick. Upjohn incorporated a terra-cotta cornice and ornamentation into his Trinity Building at 111 Broadway (demolished), which was constructed in 1851–53 (*Figure 3*). This five-story structure, one of the city's earliest buildings intended exclusively for offices, was forty feet wide and a full block (more than two hundred sixty feet) in length. The lion's head for the keystones of the building's lintels was designed by sculptor Henry Kirke Brown. The work was executed by the Hudson River Pottery and Terra Cotta Works, located at 34 Fulton Street in New York City. Edward Roche, the proprietor, felt that the sculptor's intent could be more accurately represented in terra cotta than in stone and that "the advantages of 'Terra Cotta' are best seen when we produce duplicates of the *highest order* of *artistic design*, equally durable with *stone*, and at *one half* the price."[14] Terra cotta, which was made in molds, was both cost- and labor-saving in comparison to hand-carved stone ornament. These keystones, and a series of modillions that decorated the main cornice of the building, were painted to mimic brownstone, thus creating a contrast with the buff brick of the walls.

In 1853, Upjohn chose terra cotta for the cornice of the Corn Exchange Bank Building (demolished), relying this time on the material's natural color rather than painting it in an effort to imitate stone. Unfortunately, he chose Winter and Company of Newark, New Jersey, the lowest bidder for the job. Barely a year old, they produced terra-cotta statuary, house ornaments, and drainpipes, and had participated in the Crystal Palace Exhibition of 1853. However, the firm's four partners seemed ill-suited for their work. "It is stated that among themselves, during the hours of labor, these gentleman used to sweeten their tasks by reflections upon the Renaissance—classical conversations in Latin, Greek, French, and German. This party...failed of the desired success; and it is not unreasonable to assume that if they had been possessed of less mental culture—if they had been poorer scholars and better terra cotta makers—success would most likely have been the sweet solace of their labor."[15] The terra-cotta cornice on Upjohn's building was "badly burned" because of unreliable firing methods and was destroyed by frost during the first winter.

Parallel efforts to introduce terra cotta as an alternative to cut stone were made in 1853 by James Renwick, renowned for his design of two New York landmarks, St. Patrick's Cathedral and Grace Church. He sought the help of a drainpipe manufacturer, Alexander Young, whose Manhattan company also had shown wares at the Crystal Palace. Excellent terra-cotta belt courses and cornices for the Tontine Building on Water and Wall Streets (demolished), the St. Denis Hotel on Broadway at 11th Street, and three houses on 9th Street (demolished) were made by Young (*Figures 4, 5*). Although these buildings were successfully completed, Renwick's use of terra cotta met with vigorous opposition from New York stonecutters and masons, who felt that their livelihood was in jeopardy. They argued that the terra cotta would not last, as was reported in an interesting account in *The American Architect* published almost seventy-five years later:

FIG. 5. *This house at 37 West 9th Street, New York City, was one of three built in 1853. The terra-cotta window surrounds and cornice were also produced in Mr. Young's factory.*

> Every stonecutter and mason in New York told Mr. Renwick that terra cotta would not last—in spite of the evidence in northern Italy. To realize how badly mistaken they were it is only necessary to compare the condition of the terra cotta he made with contemporary brownstone.... [T]he terra cotta is unchanged. The modeling is as fresh and crisp, though somewhat Victorian in detail, the lines as clean-cut as on the day the terra cotta came from the kiln.[16]

Renwick tried to promote the use of Young's terra-cotta ornaments, in a relationship similar to that of architect Elbridge Boyden and potter Henry Tolman a few years earlier in Worcester. However, these efforts failed, and Young, who lost money in the terra-cotta business, resumed the full-time manufacture of drainpipe. The situation was summarized by Renwick in an 1886 letter to Orlando B. Potter, founder of the New York Architectural Terra Cotta Company: "The fact is, we were ahead of the times, and could find no one who understood or would venture to use it. The buildings above mentioned, in which it was used, belonged either to my family or friends who had confidence in my judgment."[17]

These groundbreaking activities did little to convince the New York building industry to embrace this new material. One witty historian commented that "this formal introduction of terra-cotta did not set many new kilns on fire in or around New York."[18] Although a number of additional American companies have been identified as manufacturers of architectural terra cotta and/or chimney pots between the years 1853 and 1869 (See Appendix B), no truly significant use of the material was made in New York buildings until 1879.[19]

Chapter 2

James Taylor: His Impact

on American Terra Cotta

(1870-98)

P ARADOXICALLY, THE MAN WHO BECAME KNOWN AS THE
father of the American terra-cotta industry was not an American but an
Englishman. James Taylor came to the United States in 1870 (*Figure 6*). He
developed a reputation as a "coast-to-coast trouble-shooter" for the industry, and his knowledge proved essential to the success of terra-cotta companies in Massachusetts, Illinois, California, New Jersey, and New York.[20] By the age of
thirty-one, Taylor had spent five years as the superintendent of the renowned J. M.
Blashfield & Company, a terra-cotta works in Stamford, England. When he arrived
in New York in 1870, Taylor encountered serious misconceptions about terra cotta.
In an article he wrote in 1898, he described an experience he shared with Marcus
Spring, a wealthy dry-goods merchant. The two men were examining various materials used for the exteriors of buildings, and went to visit the Trinity Building just
north of Trinity Church on Lower Broadway. While standing in front of the building, Spring recognized an influential architect and explained the intent of their study
to him.[21] He asked the architect for a professional opinion about the probable success
of introducing terra cotta into the New York area. The reply was prompt and blunt:

> My dear sir, there can be but one opinion upon that subject. It would most surely
> fail. Terra cotta has been tried over and over again, and every attempt has resulted
> in loss and vexation to all parties concerned. We know all about that material; it is
> useful enough in Europe, but it will not withstand the rigors of our American cli-
> mate. If that young man intends to continue his trade of terra cotta making I would
> strongly advise him to return to England, for he will find it impossible to earn a liv-
> ing for his family at that trade in the United States. Our architects and builders will
> most certainly refuse to make any further experiments with the material.[22]

Although these biting remarks were discouraging to Spring, Taylor remained
undeterred. Taylor knew that Upjohn's Trinity Building (*see Figure 3*) served as a perfect example to contradict the architect's mistaken notions. Although it was one of
the few attempts to use terra cotta in the 1850s, the permanence of the material was
well-demonstrated by the fine condition of the lions' heads used as keystones over
the windows. However, Taylor found it impossible to obtain financing for a new
terra-cotta firm in New York, and soon headed west to become superintendent of the
Chicago Terra Cotta Company.

FIG. 6. *Portrait of James Taylor, the "Father of
American Terra Cotta," circa 1885.*

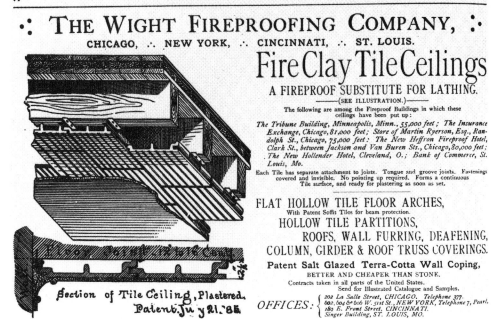

FIG. 7. *Advertisement for the Wight Fireproofing Company, 1888.*

The severe destruction wrought in Chicago by the Great Fire of 1871 provided a powerful impetus to this fledgling industry, which offered a fireproof material and new architectural forms. Prior to the fire, building professionals had believed that stone and iron were fireproof. However, inspection of the ruins taught them that cast-iron structural work needed the protection of brick or terra-cotta sheathing. "I reject everything but clay for fireproof structures....A great advantage that it has over concrete made of hard cement, so much used in Europe, is that it can be made so much lighter,"[23] claimed P. B. Wight, an architect known for his interest in fireproofing (*Figure 7*). He used the forum of the American Institute of Architects 1871 Convention to expose the inadequacies of previously accepted methods of fireproofing. Before the Chicago fire, he had warned against the weakness and limitations of unprotected iron structures, and now the proof was painfully visible: thousands of buildings had twisted, burst apart, and collapsed in ruin.

At the time of the fire, the manufacture of terra cotta was new to Chicago. The Chicago Terra Cotta Company, which had set up business in 1868, was the only architectural terra-cotta firm in the United States. One of the few commercial concerns to survive the fire, it soon received several large orders as rapid rebuilding got underway. Following the Great Fire, advances in technology and architectural design stimulated the growth and eventual widespread use of architectural terra cotta. In addition to its fire-resistant qualities, it was more durable than stone and had the same compressive strength as granite (and two to three times that of most other building stones).

Sanford Loring, an architect who joined the Chicago Terra Cotta Company as its treasurer, proved to be a key to the firm's success. Dissatisfied with the quality of its early products, he felt that the problems resulted from the company's inexperience rather than a lack of merit in the material. He firmly believed that terra cotta was an excellent building material and that it would be profitable if properly made and marketed. During its first years, the company employed a clay modeler, Giovanni Meli,

FIG. 8. *These muffle kilns, common in England, were introduced into America by James Taylor. The wall inside the kiln, seen in the drawing on the right, protects the ware from direct exposure to flames.*

to run the operation. Unfortunately, Meli's fine-arts training in Europe did not prepare him technically for the architectural products that the company needed to manufacture, and debts began to pile up. Determined to save the company, Loring was unflagging in his efforts to promote terra cotta. He intended to use steam-powered equipment, nearby clay deposits, and Chicago's excellent network of rail and water transportation. He sought advice from James M. Blashfield, proprietor of England's largest terra-cotta works. Thus, Loring learned of Blashfield's former employee James Taylor's plans to move to the United States.

Taylor's arrival at the Chicago Terra Cotta Company proved very beneficial for the floundering manufacturer. After he became superintendent in 1870, the company adopted English methods of clay preparation and production techniques, and the use of muffle kilns (*Figure 8*). Characterizing the existing molds as "clay imitation of an iron imitation of a cut stone,"[24] Taylor had more skillfully sculpted molds executed. He saw the future of terra cotta in grand terms, not simply as a material for window enframements, column capitols, and vases but rather for entire building facades.[25] Taylor's guidance led to new and improved products, and by 1876, the year he left Chicago, the company was employing seventy-five men.[26] In addition to architectural terra cotta, the firm manufactured garden ornaments, vases, and porous tiles and blocks for the fireproofing of columns.[27]

Throughout Taylor's career, the enticing opportunities offered by the burgeoning terra-cotta industry pulled him away from his family, who had settled on a farm in Port Monmouth, New Jersey. In 1876, he returned briefly to the family farm, where he helped his friend Edward Spring form Eagleswood Art Pottery on an estate near Perth Amboy.[28] The Pottery was one of the few places that offered an artistic education in ceramics, a field that had been ignored by American art schools during the second half of the nineteenth century.[29] Spring, a professor of sculpture at this new school, specialized in teaching his pupils to create sculptural plaques and medallions, an unusual opportunity at the time.

Because of the lack of trained indigenous clayworkers, European craftsmen made a significant contribution to the artistically modeled architectural terra cotta produced in the United States. American manufacturers were preoccupied with the structural and fireproofing qualities of the material, and neglected aesthetic concerns. This focus on technical proficiency with minimal emphasis on originality could also be seen in other branches of clayworking during the 1870s. The ceramic ware displayed at the 1876 Centennial Exhibition in Philadelphia clearly embodied this imbalance. With the exception of Galloway and Graff of Philadelphia, which received an award for its decorative terra-cotta wares, America's embryonic ceramics industry made an unimpressive showing.

The impact of the Centennial Exhibition, however, proved to be powerful. According to historian Edwin A. Barber, "Never before was such an impetus given to any industry. The best production of all nations was sent here and exhibited beside our own modest manufacturers, and it was only too apparent that America had been left behind in the race."[30] The exhibition also focused attention on the shortcomings of American art schools. In "Art Education Applied to Industry," a study published in 1877, George Ward Nichols lamented the lack of art training in the United States and its effect on the American craft industries. He expressed hope that the wares from abroad would have an "incalculable influence for the good upon the art education and art industry in America."[31]

One such positive outcome was the decision by the Philadelphia School of Industrial Arts to add a clayworking department in 1880. Students were given comprehensive industrial training that included experiences in local factories. Leslie W. Miller, the principal, was active in pleading with manufacturers for "increased art education and cooperation with artists in order to improve the quality of work."[32] Records show that Professor H. Plasschaert and nine assistants from the school worked in the modeling shop of Stephens, Conkling and Armstrong, an important Philadelphia terra-cotta manufacturer.[33] In the years that followed, the formation of ceramic departments at several universities helped to provide well-trained sculptors, modelers, chemists, and engineers to the ceramic industry throughout the United States.[34]

Meanwhile, in 1878, after just two years in New Jersey, the peripatetic James Taylor left Port Monmouth to continue his pivotal role in the rapidly expanding field of architectural terra cotta. The Chicago Terra Cotta Company decided to form a Boston branch after winning a large terra-cotta order for Boston's new English High and Latin School.[35] Sanford Loring, the manager, coaxed Taylor to join him, and Taylor remained with the Boston branch until it closed the following year.

Several months later, Taylor became the superintendent of the newly established Boston terra-cotta firm Lewis and Wood[36] (*Figure 9*). By October of 1880, Taylor had been recruited to join yet another new operation, the Boston Terra Cotta Company. Moving to this firm was the crucial step that eventually led Taylor back to

FIG. 9. *After the demise of the Lewis and Wood company, H. A. Lewis formed a new terra-cotta firm in 1883.*

the New York area permanently. The company's principal market was in New York, Philadelphia, and surrounding areas. George Fiske, treasurer of the Boston Terra Cotta Company, wrote that Taylor "would often go over on Wednesday or Thursday night, spend a day or two with architects and contractors in New York and Philadelphia. He made all the estimates and practically all the contracts."[37] This arrangement allowed him to spend many weekends with his family in New Jersey.

Taylor remained with the Boston Terra Cotta Company for an unprecedented duration—until 1886, when, according to Fiske, he "induced some New York parties to organize the New York Architectural Terra Cotta Company with himself as Superintendent"[38] (*Figure 10*). While at the Boston Terra Cotta Company, Taylor had overseen the production of an enormous order of 540 tons of terra cotta for a New York real-estate developer, Orlando Potter. It was used in the Potter Building on Park Row (*see Figures 20 and 21*), and shortly after its completion in 1886, Potter decided to begin his own terra-cotta company in New York. This new firm would serve the needs of both men: Taylor could be near his family farm, and Potter would have a local source of terra cotta for his future projects. Potter had a special interest in the fire-resistant qualities of terra cotta, because the previous building on the site of the Potter Building, the World Building, had been destroyed in a tragic fire.[39] When erecting the World Building's replacement, Potter sought the most fireproof material—terra cotta—for interior protection as well as for exterior ornamentation.[40]

Taylor's experience helped the New York Architectural Terra Cotta Company become one of the largest manufacturers in the country (*Figure 11*). His ideal factory layout for the company included a main building that was five stories high. Production was planned to move efficiently throughout the building: the lowest floor was used for clay preparation as well as for fueling the muffle kilns, and the highest floor included modeling studios and a plaster shop. The location of the factory, as the only New York City terra-cotta company at that time, may well have

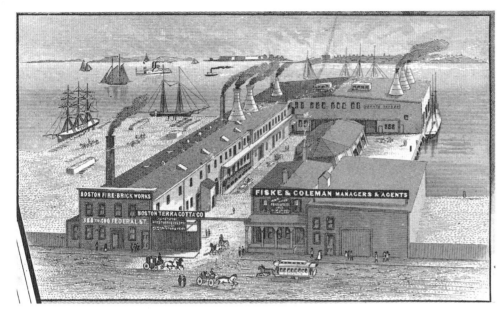

LEFT: FIG. 10. *This engraving of the Boston Terra Cotta Company's factory was featured on the company's letterhead. Fiske & Coleman owned this plant, which also housed the Boston Fire Brick Works and was located at 388–400 Federal Street, Boston, Massachusetts.*

BELOW: FIG. 11. *The New York Architectural Terra Cotta Company was located on the water's edge in Long Island City, New York. In this 1906 photo the partially completed Queensboro Bridge can be seen in the distance.*

ABOVE: FIG. 12. *One of the roof ornaments still visible on James Taylor's Port Monmouth, New Jersey home.*

OPPOSITE: FIG. 13. *Gladding, McBean & Company has been in continuous operation since 1875. This plaster model of a capital for the Fireman's Fund Insurance Building (1914, L. Hobart, San Francisco) is one of many old models that still remain in their factory.*

been a result of Taylor's beliefs. Although most manufacturers were located close to the clay pits, he favored the advantages of an urban location. He reasoned that clay was cheaper to transport than finished ware, and that manufacturers needed to maintain close contact with architects and builders, both to promote sales and to avoid delays in completing contracts. In addition, it was easier to find and hire skilled workmen in cities than in relatively remote rural areas.[41]

Taylor continued at the New York company as superintendent, until his health began to fail in 1893.[42] Apparently, he was also a guest modeler, since his signature, "Jas. Taylor," can be found on a beautifully sculpted fireplace plaque in the company's office (*see Figure 29*). For the last five years of his life, Taylor stayed close to his Port Monmouth farm. He died in 1898 and was buried nearby in the Fair View Cemetery in Red Bank. At the time of his death, Taylor left a wife, four children, three sisters, and a brother.[43] Despite his significance in the American terra-cotta industry, Taylor's family chose to place a dignified stone marker at his grave, rather than one of the terra-cotta headstones produced by local terra-cotta companies.[44]

Taylor's wood-frame and shingle farmhouse, which remains in Port Monmouth, has a roof that is embellished by a terra-cotta rooster, cat, and rabbit. Crest tiles and chimney tops are perched on the roof peaks (*Figure 12*). The current owners, proud of this fanciful ornament, have discovered that these pieces are marked "Boston Terra Cotta Company, 1880."[45] Ironically, a local historical publication, *Images of America, Middletown Township*, provides incorrect information about Taylor's farmhouse, stating that it was "occupied by a potter named Wilson. The tower is gone, but the house stands on the west side of Wilson Avenue. It is immediately recognizable by its numerous terra-cotta decorations which indicate that Wilson was a prolific potter."[46] The records of the local Monmouth County Historical Society have been amended to include the correct origins of the roof ornaments and the importance of James Taylor's achievements. One memorial tribute summed up his contribution: "The truth of the statement that 'the works that men do live after them' is fully exemplified in Mr. Taylor. There is hardly a city in the United States that has not a monument to him and his work in the form of some fine building."[47]

Like most brilliant people, Taylor had many admirers. A colleague and friend, C. A. Bloomfield, made the following comments about Taylor's generosity in a memorial speech in 1899: "He was desirous that every one who was connected with any branch of the clay industry should succeed, and how willing he was at all times to disseminate any knowledge he might have which would help some fellow-worker in that industry in which he took such great pride. He was too noble and broad-minded to refuse help to others lest their success might injure his."[48]

However, selflessness was only one aspect of Taylor's character. A less admirable quality is illustrated in a lengthy correspondence between Taylor and Gladding, McBean & Company in Lincoln, California dating from 1888 took the form of "Advice Letters," intended to solve the firm's production problems[49] (*Figure 13*). This

material indicates that Taylor was selling his expertise to the competition without the knowledge of the officers of the New York Architectural Terra Cotta Company. "I hope Mr. Gladding will be able to call on me," he wrote, "Please let me have due notice when to expect him. The company officers are jealous so please do not have him mention his business, except as a visitor to see the works. A visit will give him much practical information."[50] Indeed, he was as helpful as Bloomfield's laudatory comments suggested, but not without a large measure of personal interest.

A puzzling assessment of Taylor's character was made by Walter Geer, president of the New York Architectural Terra Cotta Company, who said, "It was due mainly to his [Taylor's] ultra-conservatism that he failed to achieve a greater measure of success. Like the Bourbons, 'He never learned and he never forgot.' He was unable to adapt himself to changed conditions and improved methods."[51] Ironically, Taylor delivered a paper at the Seventh Annual National Brick Manufacturer's Association Convention in 1893 (the year that he left the New York company) that expressly contradicted Geer's opinion that he was not adaptable: "How have we met the demands of the new school of architectural designers? How has it been done and who has done it? It has been done by the men who got out of the old ruts. It has been done by the men who saw in the clay pit something better than mud. It has been done by the men who were willing to think while they worked; who sought to elevate their craft, and thereby themselves, onto a higher plane than it or their fathers had occupied in the past generations."[52]

Human nature and the personal relationships between Taylor and his colleagues may account for some of the conflicting descriptions. James Taylor possessed great power and was regarded until the day he died as the final authority on terra-cotta dilemmas.[53] Undoubtedly, he must have been a threatening figure to some, and considering how frequently he moved from company to company, surely there must have been disagreements. An unhappy parting from the Boston Terra Cotta Company was mentioned in a newspaper article from 1886.[54] It is probable that his departure from the New York company may also have been unpleasant, since Taylor chose to omit the firm from a chapter he wrote on leading manufacturers of terra cotta, published in 1898 in *A History of Real Estate, Building and Architecture in New York City during the Last Quarter of a Century.*[55]

Although these divergent aspects of James Taylor's personality made him a complex figure, a description of Taylor from *The Clay-Worker* needs no clarification: "His experience is greatly relied upon, and as the phrase goeth, the company [the New York Architectural Terra Cotta Company] claims that what Mr. Taylor don't know about terra cotta is not worth knowing."[56] Unquestionably, he deserves the lion's share of credit for nurturing the American terra-cotta industry.

James Taylor's extraordinary influence went beyond the technical realm to include the effects of the strong artistic opinions that he expressed in a number of articles. In these, he made a sharp distinction between fired clay that imitated other building materials and fired clay that declared its distinctly clay-like properties. The former, which he deplored, he called simply "terra cotta." This could be lacquered, painted, or covered with colors to represent any material. In contrast, his definition of "architectural terra cotta" (which predates the use of glazes) stipulated that the finish be that of the natural clay. Subtle color variation was to be expected, since the tone of the clay, which resulted from mineral oxides, was strongly affected by the heat and atmosphere of the kiln.

In addition, Taylor considered it essential that terra-cotta pieces be moderate in size and textured rather than smooth, to highlight the plastic properties of clay. The use of terra cotta as a cheap material to imitate cast-iron and stone ornamentation caused Taylor much consternation. In his 1891 article in *Architectural Record,* he cuts short any discussion of this category by stating: "The pursuit of cheapness never yet had any artistic value; therefore it is useless to expend thought on the qualities of terra cotta as a substitute or sham building material."[57]

This negative response to imitative terra-cotta ornament was reinforced by a general public disdain for the artistic and technological shortcomings of some of the early material. When molds were made directly from existing cast-iron or stone ornament, the resulting forms lacked crispness and clarity. Nineteenth-century writers also objected to the use of the material on philosophical grounds. The influential British art critic John Ruskin played a central role in shaping the taste of the period. Ruskin's doctrine of "truth to materials" condemned pre-1870s American architectural terra cotta because it masqueraded as other materials, rather than expressing its own malleable properties.

A critical response to this inappropriate imitative use can be found in an 1884 article that deemed only two terra-cotta-ornamented buildings worthy of praise. Philadelphia's Pennsylvania Railroad Station (demolished), built in 1880–85 by the Wilson Brothers, and New York's Casino Theater (demolished), built in 1881–82 by Kimball & Wisedell, were considered the "only extensive examples we recall in this country of what can properly be called design in terra cotta, out of the innumerable multitudes of buildings in which terra cotta has been employed."[58] Particular design details (the same as those touted by Taylor) that were deemed appropriate to clay were lauded in these two buildings, including small-scale units, divisions within the ornament that avoided long, straight lines (which might show irregularities), and texturing of flat surfaces. Brick buildings such as these two, which incorporated terra-cotta detailing, began to be accepted and appreciated as wholly clay structures that were distinctly different from designs in stonemasonry.

Nonetheless, a stern warning was issued in "About Terra Cotta," published in 1887. This article questioned whether the increased use of terra cotta was a favorable development: "There can be no doubt that in the hands of any but conscientious architects it is decidedly 'dangerous.' We notice a growing tendency to use it indiscriminately in place of stone-carving, and the most barbarous solecisms are the result."[59] Battle lines were clearly drawn by the prominent critic Herbert Croly's "The Proper Use of Terra Cotta," published in *Architectural Record.* "Misused, clumsy, perverted, counterfeit, cheap, pretense, pretend, sham," were terms that referred to terra cotta—the substitute material. Within the same article, a contrasting bevy of glowing adjectives, including "distinctive, proper, wholesome, desirable, progressive, efficient, admirable, indispensable" describe architectural terra cotta—the independent material.[60]

The worth of terra cotta as an independent man-made material was under discussion as early as 1879 when an article in *Carpentry and Building* recognized "that the popular opinion concerning it [terra cotta] is, that it is a cheap 'manufactured' material.... It is so difficult to convince the public that man can make something harder and more durable than stone…[or] that man can improve upon Nature in her own domain…."[61] This ongoing dichotomy plagued the terra-cotta industry, since no matter how popular the material became in its own right, there remained a continuous demand for terra cotta that intentionally resembled stone.[62] Cost savings created the desire for buildings that appeared to be stone but actually relied on terra-cotta ornamentation, with stone used only for the more-visible lower stories. Examples of this common practice can be found in varied architectural styles and building types. The Gramercy, an 1882–83 apartment house designed by George Da Cunha, has a substantial two-story brownstone base with carved detailing and marble columns. Brick with figurative and geometric terra-cotta motifs is used on the rest of the facade, helping to create a striking Queen Anne-style structure. A rare surviving residence, that of J. Hampton Robb at 23 Park Avenue, was built in 1889–91. This handsome McKim, Mead & White mansion uses iron-spot brick and terra cotta on the upper floors, while the ground floor and balconies over the entrance are brownstone. Several blocks south of the Robb Mansion is the Grolier Club, designed by Charles Romeyn & Company and constructed in 1889–90. This splendid Romanesque clubhouse combines slender Roman bricks with a rusticated brownstone base and terra-cotta detailing. Smooth-faced terra-cotta arches surround the large window and doorway and are joined by a beautiful Celtic

knot motif (*Figure 14*). This clay ornament skillfully matches the color and surface of the stone and serves as an excellent example of terra cotta's chameleon-like potential.

During the 1880s and '90s, manufacturers served the demands of architects and clients by producing terra cotta that was practically indistinguishable from natural stone. This failure to capitalize on terra cotta's unique properties continued to plague the industry, and would grow to even greater proportions with the development of a reliable glaze technology at the turn of the century.

Chapter 4

The Flowering of the Terra-Cotta Industry in New York (1878-1900)

THANKS TO THE DILIGENT EFFORTS OF JAMES TAYLOR AND Sanford Loring, by the mid-1870s the Chicago Terra Cotta Company was consistently manufacturing top-quality terra cotta. The company supplied the material for two of the earliest New York buildings to use terra cotta, the Henry M. Braem Residence (demolished) built in 1878–80, and the Morse Building, constructed simultaneously.

George B. Post, the highly respected New York architect, designed the Braem Residence, located at 15 East 37th Street (*Figure 15*). He played a vital role in promoting the use of terra cotta in New York, constructing several of the earliest major buildings to use the material. "Mr. Post blazed the terra cotta trail in the face of grave warnings—criticism that was pretty close to ridicule—always the lot of a pioneer. He had the courage of conviction and events proved his judgment was justified to the fullest extent."[63] Furthermore, he helped the material achieve an independent standing by introducing a reddish terra-cotta claybody that quickly gained popularity.

Prior to 1877, most American terra cotta was a gray-buff color that was intended to match stone. Although there was no shortage of red-burning clays in the Chicago area, James Taylor's preference for a buff color had prevailed. Some Chicago architects criticized Taylor's terra cotta because of the color's similarity to stone.[64] When Post designed the Braem Residence, he specified that the color of the terra cotta should be a warm red. This particular shade of red, chosen to match the face brick, helped to make the distinction between terra cotta and stone more obvious.[65] Regional characteristics, particularly pertaining to clay color, began to develop rapidly in the terra-cotta industry during the late 1870s.

The terra cotta for the Braem Residence was hand-sculpted with wood-carving tools by Isaac Scott, a former architect and furniture maker who worked for the Chicago Terra Cotta Company. Scott created one-of-a-kind ornaments rather than the typical repeated motifs produced by traditional press molds.[66] The company arranged for James Taylor, then living in New Jersey, to supervise the installation of the terra cotta, "as they were anxious that this their maiden effort in the City of New York should prove a success."[67]

At the same time, in 1878–80, the Morse Building, designed by the New York architects Silliman & Farnsworth, was being constructed. This building, which still stands on Beekman and Nassau Streets, is considered the first important commercial building to use terra cotta in the New York area.[68] Its terra cotta was produced in

FIG. 15. *The Henry M. Braem Residence, 1878–80, was George B. Post's first New York building to use terra cotta.*

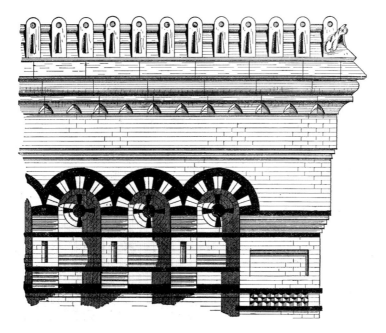

FIG. 16. *Detail of the terra-cotta cornice and the patterned brickwork on the Morse Building, 1878–80, New York's first important commercial building to use terra cotta.*

both the Chicago and Boston plants of the Chicago Terra Cotta Company (*Figure 16*). The manufacturers introduced an unusual feature, protected vertical joints, which prevented rain from wearing away the mortar, and was soon considered a necessary precaution for all exposed surfaces.[69]

The Long Island Historical Society in Brooklyn, erected in 1878–81, also made exceptional use of terra cotta. Most of the material for this exuberant building, another George B. Post design, was supplied by the Perth Amboy Terra Cotta Company.[70] The life-size Viking and Indian heads flanking the main entrance fully exploited the potential of terra-cotta ornamentation (*Figure 17*). Boston sculptor Truman H. Bartlett and his New York associate, Olin D. Warner, spent several months at the Perth Amboy plant working with modeler John Pierson on the designs. The boldness of the ornament was due in part to the fact that the artists worked directly in clay. The crispness of detail, which can be seen today in both the sculpted pieces and the molded decoration, testifies to the durability of terra cotta.

Perhaps Post's most important early contribution was the New York Produce Exchange Building (demolished) built in 1881–85 at Bowling Green and Battery Park (*Figure 18*). The Perth Amboy Terra Cotta Company supplied more than two thousand tons of terra cotta, the firm's largest job for at least the next two decades. To produce such quantities of material, the company had to erect additional buildings and kilns, nearly doubling its size. More draftsmen, modelers, modelmakers, and pressers were also hired. "There were not sufficient terra cotta men in the country at the time, so as the contract labor law was not then in force, men in all these departments were induced to come from England."[71]

The best talent that could be found was sought to execute the ornament for the building. Sculptor Edward Kemeys, known for his bronze statue *The Still Hunt* in Central Park, created heads of buffalo as well as steer, sheep, and boars, in keeping with the function of the building. Domingo Mora, one of the most renowned clay modelers of the period, created rondels with State of the Union seals. It was reported that "Mr. Mora received one hundred dollars for each state seal, a cause for great

ABOVE, LEFT: FIG. 17. *The Long Island Historical Society, 128 Pierrepont Street, Brooklyn, New York, was completed in 1881 and is one of George B. Post's most important surviving buildings.*

ABOVE, RIGHT: FIG. 18. *The New York Produce Exchange Building, 1881–85, which used over two thousand tons of terra cotta.*

RIGHT: FIG. 19. *The 1892 office of the New York Architectural Terra Cotta Company, 42–10 Vernon Boulevard, Long Island City, New York, is the only surviving structure on the site (see page 11).*

hilarity and a celebration in the [Perth Amboy] studio when he came to the State of Texas and the Lone Star comprised the entire modeling involved!"[72] Although considered a superb building by many, it was harshly criticized in the *Real Estate Record and Builders Guide* in 1884 as having "a negative disregard for the properties of the material.... [T]he design is a design for brick and stone, not translated into terra cotta, but merely, imitated in terra cotta."[73]

For the next five years, the terra cotta used in New York projects was produced in factories outside the city. It was not until 1886 that the New York Architectural Terra Cotta Company, located in Long Island City, became the city's first major terra-cotta manufacturer[74] (*Figure 19*).

REMARKABLE TECHNOLOGICAL INNOVATIONS CHANGED THE face of architecture between the 1870s and the early 1900s, and terra cotta played a key role in this transformation. As greater heights became possible, the limitations of masonry structures grew increasingly obvious. In a load-bearing structure, the wall carries the weight of the entire building. Therefore, the thickness of the wall has to increase in direct proportion to its height. This placed a sharp restriction on the maximum height that could be achieved economically, since the loss of interior space was a serious financial consideration to developers.

With the refinement of the passenger elevator, taller buildings of up to ten stories became popular, but the problem of wall thickness remained. It was generally agreed that tall buildings required a base with a wall thickness equal to twelve inches plus four inches for each story above the ground floor (i.e. sixteen inches for a two-story building, twenty inches for three stories, etc.). The highest masonry structure ever built was Burnham & Root's sixteen-story Monadnock Building, which still stands in Chicago. Constructed in 1889–91, its design followed the recommended guidelines for base thickness, and thus its walls are seventy-two inches thick at the base.[75] Not only did this minimize interior ground-floor space, but it also made it difficult to pierce the walls and provide enough windows for sufficient light and ventilation. Builders and real-estate investors began to realize that this type of construction was not cost effective.

Innovative building methods were developed that helped to solve this problem. In a relatively short period of time, the metal skeleton frame began to be used extensively in large buildings. During the years 1870–1905, a period of transition, there were three primary types of construction: bearing wall construction (metal floor beams supported by brick load-bearing walls and, in some cases, cast-iron columns); cage construction (metal frames supported the floors while the walls were self-supporting); and skeleton construction (complete metal frames supporting the floors as well as the thin curtain walls).[76]

The metal used in early skyscrapers was best protected from fire when it was surrounded with a fire-resistant material. Although brick, plaster, and cement were tried, porous terra-cotta blocks proved to be the most suitable material for fireproofing. This method was especially effective when an air space was left between the pieces of terra cotta and the structural member they encased.

FIG. 20. *The brown terra cotta on the Potter Building, 1883–86, provides a contrast to the red brick.*

The Potter Building, erected in 1883–86, was among the first in New York in which fired clay was employed to protect the columns (*Figure 20*). Tile-arched floors, along with both structural and decorative terra cotta, were used to provide state-of-the-art interior and exterior fireproofing. This eleven-story building was designed by Norris G. Starkweather, a Vermont-born architect-builder who practiced in Philadelphia, Baltimore, and Washington before coming to New York in 1880. The building's exterior walls (forty inches at the first story and twenty inches at the top), although self-supporting from the foundation to the extreme top, were considerably thinner than those of the Monadnock Building.[77] This was a result of cage construction, in which the weight of the floor is not carried by the outer walls. All of the terra cotta for this striking building was manufactured by the Boston Terra Cotta Company. An illustration of this structure is featured in the company's 1885 catalogue, accompanied by an emphatic explanation: "Please note that it [terra cotta] carries its proportion of the *entire* weight of this immense structure! Such *practical* evidence proves beyond question, that Terra Cotta when *well made*, and *properly set*, will bear any required weight."[78] Elsewhere the Potter Building was described as "an example of the best use of terra cotta for both constructive and ornamental purposes"[79] (*Figure 21*).

Skyscraper construction offered a point of departure for the most spectacular buildings of modern times. Initially dubbed "sky-supporter" and "cloud-scraper," the exceedingly tall building finally was knighted "the skyscraper." The word had been used in the eighteenth century to designate the highest sheet on a sailing vessel. In the nineteenth century it had meanings ranging from a tall person to a tall tale before it was adopted for its present use.

During this period, the term "skyscraper" described buildings that were noteworthy because of their new technology, rather than their sheer size. Most tall buildings were from twelve to fifteen stories and did not rise above the beginning suggestion of a New York skyline. Church steeples such as Trinity Church (284 feet), built in 1839–46, and St. Paul's Chapel (200 feet), built in 1764–66 were still the tallest structures on the horizon line. It was not until decades later that secular buildings such as George B. Post's Western Union Building (230 feet), constructed in 1872–75, and Richard Morris Hunt's Tribune Building (260 feet), completed in 1875, reached the height of those famous steeples. In 1889–92, Post's World Building, better known as the Pulitzer Building (with terra cotta made by the Perth Amboy Terra Cotta Company), measured 309 feet to the top of its tower. Although it became the tallest building in New York, it did not alter the skyline in the way that the dramatic departures of the Singer Building (600 feet), and the Woolworth Building (794 feet), eventually did (*Figure 22*). (With the exception of the Woolworth, all of the secular buildings mentioned above have been demolished.)

For architects, the skyscraper created a new series of structural and stylistic challenges. Technological issues included a careful consideration of the total weight of

FIG. 21. *This drawing of the Potter Building was on the back cover of the 1894 New York Architectural Terra Cotta Company catalogue.*

ABOVE: FIG. 22. *A view of New York's terra-cotta skyline from the New Jersey Terra Cotta Company catalogue, circa 1916.*

LEFT: FIG. 23. *Workmen on the terra-cotta-clad Woolworth Building, which was under construction from 1910–13.*

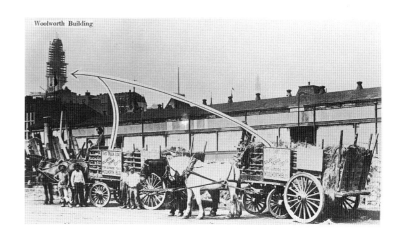

Woolworth Building

October 1.

October 29.

RAPID CONSTRUCTION

Progress Photographs
*taken at intervals of
one week*

"OUR innate modesty forbids our making any mention of the speed which we made in completing the Terra Cotta on the above building. However, we feel we can say that this job was enclosed more rapidly than any other building of a similar type which has been erected in Cleveland. It goes without saying that no progress of this kind could have been made had we not had your co-operation and your rapid delivery of materials. The manner in which you handled the work was highly satisfactory and we are all very much pleased with the results.
Very truly yours,
THE LUNDOFF-BICKNELL CO."

B. F. Keith's Theatre and Office Building, Cleveland, Ohio. C. W. & Geo. L. Rapp, Architects; The Lundoff-Bicknell Company, Builders. Atlantic Terra Cotta in glazed conglomerate with slight touches of color from sidewalk to roof. Largest building in Ohio.

Atlantic Terra Cotta Company
350 Madison Avenue, New York

Southern Factory
Atlanta Terra Cotta Company
Atlanta, Georgia

October 8.

November 5.

October 15.

November 12.

October 22.

November 19.

TOP: FIG. 24. *The Atlantic Terra Cotta Company shipped the terra-cotta pieces from New Jersey and then transported them to the Woolworth Building by horse and wagon. The metal skeletal construction of this fifty-two-story skyscraper can be seen on the left.*

BOTTOM, LEFT: FIG. 25. *Terra-cotta cladding was installed from both the top and the bottom of a skeletal frame simultaneously. This procedure is clearly visible in these progress photos of the B. F. Keith's Theater and Office Building in Cleveland, Ohio.*

BOTTOM, RIGHT: FIG. 26. *Partially clad skeleton of Daniel Burnham's Flatiron Building, 175 Fifth Avenue, New York City, as seen from Madison Square, circa 1902.*

the tall metal framework, stabilization of the foundation, and fireproof construction on a vast new scale. At the same time, it was necessary to provide proper light and air. Aesthetic concerns included the desire to express the building's framing structures and the need to unify the facade through a careful balance of proportion and scale. Ornamentation had to be designed to reflect the size and function of the new buildings. Terra cotta and metal framing provided greater possibilities for new architectural styles at considerably less cost (terra cotta was roughly one-tenth the cost of an equivalent piece of ornamental stone) and weight (terra-cotta cladding on metal framing was one-third the weight of masonry walls) than those of traditional materials.

FIG. 27. *Detail of the terra-cotta ornamentation on the Flatiron Building.*

The curtain wall, an essential element in skyscrapers, consisted of panels that extended horizontally from column to column and vertically from girder to girder. Terra cotta served as an excellent material for curtain walls: it was fire-resistant, lighter than stone, could provide repeating motifs through the use of molds, and offered many surface and color opportunities (*Figure 23*). The use of terra cotta as cladding helped to free the material from its earlier role of imitating stone or iron (*Figure 24*). "The steel frame...transferred the weight to a few points of support; the problem was so radically solved that the masonry or clay walls could be built from the top story downward, if desired."[80] This innovative technology changed the structural engineering of buildings more than any other development since the flying buttress (*Figure 25*).

One fine early example of skeletal-frame construction with terra cotta is the Flatiron Building, designed by Chicago architect Daniel Burnham and constructed in 1901–3 (*Figure 26*). Above a stone base, the building's curtain wall is a combination of brick and ornate terra cotta. Striking ornament appears on the fourth floor, where ovals with foliage alternate with rondels of a somber woman's face. The elaborate overhanging cornice and upper stories have wonderful details including lions' heads and mask-like faces. The Flatiron successfully combined the three innovations that defined the skyscraper: the elevator, fireproofing, and the skeleton frame supporting a curtain wall. Its form, which results from filling its small triangular site, makes this twenty-two-story building rise with an unusual grace and lightness. This powerful free-standing structure was, at the time of its completion, the tallest skyscraper in the city (*Figures 27, 28*).

Along with the evolution of building technology, simultaneous advances occurred in the terra-cotta industry. These changes were largely due to the collaboration between terra-cotta manufacturers, architects, and contractors. New challenges and demands made by these building professionals led to innovative solutions for the construction methods, glazing possibilities, and surface treatments of terra cotta. Having no precedent to follow, architects led terra-cotta makers in new directions. One such leader was Cyrus L. W. Eidlitz, a New York architect who frequently used terra cotta. He helped to alter its old-fashioned smooth surface by introducing a

OPPOSITE: FIG. 28. *Although there are many taller buildings in New York, the Flatiron Building retains its commanding presence and is one of the city's best-known structures.*

LEFT: FIG. 29. *A combed texture, seen in this detail from the fireplace in the New York Architectural Terra Cotta Company office, was used on many decorative pieces manufactured by the company in the 1880s and 1890s. Under the two Ts in COTTA is the signature "Jas. Taylor."*

BELOW: FIG. 31. *Detail of the upper portion of the Bayard Building, 65 Bleecker Street, New York City, showing Sullivan's complex terra-cotta ornament. The ornament was manufactured by the Perth Amboy Terra Cotta Company.*

FIG. 30. *Entrance to Louis Sullivan's only New York City building, the terra-cotta-clad Bayard Building, constructed in 1897–99.*

design technique of his own involving combed or crinkled surfaces.[81] As one writer noted in describing the type of terra cotta, "the plane surfaces are gone over with random strokes of a coarse saw, forming a surface which has evidently been wrought while it was still highly plastic.... In this detail full advantage has been taken of the extreme plasticity of the material to do what cannot be done in stone, or cannot be done so cheaply."[82] Textured surfaces became part of the standard terra-cotta vocabulary, adding a distinct feature to the buildings in which it was used (*Figure 29*). An outstanding example in New York is the 1892–93 West End Collegiate Church, designed by Robert W. Gibson. This tawny yellow brick and terra-cotta church is distinguished by a large central gable and red-tile roof. The terra cotta on the brackets, pinnacles, and entrance has subtle swirling lines that clearly show the plastic potential of clay.

The greatest display of the unique qualities of terra cotta can be found on the buildings of Louis Sullivan. Frank Lloyd Wright commented that in Sullivan's work, "background, the curse of all stupid ornamentation, ceased to exist. None might see where terra cotta left off and ornamentation came to life."[83] Although many architects contributed to early skyscraper design and technology, Louis Sullivan stands out as one of the great theorists of the skyscraper. In his now-classic essay, "The Tall Office Building Artistically Considered," Sullivan claimed that new kinds of buildings required new kinds of architectural expression, condemning the use of historical elements in the skyscraper. His belief that the skyscraper must be a "proud and soaring thing" was elegantly illustrated in his Wainwright Building of 1890–91 in St. Louis. Although only nine stories, this building nonetheless expresses an imposing sense of height. The terra-cotta spandrels and cornice are molded into delicate natural forms that contrast effectively with the simple geometry of the vertical brick piers.

The Guaranty Building in Buffalo, built in 1895–96, is another spectacular example of Sullivan's early skyscrapers, and it provides an unusual experience for its occupants. The Guaranty, along with several of Sullivan's other tall buildings, has deeply recessed windows that allow the rich red terra-cotta detailing surrounding the windows to be clearly visible from the interior (rarely can one see the exterior materials on a building while inside it). This building, along with Sullivan's 1897–99 Bayard Building in New York, uses terra-cotta cladding for the entire facade (*Figure 30*).

The facade of the Bayard Building (now known as the Bayard-Condict Building) reflects its method of construction, producing an unusual and lyrical composition. Sullivan alternated strong, imposing terra-cotta columns with slender cylindrical ones to distinguish between bearing and nonbearing members. In this way he provided a visual explanation of how the building was supported. Montgomery Schuyler considered this building "a very serious attempt to found the architecture of a tall building upon the facts of the case. The actual structure is left, or rather is helped to tell its own story.... Everywhere the drapery of baked clay is a mere wrapping, which clings so closely to the frame as to reveal it, and even to emphasize it."[84] The terra-cotta ornament that enlivens the facade consists of both intertwined geometric motifs and natural organic forms. Extensive undercutting of these designs (which was done by hand after the pieces were removed from the molds) helps to create a wonderful play of light and shadow across the building's surface. The facade terminates in a deep cornice with a remarkable series of winged figures placed just beneath (*Figure 31*).

Sullivan's achievements in terra cotta have been widely applauded. He created a highly individual system of organic ornament which was brilliantly integrated into the form of his structures. These three buildings, which so successfully embody his ability to combine new materials and technology, are still standing today thanks to the heroic efforts of a few determined preservationists.[85]

Part Two

The Factory:

From Start to

Finish

*Detail from a plaque on the front of the 1892
New York Architectural Terra Cotta Company
office building in Long Island City, New York
(also see Figure 19).*

Chapter 6

The Manufacture of

Terra Cotta

I N *The Story Of Terra Cotta,* WALTER GEER WROTE THAT TERRA COTTA, more than any other building material, offered a true reflection of the personality of the architect. Frank Lloyd Wright agreed, commenting that terra cotta was "as sensitive to a creative brain as a dry plate is to the lens of the camera. A marvelous simplifier, this material, rightly used."[86] Since architectural terra cotta was not kept in stock, every job was individually executed, with special attention paid to each set of requirements (*Figure 32*). More so than any other architectural product, terra cotta was "hand-tailored" to the highest degree. It was not simply the embodiment in three dimensions of a set of drawings, but the total expression of the architectural idea, combining colors, glazes, surface textures, and sculptural ornamentation (*Figure 33*). Early manufacturer Edward Roche described his satisfaction with making terra cotta to Richard Upjohn in a letter dated 1852: "Is there not something pleasing in the thought that when we meet a great artist we can duplicate his designs and works and give them in quantity to the world in such form as can be used for architectural purposes—so that the efforts of his genius may survive when he would be no more."[87]

The process of terra-cotta production, from the architect's blueprint to the final installation, was a complex and fascinating one. Each design passed through the hands of dozens of workmen, varying in skill and background from the finest European sculptors to untrained day laborers. Except for the modelers, some of whom achieved recognition because of their unique skills and the visibility of their efforts, most factory workers labored in anonymity. Although the architects are usually known, the fact that terra-cotta pieces were rarely signed by individuals or stamped by manufacturers leaves us with a clay legacy produced largely by unknown craftsmen.

Architects and terra-cotta manufacturers spent much time collaborating on the production of the complex and richly detailed ornament used in building facades.[88] Before the actual manufacturing could begin, the preliminary stages had to be completed, involving the creation of shop drawings, models, and molds and the selection and preparation of clay and glazes. The architect supplied the terra-cotta company with a set of scale drawings and plans for steel framing (*Figure 34*). The company's drafting department then made shop drawings showing full-size details as well as the joints and construction of the terra cotta. These were enlarged to allow for the shrinkage of the clay (typically one inch per foot). The draftsmen used a special ruler

FIG. 32. *Ten-foot-high eagles, sculpted by modelers at the New Jersey Terra Cotta Company, were proudly featured in this advertisement in the October 1928* Pencil Points. *They can still be seen on the corners at the top of 299 Madison Avenue, New York City.*

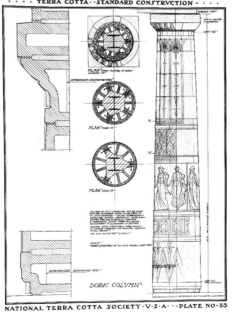

ABOVE: FIG. 33. *Thomas Lamb designed exuberant polychrome ornament and sculpture for the facade of the Pythian Temple, 135 West 70th Street, New York City, completed in 1927.*

LEFT: FIG. 34. *This page from* Architectural Terra Cotta Standard Construction *shows various methods for assembling a column, and the metal I-beams used in the center of each. At the right is a column from the Pythian Temple.*

FIG. 35. *This model of Neptune's head was sculpted at Boston Valley Terra Cotta in 1994 for a partial restoration of the Audubon Ballroom, 3940–60 Broadway, New York City. Since the original had been missing for many years, the modeler Sue Quimby had to rely upon a small historic photograph.*

that was thirteen inches long, but divided into twelve "inches" to ensure that the finished pieces would be the correct size. The shop drawings were finally submitted to the architect for approval. Small buildings required only a few shop drawings, while major ones could require somewhere between one and two hundred. The former president of the Northwest Terra Cotta Company, Trygve Kristianesen, recalled that when he joined the firm in 1924 there were approximately fifty men working in the drafting room.[89] Large sheets of linen were used, and the designs were drawn in ink.

Once the drawings were accepted by the architect, they were sent to the modeling room, where they served as a guide for the creation of full-size clay or plaster models. This step was of vital importance since a successful outcome depended on the skilled execution of the clay models (*Figure* 35). Very limited information survives about the great many modelers employed by the terra-cotta industry. However, a few interesting personalities have emerged. One modeler, Johannes Gelert, studied and worked in Copenhagen, Paris, Berlin, and Rome before he came to the United States in 1877. His first job was in the modeling shop of the Perth Amboy Terra Cotta Company. "Here his extraordinary rapidity of execution excited the jealousy of the foreman with the result that at the end of the second week, Gelert was dismissed."[90] He had managed to produce six original sculpted figurative panels, each six feet high, and a series of huge animal heads in this brief period. He eventually established his own very successful modeling studio in Chicago, but most men were not as lucky, or perhaps as gifted. "Many a man whose ambition was to be a sculptor, after working in this studio, and that, finds himself face to face with the poverty-stricken fact, that to continue waiting the arrival of an important commission…means courting a death by slow starvation."[91]

In *Common Clay*, a publication from the American Terra Cotta Company, a statement addressed to architects defined the role of the modelers. Their job was "to express your ideas, not theirs. They are responsible only that the modelling is well done, workmanlike and alive. If the ornament is not worthy of expression, it is not their fault, they are not mind-readers."[92] Each issue of *Common Clay* included a page titled "Who's Who in the American Terra Cotta Company," and in 1920 the renowned Norwegian-born sculptor Kristian Schneider was featured. He was the controlling genius and hard-working director of the modeling room, "always pleasant and affable, an artist to and in the tips of his fingers, always anxious to give you what you want, and not what he thinks in his own opinion what you ought to want."[93] Schneider executed all the models for Louis Sullivan. The American Terra Cotta Company allowed him to work for Sullivan's office when modeling was needed in materials other than clay, such as cast iron or sawed wood.[94] Sullivan's reliance on this brilliant sculptor to interpret all of his drawings helps to explain the consistently high quality of his ornament.

An 1876 article by James Taylor, then superintendent of the Chicago Terra Cotta Company, sheds light on early procedures in their modeling room: "The orna-

FIG. 36. *The modeling shop at O. W. Ketcham, Crum Lynne, Pennsylvania, 1915.*

mentation now produced is all hand wrought; that is to say, if it is a running or continuous ornament, it is first moulded nearly to the form required, and before baking is all worked over with modelling tools. The finer kinds of work, such as panellings, tympana, and capitals, are all modelled or carved in semi-dry clay, and baked just as they come from the tools. The modellers lately employed have been James Legge and Isaac Scott, both adept in the modern Gothic school."[95] Legge was a former stonecarver and Scott was responsible for the terra-cotta ornament on George B. Post's Braem Residence.

Clearly, modelers brought a variety of backgrounds and kinds of experience to the modeling room. One modeler, Nels Alling, received a gold medal of honor from the King of Denmark for his sculpting abilities at the age of twenty-five. In 1887, the following year, he came to the United States with his new bride. Years later he

FIG. 37. *A detail of the twelve-hundred-foot-long terra-cotta frieze that surrounds the Pension Building, 1882–85, in Washington, D. C.*

recalled, "I came to this country…because I heard that top-flight workers in terra cotta could earn as much as 55 cents an hour, which was a fantastic sum of money in my estimation in those days."[96] Modeling was one of the highest-paying jobs within the factory, and it continued that way, according to records from the mid-1920s, which indicated that modelers received $2 per hour while other workers were paid only about 60 cents[97] (*Figure 36*).

Terra-cotta companies relied on architects to provide information in order to execute the ornament desired. They suggested that the "architect mention the architectural style and period to be used as a precedent, possibly supplemented by rough sketches of particular details…."[98] It was up to the architect to specify in the contract either that the ornament would be modeled by the factory, or that he would supply his own models. The companies took care to see that it was to the architect's advantage both artistically and economically to have the modeling done in the terra-cotta factory.

In rare cases, well-known sculptors were hired for a special project to actually work in the company's modeling room. One such case was that of the Woolworth Building, where architect Cass Gilbert hired John Donnelly and Eliseo Ricci, of the sculpting firm Donnelly & Ricci, to do all the terra-cotta designs in the modeling shop of the Atlantic Terra Cotta Company. Montgomery Meigs, the architect for the Pension Building (1882–85) in Washington, D.C., hired sculptor Caspar Buberl to make the plaster models for a three-foot-high and twelve-hundred-foot-long terra-cotta frieze. Buberl shipped these models to the Boston Terra Cotta Company, where molds were cast and the pieces manufactured[99] (*Figure 37*).

Each terra-cotta company had a photography department which was responsible for documenting finished models (*Figures 38, 39*). If an architect was located too far away from the plant, photos of completed models would be sent for written approval so that the process could continue and the plaster mold prepared. Once all the approvals had been received, eight to ten weeks were needed for the actual

FIG. 38. *The Rookwood Pottery sent this photo-graph of clay models for the Della Robbia Bar ceiling to Guastavino Company, general contractors for the project. Approval of these models was required before the work could proceed.*

FIG. 39. *Detail of the Della Robbia Bar ceiling in the former Vanderbilt Hotel, which was designated a New York City Landmark in 1994.*

FIG. 40. *Sections of a plaster mold used to create* The Lady & The Unicorn, *a mural designed in 1957 by Elbert Weinberg for the lobby of 405 Fifth Avenue, New York City (demolished).*

manufacture. Architects frequently visited the modeling room to examine and approve the work in person. There is an interesting account of the typical visit by the well-known New York architect Stanford White to the Perth Amboy Terra Cotta Company. He would breeze into the modeling department, hastily view the clay models, and invariably pronounce them "Terrible!" "Occasionally he would fall on one particular model with his hands to make a line more sweeping or depress the relief, but in general he was secretly pleased and passed the models without change, still saying 'Terrible!' Others appreciated Mr. White's work, but as a true artist he was never satisfied."[100]

The plaster molds were allowed to dry out, and then they were sent to the pressing department, ready for the first step of manufacture. The simplest plaster molds, usually consisting of four separate sides and a bottom which fit together very snugly, were tightly bound with wire bands (*Figures 40, 41*).

While the drafting and modeling departments were hard at work, the clay was prepared so that it would be ready to use as soon as the molds were available. Despite romantic images of clay being dug from the earth's surface and effortlessly fashioned into a vast array of artistic objects, the process was not so simple, and it involved much scientific experimentation. The actual material used to make architectural terra cotta was a carefully formulated ratio of different clays known as a claybody. Since each claybody had varying characteristics, the manufacturer had to choose the one that best suited the requirements of each particular job. The most obvious distinction among different claybodies was color. When a light-colored slip or glaze finish was required, the claybody had to be made with clays that did not have metallic oxides such as iron or manganese, which would cause the clay to become brown or red during the firing. Other important considerations were the right vitrification (hardness), and the proper texture of the claybody.

FIG. 41. *After the plaster molds are filled with clay, they are left to begin hardening. In this photograph, the pieces of the plaster mold are being removed so that the stiff clay ornament can be taken to the finishing shop.*

FIG. 42. *Clay emerges from the pugmill and is cut with a thick wire into large chunks so that it can be stored and allowed to age until needed.*

Special formulas were developed to ensure that the correct amount of each kind of clay was blended with an appropriate quantity of grog (previously fired and ground terra cotta). All architectural terra-cotta claybodies required large percentages of grog to minimize shrinkage, give added strength, and reduce cracking and warping during firing. Once a claybody formula was calculated, the clays were ground to a fine powder in crushers that resembled coffee mills. This powder was then combined with water and mixed in a pugmill, or (during the earliest years of the industry) in a trough by factory workers with bare feet (*Figure 42*)! After the claybody had been blended to form a homogeneous mass that was soft enough to press into molds, it was stored, allowing it to age and become increasingly plastic.

When the molds arrived in the pressing department, clay would be packed into them carefully so that all of the ornamental details would be fully realized on each unit. A typical piece of terra cotta had one-and-one-half-inch walls and was about four to six inches deep. The pressed pieces had hollow backs with interior partition walls of clay to provide additional strength. Holes were usually put in these walls, making it easier to handle the pieces while in the factory and also providing a place where metal anchors could be inserted during installation. Following the pressing, the clay was left to stiffen in the mold. This usually occurred rapidly since the plaster walls absorbed moisture from the clay. The mold would then be disassembled by unfastening the wire bands, and the clay piece would be left to harden until it was ready to be finished.

Two alternative methods to hand pressing developed. One process, extrusion, became widely used in the late 1920s, as a desire for simpler, flat pieces of terra cotta increased. A steel die was cut to match the specific profile of the form, and clay was squeezed through the die in the extruder. (The general technique is easiest to envi-

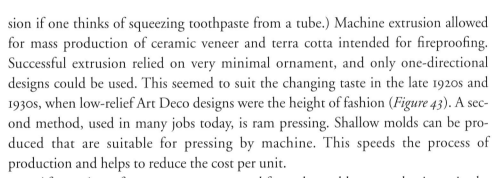

sion if one thinks of squeezing toothpaste from a tube.) Machine extrusion allowed for mass production of ceramic veneer and terra cotta intended for fireproofing. Successful extrusion relied on very minimal ornament, and only one-directional designs could be used. This seemed to suit the changing taste in the late 1920s and 1930s, when low-relief Art Deco designs were the height of fashion (*Figure 43*). A second method, used in many jobs today, is ram pressing. Shallow molds can be produced that are suitable for pressing by machine. This speeds the process of production and helps to reduce the cost per unit.

After a piece of terra cotta was removed from the mold or extruder, it received a final finishing. Edges were smoothed (workmen in one English company currently use the leather tongue of a shoe for this task), imperfections repaired, and any undercuts or final changes were made. Additional drying time was required before the piece could be glazed or fired. The length of time varied depending upon the type of piece, its size, and the method of drying. By 1913, many companies were using humidity dryers to ensure steady, even drying. A typical terra-cotta unit was allowed to dry for up to a week, while larger pieces were given at least twice that long (*Figure 44*). Uneven or incomplete drying resulted in warped, cracked, unusable ware. The foibles of clay were well-recognized, and Charles Fergus Binns, first director of Alfred University's New York State College of Clay-Working and Ceramics, respectfully warned, "Clay is very docile, but there are times when, being tortured beyond endurance, it turns upon its tormentor."[101]

The thoroughly dry terra cotta was then moved to the glaze room where the spraying department, equipped with compressed-air apparatus, applied the appropriate number and types of glazes or slips (*Figure 45*). A glaze, whether glossy or matte, combined chemicals that included large amounts of silica (glass) and oxides, which could produce a wide range of brilliant colors. Glazed surfaces tend to be slightly glassy, and all glazed surfaces (even matte glazes) have a smooth, satin-like finish. Slips are clays thinned into a liquid state with water. A slip provides a uniform color and

FIG. 45. *Glaze is being sprayed onto these blocks of terra cotta before they are stacked in the kiln and fired.*

dry surface with no evidence of glassiness. The typical finishes were called standard, matte, and full glaze. Each is described in articles of the period by comparing them to different types of stone! Standard, which had a finish "similar to smooth limestone," must have been a slip coating. Matte was a dull glaze "similar to unpolished marble" and typically used for cream, white, and all polychrome glazes. Full glaze had a glossy surface "similar to highly polished marble," and was recommended "for buildings to be erected in smoky localities because it is the surface most easily cleaned."[102] When one piece used two or more glaze colors, they were usually applied carefully with a brush to prevent them from overlapping or running together (*Figure 46*).

Glazed terra-cotta units were then loaded onto carts and moved to the kiln for stacking. Each piece was carefully lifted into the kiln and set on benches formed by blocks of fireproof material. In an attempt to limit the warping, terra-cotta pieces were not stacked upon each other. When loaded into the kiln, glazed units could not touch because the glazes would melt and the pieces would fuse together. The actual firing process took from ten to twelve days and was divided into three phases. The first three days involved a very slow and steady increase in the heat. This was followed by three days at full temperature, which was typically twenty-three to twenty-four-hundred degrees Fahrenheit. The final three to four days were used to slowly reduce the heat and cool the kiln enough for it to be unstacked. The most difficult part of firing was to maintain an even heat in all parts of the kiln. This required great skill since the largest kilns were forty-eight feet high and twenty-four feet in diameter. One method of ascertaining that the heat was even was to have draw trials in which small rings of glazed clay were placed on rods located in several parts of the kiln. Periodically during the firing, the rods were withdrawn, and the rings were

ABOVE: FIG. 46. *This photograph of women brushing glazes on polychrome terra cotta, is part of an advertisement that states, "The Northwestern Terra Cotta Company is contributing in an important measure to the advent of a new era in architecture, with colorful terra cotta the keynote." (*Pencil Points, *July 1928)*

LEFT: FIG. 49. *In the fitting department, the completed terra-cotta pieces were assembled and all measurements were checked before the work was packed for shipping.*

removed and examined. As technology developed, pyrometers were introduced, which measured the heat within the kiln, helping to chart the changes of temperature (*Figure 47*).

Muffle kilns were frequently used in the manufacture of terra cotta. As the name indicates, they were designed with muffle walls to protect the ware from any direct contact with the flames. The kiln was constructed with double walls, and the flames remained between them while the heat spread throughout the kiln walls and floor, then up through the chimney. Usually there were five or more places at the base of each big kiln where the fires were built (*Figure 48*). These fires were continually fed for the first two phases of the firing. Several kinds of fuel were available including

TOP, NEAR RIGHT: FIG. 47. *This terra-cotta block, originally used in one of the factory buildings of the Atlantic Terra Cotta Company, features their muffle kiln logo with billowing smoke—once a sign of industrial prosperity, not environmental pollution.*

TOP, FAR RIGHT: FIG. 48. *Several of the kilns used at the Rocky Hill plant of the Atlantic Terra Cotta Company stand in disrepair. The kilns were individually numbered and each of the five or six fireboxes was marked by a small ceramic number as well.*

BOTTOM: FIG. 50. *This terra cotta, which was being exported to Japan, was wedged solidly with hay into special boxes. "This method of shipping is greatly appreciated by foreign builders [helping to insure that the] Terra Cotta arrives at the building site undamaged."* (Atlantic Terra Cotta Company, *February 1926)*

OPPOSITE, TOP LEFT: FIG. 51. *These trucks and trailers were used by the Atlantic Terra Cotta Company for delivery in New York and New Jersey.*

OPPOSITE, BOTTOM: FIG. 52. *This Midland Terra Cotta Company sample box provided a foolproof way for architects to obtain the glaze color they specified. Samples were scored and numbered on the back so that the architect could break them, keeping one half and returning the other to the company to be matched.*

OPPOSITE, TOP RIGHT: FIG. 53. *This large rondel and several smaller pieces, embedded into the walls of this last surviving building, are all that remain from the Atlantic Terra Cotta Company's plant in Tottenville, Staten Island, New York.*

coal, oil, and gas. It was reported in 1901 that the Perth Amboy Terra Cotta Company had twenty-two kilns, while the New York Architectural Terra Cotta Company was operating twenty kilns in 1913. The scale of this industry is easier to envision when one realizes that the largest kilns held between thirty-five and forty-five tons of fired terra cotta, or the equivalent of two railroad cars.

After the cooling process, finished terra cotta was unloaded from the kiln to be examined and sent to the fitting department. Here all the pieces were laid out on the floor, checked for proper fit, and numbered according to the setting plan so that installation at the building site could proceed smoothly (*Figure 49*). The fitting department was equipped with large steel rubbing beds for straightening any joints that needed attention. The final step was packing the pieces in hay to protect them during the journey to their destination (*Figure 50*). This was a crucial procedure since breakage could halt the progress of a building and greatly increase the cost of a project. The importance of this matter is clearly spelled out in a twenty-page document prepared in 1910 by the Atlantic Terra Cotta Company concerning the safest way of shipping and packing a rail car with finished terra cotta pieces. It urged that the terra cotta be loaded into boxcars, padded with approximately fifteen hundred pounds of hay, and securely braced with wood to prevent any shifting in transit. The more fragile pieces were carefully crated. Still, concern remained about how the ware was unloaded and transported to the building site (*Figure 51*). One writer was understandably critical of mishandling: "Here is a material carefully made by hand, perhaps rich with expensive modeling and executed in a number of colors—and it is frequently thrown into a cart and actually dumped upon the ground as if it were common brick! Consider the result!"[103]

Trade publications carried advertising from leading terra-cotta manufacturers boasting a production time of only seven days for generic ornament from existing molds. Fulfilling this promise required a highly organized and efficient factory with draftsmen, estimators, and bookkeepers fully involved in the operation of the company. There were many different types of support staff needed in a terra-cotta company. Records from the Eastern Terra Cotta Company, active between the years 1932 and 1944, listed the names of one hundred employees with twenty different job descriptions. In addition to the types of jobs already mentioned in the description of the manufacturing process, there were also administrators, truck drivers, forklift operators, carpenters, watchmen, inspectors, machinists, coal passers, firemen, sawmen, shape fitters, hand fitters, and engineers. The work of the estimating department was to prepare the bid documents for potential jobs. Insight into the task of the sales department is provided by a description in *Common Clay*: "Selling terra cotta is not an order-taking proposition. When we sell terra cotta we are selling something we haven't got, and to make the problem more difficult, we are selling something which we have never sold before. Every job is a 'special made to order' and no two are alike"[104] (*Figure 52*).

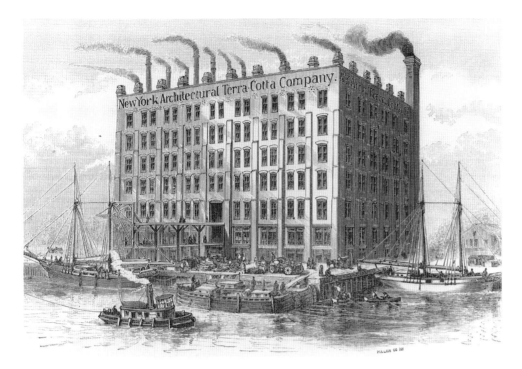

FIG. 54. *The waterfront location of the New York Architectural Terra Cotta Company's factory allowed for easy access across the East River. Frequently, visitors arrived by boat, as did the raw materials used in the plant.*

The companies played a significant part in the lives of the people whom they employed as well as those who lived in the larger community (*Figure 53*). Baseball teams, outings, dinners, and yearly picnics were documented. A chief draftsman for the Atlantic Terra Cotta Company's Tottenville, Staten Island plant, Percy Okeson, commented: "Those were good times. We were clannish, happy and had good pay. There was no commuting. After work you could go fishing, lobstering or drink a beer in a nice hotel, not in a saloon as one does now."[105] The American Terra Cotta Company had this to say about their plant in 1920: "We built, not a factory, but a place in which to create beautiful ware—the product of the skilled hands of craftsmen—and the setting has a tremendous influence on the work, there isn't a doubt about it. 'Atmosphere' is a much abused word, but there is such a thing and we have it."[106]

The factory environment described in *Common Clay* varied with each company, but many close ties formed among those in the terra-cotta industry. A surprising number of skilled workmen were employed at one firm, then moved to another, and often on to a third or fourth. The president and officers frequently met at conventions and communicated regularly about specific jobs and broad industry issues including government standards. A poignant example of the personal connections that these men developed can be found in Karl Mathiasen's obituary of August 5, 1920.[107] Mathiasen, one of the founders of the New Jersey Terra Cotta Company, started in the field as a teenager in the pressing department of A. Hall & Sons. Later he was a foreman for the Boston Terra Cotta Company and also was employed by the New York Architectural Terra Cotta Company. At his funeral the pallbearers included the presidents of the Atlantic Terra Cotta Company, the Conkling-Armstrong Terra Cotta Company, O. W. Ketcham, and the Brick, Terra Cotta & Tile Company. Flowers were sent from the National Terra Cotta Society of the Pacific Coast and the Central Terra Cotta Association, as well as from individual factories across the country.

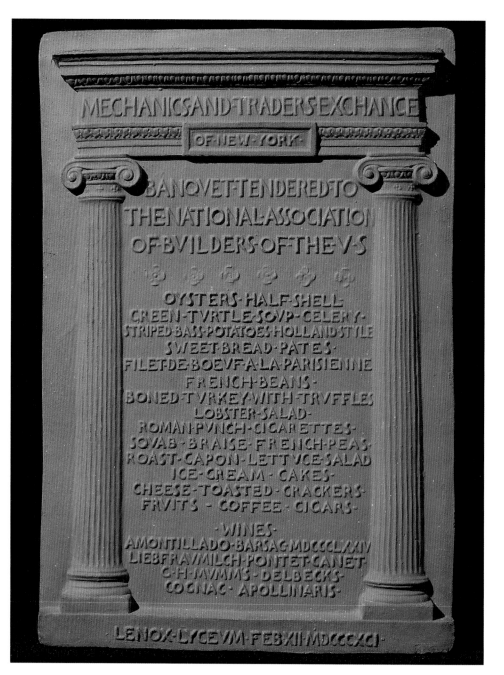

ABOVE, LEFT: FIG. 55. *This large vessel, produced by the New York Architectural Terra Cotta Company, served as a gift for important clients.*

ABOVE, RIGHT: FIG. 56. *This remarkable 1891 menu, made by the Perth Amboy Terra Cotta Company, preserves the memory of an exceptional meal that began with oysters on the half-shell and concluded with French wines and cognac.*

Active participation in professional organizations like the American Ceramic Society fostered the development of long-term friendships among many of the terra-cotta manufacturers. Established in 1899, the society's membership included scientists, educators, industrialists, government officials, a few artists, and many businessmen from the terra-cotta industry. The society provided a forum for the discussion of a wide range of ceramic concerns and sought solutions to technical problems by promoting scientific research. Numerous trips were organized by the society, and the description that follows is a small segment of a report of one such trip. Published in a 1913 issue of *The Clay-Worker*, it is titled "Midsummer Meeting of American Ceramic Society. Four Days of Sight-Seeing—Excursions Through Clay Plants and a Delightful Ocean Trip from Boston to New York"(*Figure 54*):

Immediately after dinner we boarded the rubber-neck and crossed over the Queensboro bridge to the New York Terra Cotta Co.'s plant. Messrs. F. B. Ortman and J. Clark escorted us through the factory. The first point visited was the sample room, on the fourth floor, where over 2,500 samples in different colors and surface textures were at hand. On the fourth floor are also the slip room, the modeling rooms, and plaster shop, where the molds are made. Sixty men are employed here. There is also a room set aside for the breaking in of pressers. It is absolutely necessary that a school of this character be run constantly. There are two immense pressing floors in this plant, covering 9,000 square feet of space, the ware being dried by exhaust steam and radiation from kilns. The slips are conducted from the fourth floor to the second by gravity, in pipes, and air is supplied to bottom of barrel in such a manner as to agitate the mixture continually. The slip as needed is furnished the sprayers through pipes.

Three dryers, 18 by 60 feet, are used for drying ware on the second floor.... The ware is burned in twenty kilns, sixteen of which are the old-style updraft terra cotta kiln, with network of flues in the bottom. Four other kilns, 12 to 14 feet in diameter, downdraft in construction, are used. Two are 20 feet and two are 24 feet in diameter. From eighteen to twenty tons of ware can be placed in each kiln, the ware being burned to cone 7 with oil at 4¾ cents per gallon. The kilns have six, eight, and twelve burners, and require seventy-five to ninety hours in the burning for small kilns and 120 hours for the large. New Jersey clays are used in making the body of their ware, and are ground and prepared in the usual way, automatic mixing and measuring machinery being used.

From this plant we rode back to the Fiske office, brushed up as well as we could, and went to the Battery, where we bought hat guards and prepared for a windy ride on the boat to Coney Island.[108]

As this lengthy account continues, the integration of work and play among those in the terra-cotta industry becomes apparent: "This delightful boatride was followed by a swim at Coney Island. Here Prof. Orton won fame as a high diver, while Parker Fiske showed his skill under water. The amusement places were next in line. Herford Hope took a trip through the barrel that was disastrous; Cermack cracked one of the concave mirrors smiling into it.... Full of merriment, we sat down to a splendid shore dinner at Feltman's, Prof. Orton winning the clam-eating contest with a safe 40."[109]

Although the terra-cotta business involved a vast amount of work, there was also an opportunity for a little bit of play. There are many hints at the humor and whimsy of the industry—the "Monkey-Business" of the terra-cotta business (*Figure 55*). These include cartoons, banquet menus, poems, and "after-hours pieces" (often clay pots or mementos), which were created to celebrate the fraternity of those who survived the tribulations of this remarkable material—"fired mud"—as one "lifer" in the industry called it [110] (*Figures 56, 57*).

FIG. 57. *This amusing program card from the Architectural Modelers Guild of Perth Amboy was reproduced in* Pencil Points, *July 1925.*

Part Three

Color and

Iconography in

Terra-Cotta

Architecture

Terra-cotta ornament from the facade of the Ambassador Apartments at 30 Daniel Low Terrace, Staten Island, New York (also see Figure 130.)

"WHEN ARCHITECTS FOUND THAT THEIR IDEAS COULD BE SO thoroughly expressed in form by the clayworker, they, like the Athenians of old, began 'to look for something new.' Having obtained form, why not ask for color?"[111] Stanford White and Bruce Price both expressed interest in using colored glazes, but most American architects were decidedly timid about adopting polychrome terra cotta. While production processes had not yet been perfected, there is no doubt that at the turn of the twentieth century, manufacturers were more successful in making glazed terra cotta than architects were in using it.

In antiquity, terra cotta had been applied to buildings almost exclusively for its sculptural qualities. Its plasticity allowed for the vigorously modeled designs found in Greece and Italy. But historically, brightly colored terra cotta had not been used extensively for architectural purposes. Its introduction forced American architects to address new design challenges.

Although architects in the United States were comfortable with the role of "modelers of buildings," their training offered little information about how to become "colorers of buildings." A 1912 article in *American Architect* noted that with so few historical precedents available, architects "required knowledge and pluck to lay out the scheme of, say—a projecting string course overhanging cornice, pediment, tympanum or even cap in brilliant colors—colors that shall sing as jewels in the distance! And the average architect is scared at the result, when confronted with the samples in his office. It takes years of experience to tell just how such detail will count in the facade when seen at an elevation of two, three or four hundred feet on a dull day!"[112]

The Charlesgate, a residential hotel on Beacon Street in Boston dating from 1891, was one of the earliest buildings in the United States to use glazed polychrome architectural terra cotta (*Figure 58*). Designed by Boston architect J. Pickering Putnam, it has two formal entrances and an arcaded lobby, all of which are covered in glazed terra cotta and tile.[113] This successful effort was the result of an unusual collaboration between the terra-cotta and tile industries. Atwood and Grueby, a partnership formed in 1891, was responsible for the greenish-blue glaze while the Boston Terra Cotta Company manufactured the clay forms.[114] Eugene Atwood and William Grueby had both worked for the renowned Low Art Tile Works in Chelsea, Massachusetts, where a wide variety of glazes were routinely applied to the company's tiles.

FIG. 58. *Atwood and Grueby produced the ceramic ornament for The Charlesgate, designed in 1891 by J. Pickering Putnam.*

Their innovative work was praised in *The Brickbuilder* in 1892: "Only a very few of our terra cotta manufacturers have made any serious attempt to produce and market glazed and enameled terra cottas, but the marked success which has followed the efforts of such firms as Atwood and Grueby, of Boston, has abundantly demonstrated, not only the artistic practicality of such treatment of the material, but also its commercial desirability."[115] Prior to this time, architectural ceramics with colored glazes was usually limited to tiled walls and floors. White glazed brick was used in courtyards and air shafts, applications that took advantage of the reflective property of glaze.[116] It was generally assumed that glazes could not be used without a second firing, which was prohibitively expensive and time-consuming. But in the 1890s, investigations into suitable once-fired glazes were undertaken by several companies (*Figure 59*). The

TOP: FIG. 59. *Herbert Wills Moore, Sr. in his chemistry laboratory at the Atlantic Terra Cotta Company, Tottenville, Staten Island, circa 1920.*

ABOVE: FIG. 60. *A view of the Perth Amboy Terra Cotta Company with its forty-eight-foot-high muffle kilns, circa 1904.*

American Terra Cotta Company produced red, blue, green-yellow, and flesh-colored glazes for the Bowlby Building, a music hall constructed in St. Paul, Minnesota in 1895. Cass Gilbert, the architect, was praised for his "daring attempt to relieve the dullness of street architecture and...the result is as successful as the attempt was daring."[117] Much of the credit was given to the company's chemist, W. Griffen, who "made the subject of enamels, glazes and vitrifiable colors a life study."[118]

The Perth Amboy Terra Cotta Company joined in this effort in 1894 when it employed T. C. Booth, a member of a family of English potters, who settled in Tarrytown, New York. He developed glazes that could be applied successfully to unfired terra cotta, thus requiring only one firing.[119] In the Architectural League of New York exhibit of 1896, a small storefront of highly colored terra cotta was displayed.[120] The intention, no doubt, was to impress architects and the public with the possibilities of this material for exterior designs. Although no company was

mentioned in connection with this display, it may well have been the result of Booth's early experimentation for the Perth Amboy Terra Cotta Company (*Figure 60*).

In 1898 the Perth Amboy company manufactured terra cotta that used the colored glazes developed by Booth. Shades of pink, yellow, brown, gray, and white were ordered by architects Harding & Gooch for a café in the Dun Building at Broadway and Reade Street in New York.[121] Since a successful formula for matte surfaces had not yet been developed, most of the glazes were lightly sandblasted to remove their glossy outer layer.[122] Although this building was demolished in the late 1970s, some of the same glazes made by the Perth Amboy Terra Cotta Company can be seen on the Broadway-Chambers Building, located only one block south at Broadway and Chambers Street, designed by Cass Gilbert in 1899–1900 (*Figure 61*).[123]

Immediately following the success of the Dun Building, William Hall (owner of the Perth Amboy Terra Cotta Company) decided to actively promote further use of polychrome terra cotta. He was eager to erect a complete facade of glazed ornament so that architects would have something more extensive to examine. His opportunity arose with an order that was received in April 1898 from the Kelly & McAlinden hardware store in Perth Amboy. The building, originally designed by Newark architect Harry King, was to have simple, light gray terra cotta without ornamental detail. Hall proposed to the owners that he would have the elevation redesigned, providing them with a "matt [sic] finished glazed front, elaborately ornamented and artistically picked out in color, for the same money."[124] This plan suited the store owners, and Hall asked Boston architect Thomas Fox to create a facade in polychrome terra cotta which would evoke the early Italian Renaissance. Fox's design was carefully executed, and Hall's mission succeeded by stimulating an interest among architects in polychrome terra cotta (*Figure 62*).

This seemingly obscure two-story hardware store played an influential role in Stanford White's decision to use polychrome terra cotta for Madison Square Presbyterian Church. White had long been a champion of terra cotta. As early as 1882, he

FIG. 63. *Madison Square Presbyterian Church, completed in 1906 by McKim, Mead & White, was the most well-known early example of colored, glazed terra cotta in New York City.*

had requested that the Perth Amboy Terra Cotta Company develop special colored claybodies for several of his buildings, and he was a frequent visitor to their New Jersey factory. "He would come into the modeling studio like a whirlwind," one observer recalled. "Mr. White was familiar with all the modelers and called them by Italian names, which might have been their own but never were."[125]

White's examination of the Kelly & McAlinden storefront at the Architectural League exhibit in 1898 led him to specify "brilliant polychrome" for his Madison Square Presbyterian Church (demolished), completed in 1906.[126] He wanted specific colors developed, including a golden yellow and a bright green, which were to be used side-by-side on the same pieces. While both glazes, tested on separate units of terra cotta, had proved perfectly reliable in test kilns, when the first large order for the church was fired it became evident that the two colors in close proximity produced surprisingly different results. "Only a slight indication of the yellow selected could be seen on the very highlights of the ornament, and that…shade deepened until almost brown at its meeting with the green. The factory immediately sent for Mr. White, who luckily was delighted with the accidental effect. The change was due to vaporization of the green glaze in the burning, the gases affecting the yellow and altering the expected reaction."[127]

Madison Square Presbyterian Church became the first well-known New York City building to use colored glazes, and its critical success was, in part, the result of this accident (*Figure 63*). If the fired glazes had been as strong as White had originally intended, the response to the color on this building might have been rather different.

FIG. 64. *Powerful glaze colors can be seen on the sculptural swags and ram's heads near the top of the Beaver Building, 1903–4.*

In White's completed design, the church's Corinthian capitals were cream-colored with a blue background. Pale green, rose, and yellow were used in the terra-cotta moldings, panels, rosettes, and figures in high relief, and the color scheme culminated in the low dome of green and yellow tiles.[128] As lively as the building sounds in this description, many articles praised the architect for his reserved and dignified palette. One critic commented, "In this respect [use of color] it seems to me that this building is deserving of the highest praise, and it is, I believe, destined to exercise a most salutary influence in restraining those whose fondness for color contrast might easily lead them to the other extreme."[129]

In contrast to the positive response that White's church received, the polychrome terra cotta of Clinton & Russell's Beaver Building at 82–92 Beaver Street, constructed in 1903–4 in Lower Manhattan, received mixed reviews. To critic Herbert Croly writing in 1906, the brightness of the green, cream, and russet glazes of this polychrome skyscraper was praiseworthy, but he deemed the excessive attention to the upper stories "inappropriate decoration for the top stories of a tall building"(*Figure 64*).[130] Approval of the building was expressed in *Architects' and Builders' Magazine,* which stated that "The effect of this more or less brilliant color treatment is to strengthen the outline of the building and make it a notable feature amid its

RIGHT: FIG. 65. *The Fifty-Second Police Precinct Station in the Bronx, 1904–6, combines blue and yellow terra cotta, patterned brick, and a red tile roof.*

ABOVE: FIG. 66. *Cass Gilbert's West Street Building, 1905–7, incorporates extensive polychrome terra-cotta ornament on the upper floors.*

surroundings."[131] Recent critics of the Beaver Building have considered it to be an excellent design solution in which each section of the tripartite (base-shaft-capital) scheme is differentiated by color and materials.[132]

Other early-twentieth-century architects also turned to color. The 52nd Police Precinct Station House, erected in 1904–6 in the Bronx, relies on strong yellow and blue glazes in combination with the patterned-brick facade and tile roof. Responding to the semirural setting of that era, the architects Stoughton & Stoughton created a romantic Tuscan-villa-inspired composition (*Figure 65*). Another very successful structure using color was Cass Gilbert's West Street Building, constructed during the years 1905–7. This was Gilbert's third building to feature polychrome ornament, and

FIG. 67. *A detail of several remarkable terra-cotta motifs used in the facade of St. Ambrose Church, 1905–6, in Brooklyn.*

it is one of the most beautiful and significant early-twentieth-century skyscrapers in New York. The structure is clad in Gothic-inspired terra-cotta ornament massed in a strongly vertical manner. The building's white terra-cotta shaft consists of clustered piers and colonettes that rise from the fourth to the fifteenth floor. Yellow, blue, pink, green, and black glazed details are abundant on the upper floors, which are crowned with a dramatic copper mansard roof (*Figure 66*). When constructed, it was near the Hudson River shoreline and created a powerful presence. With the development of Battery Park City, built on land-fill, the West Street Building is no longer at the water's edge. However, it has recently become visible once again because of dramatic night lighting.

As the use of bright glazes continued during the first decade of the twentieth century, a better understanding of scale and massing for maximum color effect developed. St. Ambrose Church in Brooklyn, designed in 1905–6 by George H. Streeton, used yellow and green glazes similar to those specified by White for Madison Square Presbyterian Church (*Figure 67*). Unfortunately, on both of these churches the background colors of some of the ornamentation were lost because the shadow cast by the ornament was darker than the color. In addition, some of the background areas were too small to be visible from the street. Architects began to realize that dark

FIG. 68. *Herts & Tallant received much praise for the success of their brightly colored glazes on the Brooklyn Academy of Music, completed in 1908.*

colors tended to accentuate the tones of the modeling rather than producing a colorful effect.

Attention was paid to solving these problems in two subsequent buildings: the 1907–8 Brooklyn Academy of Music by Herts & Tallant and the Brooklyn Masonic Temple, built one year later to the plans of Lord & Hewlett and Pell & Corbett (*Figures 68, 69*). The ornament on both was designed with broad fields of color, which provided a more satisfying color experience from a distance. These trendsetting buildings led to widespread agreement that glazed and colored terra cotta created unique polychromatic effects, and critic Herbert Croly felt that if terra cotta were properly employed, its "great future success…in this country will be associated with its enlarged and improved use as highly colored material."[133]

In 1907, the *New York Times* reported a growing interest in the use of color in architecture: "Color Spreads Glories on City's Architecture." Just below was a slightly smaller headline that declared "New Decorative Movement, Employing Colored Glazed Terra Cotta and Faience, Promises to Make Manhattan Blaze With the Loveliness of Azure and Ruby, Topaz and Gold." The article praised recent achievements including the colored terra cotta by Heins & La Farge in the 1904 New York City Subway and in the 1903 Lion House at the Bronx Zoo.[134] Highly visible colored ornament was felt to be especially valuable in helping to popularize

FIG. 69. *The wide range of glaze colors used to ornament the Brooklyn Masonic Temple, 1908–9, helps make this one of Brooklyn's most striking terra-cotta buildings.*

American architecture. Emphatic color detailing in settings frequented by the average citizen was expected to result in attention to good design and a more widespread awareness of architecture.

The success of glazed ceramics in new construction helped architects to recognize that "the art movement in which pottery takes the place of stone is one of the most important of the day in their profession. More, some of them prophesy that this painting of buildings has merely begun, and that a general transformation will result from it."[135] Emphasis was also placed on the "artistic" quality of clay products in a 1910 advertisement that glowingly described the soft tone, beautiful texture, and varied shades of matte glazes. "It [the glaze] is *not* 'absolutely uniform in color,' therefore it does *not* present the monotonous appearance of painted metal so disappointing to the artistic architect."[136]

Highlighting an increased use of polychrome terra cotta, a 1911 article in *The Brickbuilder* predicted that "a general sentiment will be forming as to the suitability of these materials for exterior design. If this follows the course of most similar manifestations excessive indulgence will be succeeded by nausea and subsequent distaste. This would be unfortunate. The material possesses so much intrinsic merit as a medium of architectural expression,...that we have, I believe, good grounds for expecting a gradual, wholesome and beautiful development of its possibilities."[137]

Chapter 8

Glazes that

Simulate Stone

OPTIMISTIC PREDICTIONS OF THE WIDESPREAD USE OF COLored glazes must have been heartening to manufacturers, who had long been faced with demands for unglazed terra cotta that replicated other materials, as on the 1851–53 Trinity Building, where it imitated brownstone. By the 1890s, as numerous claybodies including brown, red, gray, yellow, and tan became available, unglazed terra cotta began to be appreciated for its own distinctive qualities.[138] However, at the turn of the century, as new glaze textures and finishes became available, once again the issue of terra cotta as a substitute material arose. This time *glazed* terra cotta was produced to intentionally mimic other building materials.

The architectural journals of the period repeatedly stressed that stone and terra cotta were very different materials serving distinct functions. Nonetheless, practitioners frequently used them interchangeably. Since terra cotta was cheaper than stone, it was often chosen as an economic substitute and was made to look as much like stone as possible. Company advertisements boasted of new glazes with names like "Granitex" that replicated the texture and color of granite and other natural stones. The terminology used by the terra-cotta industry in trade journals and correspondence did nothing to help distinguish terra cotta from stone. On the contrary, it seems to have exacerbated matters. A letter sent to the New York Architectural Terra Cotta Company in 1916 by an architect in Fall River, Massachusetts inquired, "I would like to know if you manufacture a terra cotta product to imitate granite...." and a notation on the page from the company indicates that three "granite samples" were sent.[139] The following year, an advertisement in *Architectural Record* claimed that "Federal Granite Terra Cotta is the logical material for domes on buildings where natural granite is used below"[140] (*Figure 70*). This practice continued, and in 1948 even the president of the Federal Seaboard Terra Cotta Corporation described terra cotta as "a piece of granite that's been made in two weeks."[141]

Ironically, while the production of wares that imitated stone continued to thrive, the industry recognized that long-term survival revolved around a product that was unique and therefore would not be affected by competition. Although some feared that a cement composition might eventually compete with terra cotta as cladding for tall buildings, most were confident that nothing could ever replace strongly colored terra-cotta glazes.[142] In 1900, Herman Carl Mueller, an innovative figure in the American terra-cotta and tile industries, addressed a meeting of the

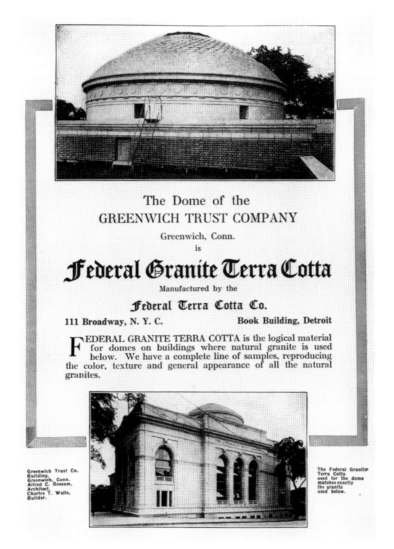

The Dome of the
GREENWICH TRUST COMPANY
Greenwich, Conn.
is

𝔉ederal 𝔊ranite 𝔗erra 𝔠otta
Manufactured by the
𝔉ederal 𝔗erra 𝔠otta 𝔠o.
111 Broadway, N. Y. C.   Book Building, Detroit

FEDERAL GRANITE TERRA COTTA is the logical material
for domes on buildings where natural granite is used
below. We have a complete line of samples, reproducing
the color, texture and general appearance of all the natural
granites.

Greenwich Trust Co.
Building,
Greenwich, Conn.
Alfred C. Bossam,
Architect,
Charles T. Walls,
Builder.

The Federal Granite
Terra Cotta
used for the dome
matches exactly
the granite
used below.

FIG. 70. *This 1917 advertisement in* Architectural Record *recommends a product called Federal Granite Terra Cotta and states that the company has "a complete line of samples, reproducing the color, texture and general appearance of all the natural granites."*

American Ceramic Society. He presented a paper titled "The Independence of Burned Clay as a Decorative Building Material" that stated:

> We may, therefore, say that clay offers its colors to the painter and its plastic conditions to the sculptor to make the most of it; that the unlimited range of color, and the pliable condition of the plastic material, affords the highest artistic conception and execution of the work and therefore places the clay in the front rank as an independent decorative material. It is certainly in the interest of the claymaker to induce the architect to become familiar with polychrome architecture because this is the field where nobody can follow us.[143]

The terra-cotta industry never successfully developed a marketing strategy to propel polychrome architecture into prominence. Rather, brightly glazed terra cotta remained the exception, not the rule. Approximately seventy-five percent of all terra cotta that was produced was intentionally made to look like stone. In 1913, the complex glaze finishes that were available were described in *The Brickbuilder.* The article reported that the upper stories of one of New York's newest structures were intended to be made of a terra cotta that simulated granite. When the samples were submitted for this unnamed building, they proved to be an excellent match, "even to the

FIG. 71. *The glaze on the terra-cotta ornament at 81 Irving Place, New York City, has a textured, matte surface that resembles stone.*

patches of quartz and mica." However, plans to use this finish were abandoned because of "their ethical influence on architects, builders and manufacturers....If manufacturers were tempted to push this clever making of facsimiles to its uttermost, a material really beautiful in itself would soon lose its identity."[144]

Thousands of New York buildings relied on terra cotta with granite- and limestone-like finishes to provide a sense of opulence when builders found that natural stone was too expensive. An interesting example is an apartment house at 81 Irving Place that combines terra cotta glazed to resemble stone and dark, rough cut brick. Designed by George Pelham and constructed in 1929–30, the sculpted grotesques are easily mistaken for stone (*Figure 71*). Terra-cotta manufacturers were obligated to produce a "false" material—one for which they obtained no credit and which offered no unique qualities besides saving the client money. They disliked this situation and were convinced that the "field of its [terra cotta's] application is large enough without trying to make it, as we might say 'play second fiddle' while it can most successfully play first."[145]

However, the historical validity of imitation was expressed in *The Brickbuilder* of 1913, which concluded that all building materials from ancient times have been "so frankly imitated from each other,...[that] we begin to criticize the Egyptians for cutting and painting their stone columns to imitate bundles of reeds tied together...."[146] No resolution to the question of imitation was reached, but architecture and ceramics professionals argued about it for years. A particularly heated debate took place in 1922 among members of the American Ceramic Society. The Society's journal printed a lecture by Professor Gabriel Ferrand addressing this question, and the discussion that followed. Fritz Wagner, former president of the National Terra Cotta Society and vice-president of the Northwestern Terra Cotta

FIG. 72. *The material in the upper portion of this photograph is terra cotta, coated with a granite-like glaze, while the lower portion is the actual granite base of the building, at 148–50 Madison Avenue, New York City.*

Company, commented that "simply because a combination of colors has been placed together before [to imitate stone], was no reason why, when we made up a model sample of various colors, they should be called imitation."[147] Albert Sheffield, secretary of the American Terra Cotta Company, agreed with this view and added: "Instead of matching granite we have given our samples a mottled effect that was never seen in granite and could not be had in granite.... [W]e have been asked very seldom to imitate granite, instead, the architect will ask for a mottled combination that will harmonize with his building."[148] But Professor Ferrand again asked the

The added vigor of

COLOR

can best be given

MODERN ORNAMENT

by designing in

TERRA COTTA

NATIONAL TERRA COTTA SOCIETY
230 PARK AVENUE · · NEW YORK, N. Y.

FIG. 73. *The glaze surface on the top and bottom borders of this terra-cotta unit is an excellent example of the mottled effect that the Pulsichrometer could produce.*

question: "Is it not wrong though, to continue the use of certain kinds of terra cotta to deceive and make people believe that stone or some other material has been used instead?"[149] (*Figure 72*)

There was general agreement that the "false use" of terra cotta was wrong, but clearly there was no agreement about just what constituted "false use." The exchange quoted above centered around the "mottled effect" that had gained popularity after the invention of the Pulsichrometer (*Figure 73*). The traditional method of applying glazes to produce a mottled effect required experienced workers who could instinctively apply the correct pressure on the hoses carrying the slip or glaze; consistency was difficult and labor costs were high with this procedure. The Pulsichrometer sprayed varied glazes or slips at a controlled pressure and speed so that the same color combinations and textured surfaces could be repeated. This method allowed two to six different colors to be applied in one operation. The minute particles that were sprayed resulted in variations of shade and depth of tone, preventing the monotony

FIG. 74. *The malleability of clay is very apparent in this elaborately sculpted covered jar manufactured by the Federal Terra Cotta Company as a gift for special clients.*

of flat colors. This invention resulted in the widespread use of glaze effects that were considered by some to be too imitative of stone.

On the other hand, Fred Ortman, a ceramic engineer with a great deal of experience, viewed the Pulsichrometer as a positive innovation. He considered it "a distinct addition to the terra cotta industry in that it has enhanced the architect's opinion of the material by making it possible for him to secure effects not hitherto available.... There is no doubt that Pulsichrome material appeals to a large majority of the architects who are anxious to develop something new in color and texture effects for building facades."[150]

Using terra cotta to simulate marble, limestone, or granite offered little opportunity to highlight color and plasticity, two of its unique qualities (*Figure 74*). As a result, it proved difficult for the industry to create and maintain a separate identity which could have helped protect terra cotta from direct competition with newly developing materials.

LEFT: FIGS. 75 A & B. *George Pelham designed both of these examples of terra-cotta ornament for New York apartment buildings constructed in 1928–29. Although they were modeled within weeks of each other by Isadore Kaplan at the New York Architectural Terra Cotta Company, they represent architectural styles from extremely different periods.*

BELOW, LEFT: FIG. 76. *This massive grotesque, which weighs nearly a ton, was designed by Starrett & Van Vleck for the Farmers Loan & Trust Company Building at 475 Fifth Avenue, New York City.*

BELOW, RIGHT: FIG. 78. *This detail of the Woolworth Building provides a close look at yellow and blue glazed terra cotta, which usually goes unnoticed on this fifty-two-story tower.*

W ILLIAM H. POWELL, PRESIDENT OF ATLANTIC TERRA COTTA company, writing in 1909 for the *Real Estate Record and Builders Guide*, firmly believed that "polychrome terra cotta is beyond the pale of competition. No other building material can, for the same practical or aesthetic purposes, be used, since no other building material possesses the same qualities or answers the same ends."[151] If Powell's comment had been as accurate as it was assertive, historic sections of our cities would be far more dazzling and colorful than they are today. Long-lasting exterior color—the truly unique characteristic of terra cotta—should have resulted in a far broader use of polychrome. Where are the rainbows of brilliant ornament that were anticipated? The answer is complex and requires a careful investigation of the evolving styles in architecture in the early twentieth century.

Despite some notable examples, colorful terra cotta remained an exception rather than the rule throughout the teens and early 1920s. During these years, a strong dichotomy existed between the revival of historic styles and the exploration of new decorative forms. This is underscored by historic photographs owned by the daughter of Isadore Kaplan, a modeler for the New York Architectural Terra Cotta Company. Trained as a sculptor at Cooper Union, he worked for the company from the early 1920s until 1931. The photographs show details that Kaplan modeled for the company. Since they each have job numbers that correspond to existing records, the specific buildings, dates, and architects can be identified.[152] Two examples from 1928–29, which are only fourteen order numbers apart (and thus were probably modeled within a week or two of each other) are a detail from an apartment house at 944 Park Avenue and a detail from an apartment building of similar size at 30 Beekman Place[153] (*Figure 75 a and b*). The latter harks back to traditional architectural styles, while the former has more contemporary Art Deco characteristics.

Buildings that relied on historical styles often used bold, sculpted relief rather than colored glazes to provide surface ornamentation (*Figure 76*). Perhaps New York's most famous structure of this type is the 1910–13 Woolworth Building, clad almost entirely in Gothic-inspired terra cotta[154] (*Figure 77*). The overall appearance of the Woolworth Building is that of a uniformly white surface. Although Cass Gilbert introduced blue, green, tan, and yellow glazes into many architectural details, his intention was to heighten the surface articulation rather than to create a colorful facade (*Figure 78*). Following the completion of the Woolworth, the popularity of monochromatic cladding increased greatly.

FIG. 77. *The Woolworth Building, 1910–13, surrounded by six of New York's other notable terra-cotta towers. From the top left, counterclockwise: the Broadway Chambers Building, the Times Tower, the Flatiron Building, the West Street Building, Liberty Tower, and the Chanin Building.*

The Woolworth, the world's tallest terra-cotta building, was acknowledged as a masterpiece of American architecture. But its impact on building design was, in many ways, regrettable. It created such an indelible image, complained one critic in 1926, that "the first impulse of a draftsman, facing the problem of the tall unit, is often to start with the Woolworth tradition and perpetuate whatever need of Gothic may still be his. It has seriously held back the development of fresh design."[155] So, too, did it hold back the increased use of polychrome terra cotta. This newest symbol of progress in architecture was perceived to be monochromatic.

In 1912, the Art Nouveau architect Hector Guimard traveled from France to visit New York City. "I came to see if it is possible for the lofty buildings you have here to be

pleasing to the eye as well as useful in housing their many business tenants," he wrote, predicting that the Woolworth Building "will be pleasing and harmonious, but some of the other high office buildings, notably the Singer building, emphasize too much the idea of decoration as they ascend. The lines of a lofty building, it seems to me should be less pronounced and decorative the higher they go, and should finally blend or be lost in the sky."[156] Guimard urged American architects to share ideas and to remember that little is gained from copying the past. He believed that a distinctive type of American architecture would soon evolve. Other architects who agreed with him appreciated the wide range of possibilities that terra cotta offered. They found the material flexible enough to meet the dramatic change that was occurring in American architecture. One architect, Ely Jacques Kahn, called this new direction in architecture the "New York Style," acknowledging that it "also contained something essentially American."[157] An article in *Buildings and Building Management* titled "Clothing Modern Skyscrapers" described this modern form as "a proud and soaring thing that eloquently voices the spirit of today. Instead of imitating masonry, it frankly expresses the steel frame. The facing, while it must, of course, be fireproof and must safeguard the framework and be pleasing in appearance, does not pretend to have any structural value."[158]

The introduction of steel caused a profound shift in the character of building design. The comparative thinness of the walls of steel-frame buildings helped force architects to move out beyond the need for stylistic precedent. Kahn wrote that "as buildings have reached toward the sky they have sloughed off, by a natural process of refinement, the cluttered detail of the past. The tall building has shed the old-fashioned cornice.... Decoration becomes a far more precious thing than a collection of dead leaves, swags, bull's heads and cartouches. It becomes a means of enriching the surface with a play of light and shade, voids and solids."[159]

ABOVE, LEFT: FIG. 79. *Model of the eighteen-foot-high frieze from the Chanin Building at the Atlantic Terra Cotta Company factory, before it was cut and used to make plaster molds. Terra cotta was frequently used in the brick skyscrapers of the late 1920s to provide texture, color, and surface variation.*

ABOVE: FIG. 80 A & B. *Two views of the terra-cotta frieze being installed on the Chanin Building, 122 East 42nd Street, New York City.*

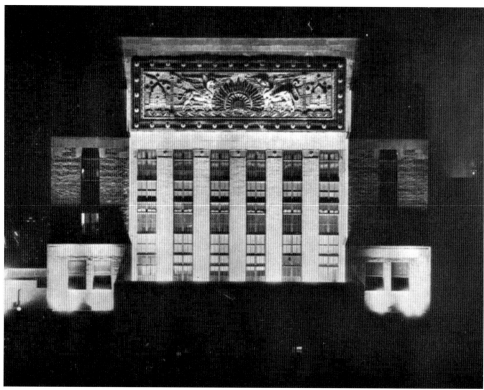

ABOVE: FIG. 81. *Although the Chanin Building frieze consists of many terra-cotta units, the joints between the irregular pieces work into the overall design and are nearly invisible.*

RIGHT: FIG. 82. *The top of the Fred F. French Building was floodlit from a setback below, reversing the normal shadows and accentuating the low relief.*

The cladding for skyscrapers, although constructed of masonry, was flatter than the sculpted ornament of the past. This offered the architect an opportunity to investigate polychrome ornament, sculpture in low relief, and the use of materials with interesting surface textures (*Figure 79*). Brick and terra cotta were recommended for the outer surface of the building, to enclose the framework. They were supplied in units small enough to be easily handled. In addition, fired clay was valued for its fire-resistant qualities (*Figures 80a and b, 81*).

New York's first zoning law, passed in 1916, changed the rules for skyscraper design. The law limited the height and bulk of tall buildings, thus protecting air,

FIG. 83. *The National Terra Cotta Society created advertisements of this type, which were intended to promote the use of color in architecture.*

light, and property rights. These restrictions, which required setbacks, led to innovative buildings composed of stepped masses often visible from a distance. Architects placed great emphasis on the shaping of these towers, creating silhouettes that were recognizable at a glance. A number of skyscrapers with distinctive towers were lit at night to increase their dramatic impact, including Cross & Cross's RCA Victor Building, H. Douglas Ives and Sloan & Robertson's Fred F. French Building, and Sloan & Robertson's Chanin Building. Floodlights were easily placed in the setbacks, and the reflective terra cotta used on the tops of these three buildings (as well as many others) aided in providing excellent night illumination[160] (*Figure 82*).

Night lighting of skyscrapers and the ornamental possibilities for sculpted forms in low relief were featured in the promotional literature of the National Terra Cotta Society during the 1920s. Efforts were made to inspire architects, reminding them that "the ceramic industry holds within the nature of its material unexploited resources of the most promising nature"[161] (*Figure 83*).

ABOVE: FIG. 84. *A detail of the boldly colored terra-cotta motifs on the upper stories of 2 Park Avenue, New York City, by Ely Jacques Kahn.*

RIGHT: FIG. 85. *Kahn's terra-cotta patterning is an integral part of the ornamental surface of this 1927 office building.*

Chapter 10

Innovative Color

(1927-1931)

Ely Jacques Kahn

ELY JACQUES KAHN USED TERRA COTTA IN A MORE CONSIS-
tently personal style than any other architect since Louis Sullivan.
Whether creating brightly colored or quietly monochromatic schemes, his
rigor and handling of the material as well as his overall building designs
were very unusual. The highly stylized floral motifs and chevrons typical of
the period did not influence his strong sense of geometry and repetition. The rich
color and texture found in his remarkable buildings are unique.

Kahn's Two Park Avenue, completed in 1927, is a freestanding brick structure
with two differing terra-cotta designs. A linear band with ochre glaze was used on the
lower setback, which provided a visual transition between the tan brick and the
brighter glazed terra cotta above. Strongly colored matte glazes of red, green, and
blue geometric designs, capped by a band of glossy black terra cotta, were used at the
higher level (*Figure 84*). The coloring was so important to Kahn that he consulted
with Leon Solon, a friend and expert in architectural color. They agreed that full-
scale plaster models should be painted to match the proposed glaze colors and set on
the roof of the unfinished building. This experiment provided some idea of how the
colors would change under differing light conditions and what their impact would
be from street level (since the terra cotta did not begin until the seventeenth story).
Even having taken this precaution, Solon reported that they had miscalculated the
effect of the black terra cotta. Because its shiny surface reflected more daylight than
expected, it did not appear to be as dark as had originally been intended.[162]

The main difference between the decorative details on Two Park Avenue and
those of more traditional buildings was that Kahn's ornament became an integral
part of the facade rather than being merely applied to the surface. Kahn considered
the mass as a whole, dividing it into areas of colored terra cotta appropriately scaled
to the building. The architectural detail was created by varying the surfaces of the
terra cotta so that shadows or holes would be produced by their projections or
recesses. This method was like cutting into a block of clay and allowing the cuts to
enliven the surface (*Figure 85*). It differs from traditional decoration because the
blocks of carved color are part of the building plane, not mere encrustation. A 1933
article titled "Recent Developments in Architectural Ceramics" praised Two Park
Avenue, stating that the "resulting forms were more appropriate to terra cotta than

OPPOSITE: FIG. 86. *This striking polychrome facade, also designed by Kahn in 1927, is located at 42 West 39th Street, New York City.*

LEFT: FIG. 87. *The gold-lustered ornament on 261 Fifth Avenue is an outstanding example of the eye-catching potential of metallic glazes.*

had been designed for some time. Kahn has continued his studies of the use of color in architecture and has pioneered in this field."[163]

Although the clients did not voice objections to Kahn's plans for Two Park Avenue, they quietly hired architect Raymond Hood to review the project before giving final permission to proceed. Kahn reports in his unpublished biography that his friend Hood reassured the clients that they were "in perfect hands."[164] Another hurdle that Kahn faced was a meeting with S. W. Straus, head of the loan company that was financing the construction. Kahn wrote that Straus had asked, "Why did I affront the clients and endanger my own career by such outrageous experiment?" Straus continued by suggesting that "walls of brick were of little interest where marble could be used." He offered to increase the loan so that the building could have "the extravagances he was accustomed to see."[165]

Kahn's efforts did not go unnoticed. Lewis Mumford wrote that Two Park Avenue "strikes the boldest and clearest note among all our recent achievements in skyscraper architecture."[166] Because of its height and setting, the building can easily be appreciated from many midtown locations. Fortunately, this continues to be true today, because most of the surrounding buildings are of a similar size and the facade is now strikingly lit at night.

In contrast, another building by Kahn, 42 West 39th Street (also built in 1927) is easy to overlook. It is tucked into a narrow mid-block location on a busy commercial street. The building has a series of handsome brick setbacks and a very unusual geometric terra-cotta border that uses pink, buff, and black matte glazes (*Figure 86*). The structure Kahn designed at 261 Fifth Avenue, New York City, built in 1928–29, is a corner building that also combines brick and terra cotta. It has two distinct and powerful areas of ornament, one at the street level and the other at the roofline. The lower design is very complex and makes excellent use of gold luster glaze (*Figure 87*). The upper area combines red, blue, and beige terra cotta in a striking and abstract pattern with similarities to motifs used by Frank Lloyd Wright.

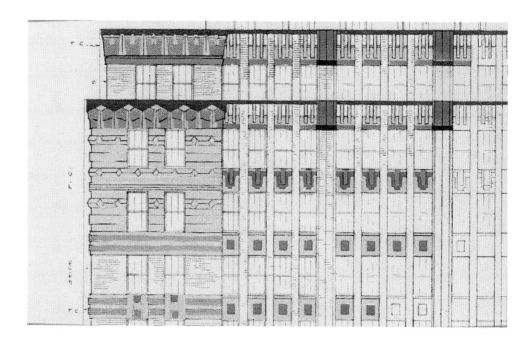

FIG. 88. *A small section of the color study for 2 Park Avenue, which was published in* Architectural Record, *April 1928.*

Kahn commented on the difficulty of trying to introduce color into architecture: "I had been trying for some time to incorporate color as I tried in Two Park Avenue. There were few efforts to find color beyond the few I had found possible. The architectural press was not interested, for illustrations in color—to begin with—were costly. I had done a building on 28th and Fifth Avenue [261]—several on 39th between Fifth and Sixth avenues—not important but continued efforts to find color masses."[167] Although Kahn complained about the architectural press, black-and-white photographs of his buildings were included in frequent articles about his work and many of his own essays were published. In addition, a color drawing showing the upper stories of Two Park Avenue was the frontispiece of the April 1928 issue of *Architectural Record* (*Figure 88*).

Few of Kahn's other buildings used polychrome glazes, but his fascination with terra cotta continued. In 1930, he wrote a brief promotional pamphlet edited by Leon Solon, titled "Terra Cotta Futurities." Published by the Federal Seaboard Terra Cotta Corporation, it pictured four "directional textures" designed by Kahn. His text made clear his hopes for the material: "The use of clay products in the entire field of surface texture and color is yet to be scratched. The development of surface, the opportunity for light refraction, the beauty of low tones in delicate relief, will come with increasing interest to the designer as he appreciates their possibilities."[168]

By the end of the 1920s, Kahn's work became increasingly simplified and abstract. His elevations no longer used bright colors, but relied instead on pattern created by tonal variation. He enlivened the building surfaces, organized the fenestration, and created a coherent facade. Kahn combined glazed brick and terra cotta with natural stone in these new, ever-taller structures—120 Wall Street, built in 1930–31, rose to thirty-three stories. One of his last projects, also completed in 1931, was the Squibb Building on Fifth Avenue and 57th Street, New York City. Kahn, who had been involved with many of the decorative details, expressed pleasure at its outcome. The entrance and lobby were richly ornamented with painted murals and bronze elevator doors from models in clay by Kahn. In contrast, the exterior was a study in monochrome. White marble was employed on the lower portion, with

FIG. 89. *Overview of the top of the Fred F. French Building at 551 Fifth Avenue, New York City, among the city's most fanciful skyscrapers.*

glazed white brick on the upper floors and geometrically patterned terra-cotta spandrels. Mumford wrote that if Two Park Avenue was Kahn's "most successful attempt to use warm tones and full color in a large office building, perhaps the most satisfying essay in color to be seen in New York so far," then the Squibb Building "shows equally what can be done in pure white."[169]

Color in Tall Buildings

After Kahn's striking examples, it might seem natural to expect that color in architecture would have been widely explored in new tall buildings. However, this was not to be the case. The Fred F. French Building, constructed in 1926–27, is the most noteworthy of the few efforts during the late 1920s. Located at 551 Fifth Avenue, this brick office building incorporated large areas of black and red terra-cotta ornament into the facade at each setback and in all of the window spandrels. Numerous colors, including gold and vermilion, were used in the extensive murals on the north and south elevations of the tower. These polychrome panels of terra cotta represent Progress (in the form of a rising sun), flanked by two winged griffins, Integrity and Watchfulness. On both sides of these panels are golden beehives, the symbols of Thrift and Industry (*Figure 89*). Smaller panels on the east and west elevations show "Mercury spreading the message of the French plan."[170] The building was recently restored, and deteriorated terra cotta was replaced with new units manufactured by Boston Valley Terra Cotta. Although the intricacy of this rich iconography is difficult to fully appreciate without the aid of binoculars, the building provides a fine example of architectural color executed in a traditional style (*Figure 90*).

In 1927, the same year the French Building was completed, New York was the site of the Architectural and Allied Arts Exposition. One of the events associated

RIGHT: FIG. 90. *The French Building mural showing Progress (in the form of a rising sun flanked by winged griffins), Integrity, and Watchfulness.*

BELOW: FIG. 92. *This bold combination of red brick and blue glazed terra cotta can be seen on the Bowker Building, 1926–27, located at 419 Park Avenue.*

FIG. 91. *Mecca Temple, 1922–24, located at 131 West 55th Street, New York City, is an excellent example of the successful use of color throughout a building's facade.*

with the exposition was a forum that discussed "modernistic views on color schemes in skyscrapers."[171] Participants included architects Raymond Hood and Julian Clarence Levi, architectural colorist Leon Solon, and sculptor John Gregory. Hood predicted that whole buildings "will eventually have a distinct color. To color only the architectural embellishments and a few outstanding cornices and facades will appear like the rose decorations on a woman's white dress. They are hardly notice-able. It is best for the whole building to be of one color, harmonized, of course, by some medium or break at a suitable distance from its base, the top, or the top only....New York of the future, I believe, will consist of gayly colored buildings"[172] (*Figures 91, 92*).

Solon strongly disagreed with Hood, saying: "The tendency will be to color the embellishments. It is not likely that one color will predominate in the entire building. One must be careful of the visibility of his colors. The areas of ornamenta-tion will be carefully judged so the color will carry for a good distance....Our

FIG. 93. *This simple brick structure at 1220 Broadway, New York City, is very noticeable because of the splashes of color that the terra-cotta ornament provides.*

future buildings will provide many freaks in color, but others will show a stroke of genius"[173] (*Figure 93*). Leon Solon, an English trained ceramist, had immigrated to the United States in 1909. His years of experience at Minton China Works had enabled him to work successfully for many American ceramics companies including the American Encaustic Tiling Company (1912–28), the Mosaic Tile Company (1930), Ravenna Mosaics (1932), the Robertson Tile Company (1929–30), and the United States Quarry Tile Company (1932). His varied skills also had led him to work as an illustrator, portrait painter, ceramic designer, architectural critic, and colorist.[174]

Hood's 1927 prediction that a whole building of one color was to be part of New York's future came to fruition in just four years. In 1930–31 his McGraw-Hill Building, a potent blue-green "proto jukebox" rose thirty-seven stories on the western edge of 42nd Street (*Figure 94*). This streamlined structure was the first New York skyscraper to express Modernist ideas. Its strong horizontal bands of metal-framed windows alternate with panels of turquoise terra-cotta cladding. The impact of the building depends on overall color, not on ornamental details and patterning. The use of Art Deco elements at the entrance and the eleven-foot-high letters (originally painted white with an orange stripe, now painted out), spelling out "McGRAW-HILL" at the top of the buiding, provided relief from the austerity of the design (*Figure 95*). The smooth terra-cotta ashlar blocks offered none of the decorative

ABOVE, LEFT: FIG. 94. *The streamlined McGraw-Hill Building at 330 West 42nd Street is clad in turquoise terra cotta.*

LEFT: FIG. 95. *The eleven-foot-high letters on the top of this building provide decorative relief from Hood's otherwise austere design.*

ABOVE, RIGHT: FIG. 96. *A wall section of the McGraw-Hill Building showing how the terra-cotta ashlar blocks were installed.*

qualities that had come to be expected of terra cotta. The demands of Art Deco for a new flatter look led to the introduction of machine-extruded terra-cotta units. These pieces, compared to the earlier, more sculptural ones, required less hand labor and could be produced more economically.

During construction of the McGraw-Hill Building an interesting problem developed. The blue-green glaze, which was chosen to blend with the color of the sky, varied from firing to firing because of the uneven heat and atmosphere in the large kilns. This was the largest application of terra-cotta ashlar blocks ever tried, and the Federal Seaboard Terra Cotta Corporation could not afford, at the contract price, to impose strict color-quality controls on the product. A young designer in Hood's office, Bob Carson, set up an office in a window across the street from the McGraw-Hill Building site. As each block was installed, it was faced in his direction, and by prearranged signals, he would indicate where along the wall that particular block could be placed to keep an overall harmonious color blend[175] (*Figure 96*). After completion, the building met with harsh criticism, particularly of the color, which was pronounced "perfectly awful" by the owner James McGraw. He claimed he must have been sick on the day he chose it! It has come to be appreciated by a great many New Yorkers, and eventually even James McGraw grew to like it. He implied that the color was connected with his Irish ancestry.[176]

Hood's interest in the placement of his buildings on their sites led him to consider massing as a first priority. He claimed that "to worry about the details of something as huge as a modern office building is like wondering what sort of a lace shawl you should hang on an elephant."[177] Hood was, however, particularly concerned with the clean appearance of the McGraw-Hill's facade, and chose his surface material accordingly. As a designer, Hood was thinking in terms of clean lines, but a critic for *The New Yorker* addressed another aspect of cleanliness: "What do they do with that building when it gets dirty? It's all green tile. They don't paint it. They don't sandblast it. They just run over the whole thing with a damp cloth the way you would the inside of a bathroom."[178]

The McGraw-Hill was the only New York skyscraper selected by Henry-Russell Hitchcock and Philip Johnson for inclusion in the Museum of Modern Art's 1932 exhibition, *The International Style*. They felt that of the skyscrapers in New York, it came closest to achieving the true aesthetic expression of the enclosed steel cage. The *New York Herald Tribune* reported, "The colored skyscraper is here. On the fringe of Times Square the steel framework of a large structure is rapidly being sheathed in color. Not content with the mere introduction of colored ornament, this building shows large surfaces of sea-blue green, the glaze of the terra cotta lending additional interest by giving the walls the appearance of shimmering satin. By its bold approach this new skyscraper constitutes an answer to the question of using color in exterior architecture."[179]

Two years later, in 1933, an article titled "Recent Developments in Architectural Ceramics" stated, not surprisingly, that both Ely Jacques Kahn and Cass Gilbert were opposed to using color as an embellishment for tall buildings. "The experience which Mr. Kahn has gathered from actual construction makes him feel definitely that spotting a building with little masses [of color] is more dangerous and less important than the use of monochrome, whether it be brick or terra cotta. It is largely for this reason that during the past few years he has experimented with a number of buildings in white with a certain amount of black brick or terra cotta as a contrast."[180]

Opinions differed over the aesthetic questions concerning color in architecture, but the issue itself remained a vital one for the future of the American terra-cotta industry. As skyscrapers reached new heights, color became increasingly difficult to see and consequently its impact diminished. A new wave of extremely tall buildings brought with it the abolition of the cornice and much decorative detail. Thomas Tallmadge's 1930 article in *Architectural Forum* ridiculed the use of decoration. "Classic columns, chased out of New York's thoroughfares, are reported to have taken a final refuge on the top story of the New York Central Building (*Figure 97*), where they hang by the skin of their acanthus leaves. The unprecedented forms that the skyscraper has taken are so lovely, as witnessed in the proposed Empire State Building in New York, that we have no reason or desire to look immediately for further change."[181] With ornament nearly eliminated, the tonal massing of the building form became the predominant design concern.

Terra cotta was certainly able to serve a valuable function in the taller towers that continued to be constructed until the early 1930s, but in such buildings the role of polychrome disappeared. Skyscrapers such as the 1927–29 Chanin Building at 122 East 42nd Street, the 1928–29 Fuller Building at 41 East 57th Street, and the 1929–31 RCA

FIG. 98. *A web of undulating terra cotta creates an eccentric roofline on the RCA Victor Building at 570 Lexington Avenue, New York City.*

Victor Building at 570 Lexington Avenue each used terra cotta in a distinctive way, but the emphasis was on tonality or linear pattern, and not on color (*Figures 98, 99*). An advertisement that featured a photo of the Fuller Building claimed: "Jet black glazed Atlantic Terra Cotta emphasizes the design of a building as *italics* emphasize text. Features that would be blurred by distance can be clearly defined with Terra Cotta."[182]

Under construction during the years 1931–39, Rockefeller Center used no colored terra-cotta ornament.[183] This is particularly mystifying since Leon Solon had been hired as the architectural colorist for the overall project. Surely the terra-cotta industry

FIG. 99. *The overscaled black and white terra cotta on the Fuller Building at 41 East 57th Street, New York City is visible from a great distance.*

would have been eager for a chance to participate in such a momentous project, where color highlighted some facades in the form of glass mosaics and enamels on metal.[184] If terra cotta had been an integral part of the Rockefeller Center color scheme, the business outlook for that industry probably would have improved in the years that followed. Such a visible use of the material would have been a potent reminder that terra cotta was versatile enough to serve the needs of modern design. Comments from correspondence by Aslag Eskesen, a shareholder and future president of the Federal Seaboard Terra Cotta Corporation, reinforce this impression. "Business in the 1930s would, in any event, not have been so good as in the 1920s, because of the building depression, but, at some point in this period, I feel, the terra cotta *industry* got lost in the shuffle...twenty years ago it was seldom necessary to explain to anybody what architectural terra cotta was used for, but now it generally is...it seems to me, the postwar leaders of that [the building] profession will probably be the men who were the youngsters of the depression years when the uses of terra cotta began to be overlooked—for example, Radio City."[185] This 1944 letter stands in stark contrast to a remark made in the 1909 *Real Estate Record and Builders Guide*: "Architectural Faience has come to be so extensively used in recent years that no description of it as a material is necessary to the circle whose interest will be reached by the recent issue...."[186] Over a period of thirty-five years, a great many things had changed.

ABOVE: FIG. 100. *Terra-cotta bas relief over the entrance to the Prudential Savings Bank, 1946–48, located at 1954 Flatbush Avenue, Brooklyn, New York. The* Ridgewood Times *(2 October 1958) described it as "a tribute to thousands of mothers who, throughout the history of this community have taught their children the habit of thrift."*

RIGHT: FIG. 101. *The terra-cotta-clad Lyceum Theater, 1902–3, New York's oldest theater still used for legitimate productions, was designed by Herts & Tallant.*

Color

WHILE THE SKYSCRAPER STRETCHED HIGHER AND HIGHER,
sharply curtailing the role of color, widespread use of polychrome terra
cotta increased in many other more modestly scaled building types,
including hotels, garages, restaurant chains, banks, museums, and commercial structures (*Figure 100*). In New York, three of the most popular
kinds of structures to feature terra cotta were theaters, apartment houses, and
schools. Brightly glazed ornament was introduced as an emphatic element in entry-
ways, street level facades, cornices, and lobbies. An enormous range of glazes was
developed including metallic lusters, vivid yellows, cobalt blues, and fashionable Art
Deco shades such as lime green, lavender, and ebony.

The firm of Herts & Tallant was highly regarded for the great theaters it
designed. Two of their theaters in the Times Square area are the Lyceum Theater, the
oldest New York theater still used for legitimate productions, and the New
Amsterdam Theater, both built in 1902–03 (*Figure 101*). The facade of the Lyceum
Theater is dominated by powerful French Baroque columns and a series of arched
windows. Large terra-cotta heads are placed above the columns and a pair of masks is
set between the two end columns on each side of the building. The New Amsterdam
has a remarkable interior that includes the finest existing examples of terra-cotta
newel posts and staircase banisters, designed by the Norwegian architect Thorbjorn
Bassoe and executed by the Perth Amboy Terra Cotta Company. Their rich green
glaze and intricate Art Nouveau styling make them unique (*Figures 102, 103*). The
1982 demolition of one of Herts & Tallant's finest theaters, the Helen Hayes Theater
(originally Folies-Bergere Theater), built in 1911, served as a catalyst for the landmark
designation of many theaters in the Times Square area.[187]

Movie houses as well as legitimate theaters were frequently built with elaborate
terra-cotta-clad facades. The glamour and exotic fantasy of the theater made it an
ideal building type in which to exploit the rich color and imagery so readily achieved
in terra cotta. Thomas Lamb, an important theater architect, designed the Regent
Theater, New York City's most significant surviving early movie palace. Dating from
1912–13, the facade was executed in polychrome terra cotta incorporating Italian and
Northern European Renaissance motifs. The following year, Lamb combined
mythological iconography, theatrical references, and icons for the owner, William

ABOVE, LEFT: FIG. 102. *This terra-cotta newel post is part of the staircase inside the New Amsterdam Theater, 214 West 42nd Street, New York City.*

ABOVE, RIGHT: FIG. 103. *These heads, which represent characters from Shakespeare, are also from the New Amsterdam Theater staircase and were modeled by Thorbjorn Bassoe.*

RIGHT: FIG. 104. *Thomas Lamb used a rich variety of terra-cotta imagery on the Audubon Ballroom, completed in 1912.*

Fox—in the form of fox heads—on the Audubon Ballroom at 165th Street and Broadway (which became infamous as the place where Malcolm X was assassinated in 1965) (*Figures 104, 105*). His 1930 Loew's Theater at Broadway and 175th Street covers nearly an entire city block. The "Magnificent Moroccan" decor is beautifully exe-

RIGHT: FIG. 107. *The seahorse motifs found on the lower portion of 340 East 57th Street, New York City are glazed in black and silver. "The black will always retain its richness and the silver, being real silver on a platinum base, fired into the clay, will never tarnish and will never need polishing."* (Atlantic Terra Cotta, *June 1932*)

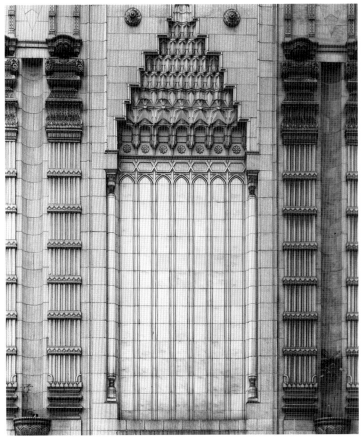

cuted in a white glazed terra cotta. The building is currently the home of Reverend Ike's United Church (*Figure 106*).

Apartment buildings were designed in surprisingly varied architectural styles. Some of the earlier ones, from 1905 to 1915, were completely clad in traditional terra-cotta ornament, while many from the late 1920s used streamlined geometric designs at the entrances and rooflines (*Figure 107*). The architectural firm of Harde & Short was responsible for three early and unusual apartment buildings. In 1906, they designed 45 East 66th Street, a brick and terra-cotta structure with rich Gothic ornament that was echoed several years later in the Studio Building at 44 West 77th Street. During this same time (1907–09), their Alwyn Court at 182 West 58th Street

ABOVE, LEFT: FIG. 105. *One portion of the Audubon Ballroom facade, 3940–60 Broadway, New York City, was recently restored, and the Neptune's head, which had been missing for many years, was re-created.*

ABOVE, RIGHT: FIG. 106. *Exotic terra-cotta patterning on Thomas Lamb's Loew's Theater, at Broadway and 175th Street.*

RIGHT: FIG. 108. *Alwyn Court is clad in elaborate terra-cotta detailing, although the base of the building, including the arch with salamanders, is stone.*

BELOW: FIG. 110. *This geometric Deco band is incorporated into handsome brickwork on the Blums' apartment building at 235 East 22nd Street, New York City.*

FIG. 109. *An exuberant terra-cotta border on George & Edward Blum's apartment house at 210 East 68th Street, New York City.*

was constructed. It is New York's most elaborate terra-cotta-clad apartment building, richly encrusted in French Renaissance details (*Figure 108*). During the years 1910 to 1930, two brothers, George & Edward Blum, designed a striking group of apartment houses that combined unusual facade detailing. Their buildings are superbly embellished with complex brick patterning and highlighted by exceptional motifs in terra cotta and art tile. Several of their apartment houses from the 1920s incorporate unusual geometric Art Deco ornament. Two such examples that also illustrate their unusual color sensibility and handling of brick are 210 East 68th Street, constructed in 1928–29, and 235 East 22nd Street, of the following year (*Figures 109, 110*).

Emery Roth produced dozens of brick apartment buildings that were highlighted by glazed terra cotta. One of his earliest buildings that uses polychrome terra cotta and patterned brick is 45 Tiemann Place, constructed in 1909 (*Figure 111*). The building also has a remarkable tiled lobby executed by the Hartford Faience Company. Two additional polychrome apartment buildings are 39 Fifth Avenue,

ABOVE, LEFT: FIG. 111. *These details are from one of Emery Roth's earliest polychrome facades, located at 45 Tiemann Place, New York City.*

ABOVE, RIGHT: FIG. 112. *The terra-cotta-clad Manhattan Trade School for Girls, 1915–19, is located at 127 East 22nd Street, New York City.*

RIGHT: FIG. 113. *A vintage postcard showing the Collegiate Gothic terra-cotta-clad buildings at the City University of New York.*

built in 1922, and 24 Fifth Avenue, completed several years later in 1925–26. Particularly notable is Roth's 1929–30 apartment house, the San Remo, at 145–46 Central Park West, which changed the skyline of the Upper West Side with its twin towers encrusted in richly sculpted terra-cotta ornament.

Many public buildings, including libraries, post offices, and museums, consistently used terra cotta. Educational institutions in New York provide particularly impressive examples of such structures. The architect C. B. J. Snyder is responsible for many of New York City's most exceptional public high schools. Two of his early Gothic Collegiate buildings that used brick and terra-cotta trim are Morris High School in the Bronx, constructed in 1900–04, and Erasmus Hall High School in

FIG. 114. *This 1928 building on the Yeshiva University campus combines exotic terra-cotta motifs with metallic lusters and colorful glazes.*

Brooklyn, begun in 1905. In 1915, he designed a white terra-cotta-clad structure for the Manhattan Trade School for Girls. The school is unusual because it combines traditional Collegiate Gothic styling with a loft-like structure (*Figure 112*). Such a blend was appropriate for a building where students were trained in trades related to the garment industry, which was located primarily in lofts. At the cornice, above the tenth-story windows, is a series of figures holding books and tools. In the mid-1980s, some of the gargoyles and cornice units were replaced with new terra-cotta pieces made by Gladding, McBean & Company.

The first buildings for the uptown site of the City University of New York, located on Convent Avenue between 138–140th Streets, were constructed during the years 1903 to 1908. George B. Post designed them in a Collegiate Gothic style using dark Manhattan schist excavated from the site, with white terra-cotta trim that created a dynamic contrast. The early campus consisted of six buildings and three terra-cotta arched gateways (*Figure 113*). All are designated landmarks, and a restoration plan is in place that will ensure their continued preservation. Baskerville Hall (originally the Chemistry Building) has been impressively restored with more than one million dollars worth of newly manufactured terra cotta, also from Gladding, McBean & Company. In contrast to the traditional design of the education buildings mentioned above, the main building on the Yeshiva University campus in Upper Manhattan uses a different stylistic approach. Designed in 1928 by Charles Meyers, this exotic structure with domes, towers, and turrets is covered with polychrome terra-cotta ornament and metallic luster glazes and would be very much at home in the Middle East (*Figure 114*).

TOP, LEFT: FIG. 115. *This rondel of Neptune, dripping with seaweed, is one of many sea-related terra-cotta designs used on Child's Restaurant, located on the boardwalk at Coney Island, New York City.*

TOP, RIGHT: FIG. 116. *A color rendering of window ornaments at Child's Restaurant, published in the National Terra Cotta Society's* Color in Architecture, *1924.*

ABOVE: FIG. 117. *Throughout the United States, "moderne" terra-cotta designs can still be found on chain stores such as Kress and Woolworth.*

Iconography

In addition to reflecting different architectural styles, terra-cotta ornament frequently incorporated references to a building's owner or its purpose. Through these symbols, terra cotta helped to capture the wit and humor of many owners and architects and has added whimsy to many of New York's buildings.

Varied commercial ventures sought to express their identities through the buildings that housed them. Eating establishments like Child's, a chain of family restaurants with an elaborate dining facility on the Coney Island Boardwalk, used many marine images, including rondels of Neptune with seaweed in his beard and ornamental bands featuring seahorses, snails and crabs (*Figures 115, 116*). Horn & Hardart Automats chose to use a more generalized type of imagery for both interior and exterior detailing—stylized floral motifs in a deco mode. For many years automats were a common sight in New York City, but few of the buildings are still standing. The finest remaining example, with brightly colored deco motifs, dates from 1930 and is located at Broadway and 104th Street. Chain stores such as Kress, Woolworth, Lerner Shops and A. S. Beck designed simple, monochromatic but recognizable buildings, which appeared on main streets throughout the country. A neat, clean, streamlined look with slight deco stylization was characteristic of these three companies (*Figure 117*).

Iconographic references can be found in the ornament of buildings that served more generic functions. Parking garages often had steering wheels and automobile tires (sometimes with wings); theaters displayed masks portraying comedy and tragedy in a wide variety of styles (*Figure 118*); and concert halls such as Carnegie Hall and the Brooklyn Academy of Music have musical imagery such as instruments or notes incorporated into their decoration (*Figures 119, 120*). A more complex reasoning exists behind Cass Gilbert's use of salamanders on the Woolworth Building:

SUN WILDER'S SOME LIKE IT HOT AND
DUDLEY MOORE IN ARTHUR
MON DAY FOR NIGHT AND WOMAN NEXT DOOR

LEFT: FIG. 118. *This rondel, portraying Comedy and Tragedy, is the focal point of the Metro Theater, 1932–33, at 2624–2626 Broadway, New York City.*

BELOW, LEFT: FIG. 120. *A detail of the musical imagery created in terra cotta on the Brooklyn Academy of Music, 30 Lafayette Avenue, Brooklyn, New York.*

BELOW, RIGHT: FIG. 121. *Athletes playing golf, baseball, and tennis are integrated into the terra-cotta doorways of the 63rd Street YMCA, New York City, by Dwight J. Baum.*

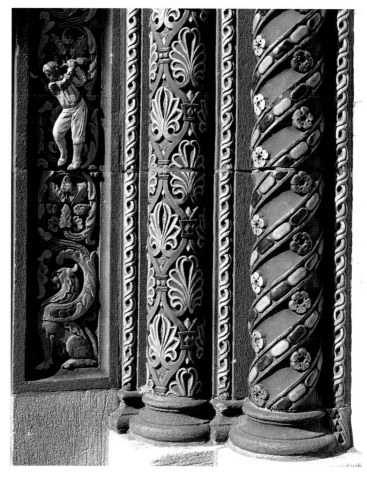

FIG. 119. *Carnegie Hall was originally called the Music Hall, and the initials "MH" are easily visible in the terra-cotta decorations near the entrance of the building.*

"The salamander in the ancient world, believed to be unharmed by fire, became the symbol in alchemy for the transmutation of base metals into gold. Gilbert used the lizardlike creature in the Woolworth Building as the symbol for the transmutation of iron and clay into steel and terra cotta, the two basic structural components of the building."[188] Other architects used salamanders as well; they can be found on a number of New York's terra-cotta buildings including Liberty Tower and Alwyn Court.

Some of New York's most fanciful examples of iconography were unique. The 63rd Street YMCA by Dwight J. Baum, built in 1929–30, has portals that portray athletic figures in multicolored glazed terra cotta including a baseball player, a tennis player, and a golfer (*Figure 121*). Above the entry of an apartment house at 32 Washington Square West by Deutsch & Schneider, built in 1925, are terra-cotta rondels with the busts of George and Martha Washington. The facade of the International Tailoring Company by Starrett & Van Vleck, completed in 1921, includes white terra-cotta figures sitting cross-legged, sewing and wearing half-spectacles (possessing an uncanny likeness to Ben Franklin) (*Figure 122*). One New York skyscraper ornamented with many symbolic images is the former RCA Victor Building, now the General Electric Building (*see Figure 98*). It incorporates terra-cotta radio waves, stylized human figures, and phonograph needles into the exterior facade and top of the building. Perhaps the most unusual architecture-related imagery can be found on the Park Plaza, an Art Deco apartment house at 1005 Jerome Avenue by Horace Ginsbern. A terra-cotta panel depicts a kneeling figure symbolically offering a skyscraper before an architectural altar on which the Parthenon is placed! Additional polychrome plaques showing the city skyline and the rising sun also embellish this 1929–31 building (*Figures 123, 124*).

This selection from the city's wonderful architectural heritage makes it obvious that colored terra-cotta ornament thrived in structures where it could be readily seen

FIG. 122. *This cross-legged tailor on the International Tailoring Company facade, located at 111 Fourth Avenue, New York City, is one example of terra-cotta iconography.*

from street level. Modestly scaled buildings meant moderate-size job orders for the terra-cotta companies, not the vast tonnage used in the cladding of the McGraw-Hill Building. One wonders what the New York skyline might have looked like had Raymond Hood's turquoise skyscraper begun a fashion for brilliantly colored towers. *Color in Architecture*, a 1924 publication by the National Terra Cotta Society, featured a variety of drawings of imaginary colored skyscrapers (*Figure 125*). The aim of the book was "to contribute in some small measure to the splendid results which await a confident employment of more color in our contemporary architecture."[189] Although this goal was admirably achieved in a wide array of buildings from the 1920s and 1930s, the manufacturers never produced the volume of work that they had hoped would materialize from the construction of tall buildings. The terra-cotta industry faced a difficult struggle to gain recognition in the changing architectural climate of the decades that followed.

RIGHT: FIG. 123. *One panel on the Park Plaza Apartments at 1005 Jerome Avenue, Bronx, New York, displays a kneeling figure symbolically offering a skyscraper before an architectural altar on which the Parthenon is placed.*

BELOW: FIG. 124. *The rich polychrome imagery on the Park Plaza Apartments combines unique details with conventional Art Deco motifs such as stylized fountains.*

OPPOSITE: FIG. 125. *This visionary drawing, published in the 1924* Color in Architecture, *is described as a "suggestion for color treatment of a skyscraper conforming in design to the requirements of recent municipal zoning laws."*

Part Four

The Business of

Terra Cotta

Detail from "Group Photo of 26 of America's Finest Buildings," a montage of buildings that are faced or trimmed with Northwestern terra cotta. (Northwestern Terra Cotta Company catalogue, November 1937)

Chapter 12

A NDREW CARNEGIE'S OBSERVATION THAT "MORE BIG CON-
tracts are closed over nuts and wine than across a desk" was not lost on
leaders of the terra-cotta industry. They recognized the value of orga-
nized business efforts as early as 1886. At that time, the First Brown
Association was formed by five East Coast companies: the New York
Architectural Terra Cotta Company, the Perth Amboy Terra Cotta Company, the H.
A. Lewis Architectural Terra Cotta Works, the Boston Terra Cotta Company and the
A. Hall Terra Cotta Company.[190] After several successful years, a serious problem
developed when the association lost three important jobs to the recently formed
Philadelphia company, Stephens, Conkling and Armstrong. Since the association
could not entice this newcomer to join it, the decision was made to disband. Plans to
formulate the Second Brown Association began in 1889 and were consummated in
1893. By this time the New York and Perth Amboy companies had succeeded in controlling the East Coast competition (including Stephens, Conkling and Armstrong)
through leases, purchases, and partial mergers.[191]

This association remained active for the next few years and was followed by
a succession of ill-fated organizations that came and went over the next quarter-
century.[192] Most lasted for a number of years, although the Terra Cotta Manufacturers Association survived for only two years, from 1902 to 1904. A plaintive
verdict for this group, arrived at by Walter Geer of the New York Architectural Terra
Cotta Company, was that of an epitaph found on a child's tombstone: "If I was so
soon to be done for, I wonder what I was begun for."[193]

The need for a broad-based organization that could serve the interests of manufacturers across the country was finally met in 1911, when Geer corresponded with all
of the manufacturers to obtain support for a national organization. The replies were
so positive that a meeting was arranged in Chicago. Fifteen companies sent representatives to this initial gathering in December, 1911 (five more sent pledges of support),
which led to the formation of the National Terra Cotta Society. Twenty companies
were charter members, and by 1920 that number had risen to twenty-four.[194] The
goals of this powerful and long-lived organization were:

1. To encourage uniform standards and high quality in the production of terra-cotta
products. [Inspiration sprang, in particular, from the great Della Robbias of
fifteenth-century Italy.]

SUGGESTIONS FOR COLOR EF TERRA CO

SUGGESTIONS FOR COLOR EFFECTS IN TERRA COTTA

A   B

FIG. 126A & B. *This color wheel was another creation of the National Terra Cotta Society. The cutout areas (which appear white in image A) can be colored in various ways (see image B) by moving the wheel behind the architectural drawing.*

2. To spread knowledge of the merits of terra cotta through advertising, publications, and trade literature. [Handsomely executed books and brochures included: "Standard Terra Cotta Construction" (1914, 1927), "Color in Architecture" (1924), and a series on specific building types: "The School," "The Bank," "The Store," "The Theater," and "The Garage."] (*Figure 126a and b*)

3. To cooperate in a study of important technical problems. [During the 1920s, the Society worked with the United States Bureau of Standards to investigate the causes of terra-cotta failure and to standardize testing procedures. Lengthy reports were printed as a result of this work.]

4. To advance mutual business interests and review business practices without controlling prices or suppressing competition. [Evidently this strategy was imperfect, since the Society was fined for price-fixing in 1918 under the Sherman Anti-Trust Law.[195]]

5. To promote friendship and communication among the member companies. [This seems not to have included social interactions, since relatives were excluded from the Society conventions.[196]]

The scientific exploration of terra-cotta manufacture was one of the most vital aspects of the National Terra Cotta Society. This effort was enhanced by the active participation of the American Ceramic Society. A Terra Cotta Division of the Society, created in 1919, developed a plan to study fifteen separate subjects, which covered nearly all phases of the manufacturing process. Collaboration on these studies also extended to a number of ceramics departments at state universities, including the two earliest, Ohio State University (founded in 1895 under the leadership of Edward Orton, Jr.) and Alfred University's New York State College of Clay-Working and Ceramics (founded in 1900 with Charles Fergus Binns as director).

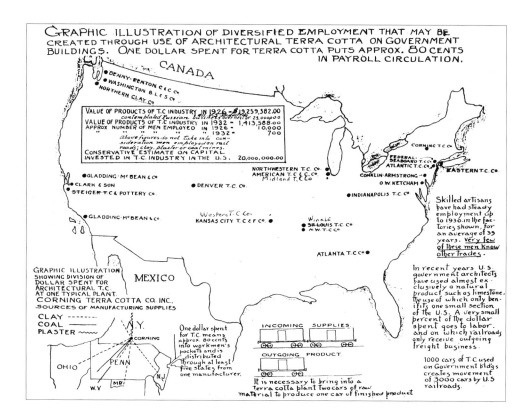

FIG. 127. *This chart was prepared by the National Terra Cotta Society, circa 1932.*

Surely the most visible work of the Society was promotional campaigns, including publications, advertisements in magazines, educational programs, films, and direct mail. In order to maximize these activities, yearly records were compiled which included the number of terra-cotta jobs, the tonnage and dollar amounts involved, the architectural firms, the type of structures, and the geographic distribution (*Figure 127*). The numbers were quite dramatic and provided a valuable record of economic trends in the industry. During 1912, for example, 1,309 of the 6,000 registered architectural firms in the nation used terra cotta for at least one project.[197] Statistics of this type served as a reference point for major public-relations efforts, including one that began in 1930. In that campaign, questionnaires were sent out to 8,250 architectural offices requesting an indication of interest in receiving the National Terra Cotta Society literature. More than 5,000 positive responses were received.[198] Little did architects know the extent of the marketing effort that was planned.

The Society decided to begin a "high grade personal promotion" over an extended period of time.[199] This included a comprehensive strategy to send out twenty-eight mailings per year providing information on standard construction detailing of terra cotta, contemporary ornament available in terra cotta, and reprints from professional journals. It was calculated that architectural firms would receive the National Terra Cotta Society mail on an average of once every ten working days throughout the year!

Member companies were reminded that photographs were their most powerful ammunition and that "we cannot shoot unless you furnish the ammunition."[200] Strong recommendations were made to follow these frequent mailings with personal meetings arranged by the companies or their local sales representatives.

This information blitz was in response to the decreasing use of terra cotta and the consequent closing of companies. In 1929, the number of active the National

FIG. 128. *The 1928 Richfield Oil Building in Los Angeles used terra-cotta cladding to create an elegant, modern skyscraper (demolished).*

Terra Cotta Society members was down to eighteen and the following year it dropped further to thirteen.[201] The severity of the situation is reflected in a memo circulated by the Society: "We find a consistent drop in the use of terra cotta per $1 of construction regardless of yearly fluctuation in total tonnage, which reaches its present low at a level but slightly over ⅓ of the 1923 ratio. This emphasizes once again the need for drastic action on the part of the industry."[202]

These intensive efforts proved futile during the depressed economy of the 1930s, and by 1933 the membership had dropped to eleven companies. The following year brought an end to the Society. A succession of other organizations sprang up after 1934: the National Terra Cotta Manufacturers Association (mid-1930s), the Architectural Terra Cotta Institute (1947–1959), the Structural Clay Products Institute (mid-1960s), and the Brick Institute of America, which is still in existence.

The end of the National Terra Cotta Society went hand-in-hand with the dwindling use of terra cotta. E. V. Eskesen, president of the Federal Seaboard Terra Cotta Corporation, succinctly described one of the factors which had led to this situation: "The dream of the modern architect is to build houses entirely out of metal, glass, and cement.... In this construction, brick, tile, or terra cotta has no place."[203] These new mass-produced materials were economical and readily available in very large quantities. Terra-cotta production was labor-intensive and thus more expensive. It took longer to get to the job site, because it required time for hand finishing, proper

RIGHT: FIG. 129. *Sculptor C. Paul Jennewein standing next to a model of the pediment for the Philadelphia Museum of Art.*

OPPOSITE: FIG. 130. *The metallic finish in combination with brilliant glaze colors creates a stunning entry to the Ambassador Apartments at 30 Daniel Low Terrace, Staten Island, New York.*

drying and firing, and packing for shipment. Ironically, in the 1880s *economy* had been one of the selling points of terra cotta. It had been easy to produce in comparison to the laboriously carved stone ornament that it replaced.

The Bauhaus School, as well as European modernists who moved to the United States such as Ludwig Mies van der Rohe and Walter Gropius, had a significant influence on American architects and architectural education. The introduction of the International Style, which featured a clean, unadorned aesthetic, led to a further diminution of interest in terra cotta. Architects believed that the sleekness of transparent glass and metal could not be achieved with terra cotta. They ignored the fact that large extruded terra-cotta units, suitable for the unornamented lines and flatter motifs of the prevailing architectural taste, were already being manufactured. The black and gold Richfield Oil Building in Los Angeles, designed in 1928 by Morgan, Walls & Clements (*Figure 128*); the turquoise blue Eastern and Columbia Outfitting Building, also in Los Angeles, designed by Claude Beelman in 1929; and the thirty-seven-story blue-green McGraw-Hill Building in New York (*see Figures 94–96*) are several fine examples of the streamlined look that could be created by using terra-cotta cladding. However, it was difficult to shake the perception of many architects that terra cotta was an old-fashioned material.

One colossal project completed 1932 was the seventy-foot-long pediment for the Philadelphia Museum of Art. It contained thirteen free-standing figures in brilliant polychrome and gold glazes. Although it was an exercise in antiquity, looking backward toward Greece rather than forward toward modern architecture, it received widespread publicity. The design and execution, requiring more than two years, were the result of a collaboration between the sculptor C. Paul Jennewein, the colorist Leon Solon and the architects C. C. Zantzinger, Horace Trumbauer, and C. L. Borie, Jr. (*Figure 129*). The Atlantic Terra Cotta Company was so proud of the completed work that it erected the pediment at the plant and invited the public to a viewing. They announced this display in an advertisement in the pages of *Ceramic Age*. Following this event the magazine ran a brief commentary, titled "Architectural Terra Cotta Lesson for Thousands." In it they lauded the aggressive tactics of the manufac-

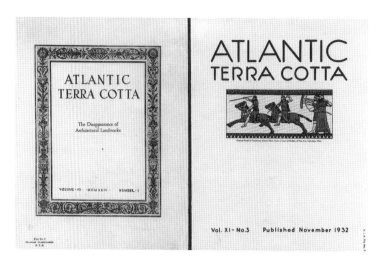

turer that "brought throngs from far and near to see what is regarded as a milestone in terra cotta art...."[204]

That same year, an issue of *The Clay-Worker* noted that terra cotta was being overlooked and that "substitute materials were gaining a strong foothold" in recent New York construction projects. However, with the assumption that building activities would soon return to normal, it was expected that terra-cotta manufacturers would again be "placing themselves in position to meet competition to better advantage."[205]

Terra-cotta companies were confident that the industry could adapt to changing needs. "With the development of new architectural styles and the creating of an entirely new system of ornament, metals are playing a part of constantly increasing importance in architecture (*Figure 130*). Metallic finishes are attained easily in terra cotta, with textures which would be difficult or impossible to obtain in the metals themselves. This is important for effective flood-lighting. Furthermore, expensive polishing is not needed to maintain their brilliance. Simple washing with soap and water will restore the metallic surfaces to seeming newness."[206] An obvious attempt to be more modern can be seen in the updated cover of the Atlantic Terra Cotta Company's 1932 bulletin, which replaced its traditional motifs and typography with a very contemporary design (*Figure 131*). The desire to participate in current architectural trends was reflected by the fact that terra-cotta manufacturers endorsed the frequent stripping of ornamental terra cotta from old facades and their resurfacing with a newly made ceramic veneer (*Figure 132*). Gladding, McBean & Company praised this action when it occurred on the Pacific Mutual Building, which used a new grayish-buff ceramic veneer in its "renovation" effort. The company expressed pleasure in terra cotta's adaptability to new styles and praised the architects: "Practical modernity is the keynote of the remodeled Pacific Mutual Building in Los Angeles' busiest street corner. The simple severity of its new lines, the modern feeling of its fluted piers, and the ground-floor shops…are a threefold tribute to the creative genius of its architects."[207] They further suggested that "modernizing old buildings means new work for architects; greater values for real estate. Refacing with terra cotta or tile means a modern and up-to-date exterior."[208]

Surviving companies were eagerly looking for ways to adapt to the changing times. "Some Products Which Might Be Made in Terra Cotta Plants as Now Built or With Slight Changes in Present Equipment,"[209] a document compiled in 1935, made this painfully evident. Written by H. G. Schurecht, a Professor of Ceramics at Alfred University, it was divided into three major sections. The "Exterior Ware" portion suggested the manufacture of such disparate items as golf tees, caskets, bleacher seats, and septic tanks! Several other ideas from the "Interior Ware" section were freestanding terra-cotta furniture, radiator covers, and terra-cotta mantels. Finally, under "Miscellaneous" there were categories of an entirely different nature, including porcelain electric fixtures, plumbing items, sanitary ware (such as sinks, tubs, or toilets), and chemical stoneware. Although many of these suggestions seem farfetched, the seriousness of the situation is clear from a questionnaire filled out in 1937 by the Federal Seaboard Terra Cotta Corporation. The company had been employing between 750 and 800 men in their three plants but, "was at present, with 2 plants shut down, employing approximately 200 to 240 men."[210]

Terra cotta was used in a number of the Federal Government's public works projects, which were undertaken to help the widespread unemployment caused by the Great Depression. Many new post offices were erected throughout the country during the 1930s, including fourteen new facilities in Manhattan alone. Most of these were designed in the Colonial Revival or Classical Revival style, but several New York buildings that used terra cotta relied on forms created in an Art Deco or International Style.[211] Two of the most unusual are the Forest Hills Station Post Office in Queens, designed by Lorimer Rich and constructed in 1937–38, and the Canal Street Station Post Office, completed a year later under the guidance of architect Alan B. Mills. Large, smooth pieces of ceramic veneer clad the buildings' surfaces. The post office in Forest Hills used terra cotta made by the Atlantic Terra Cotta Company; the material at the Canal Street Station was from the Federal Seaboard Terra Cotta Corporation.

A two-page advertisement from the Atlantic Terra Cotta Company featured photographs of the Forest Hills building and claimed: "Our Laboratory, in collaboration with Mr. Rich, succeeded in producing a terra cotta reddish brown in tone well suited to the environment and with just enough texture to give life and warmth to the flat surfaces."[212] The Canal Street Station had a glaze palette of rosy-buff,

FIG. 133. *The terra-cotta-clad Forest Hills Station Post Office, 1937–38, with Sten Jacobsson's sculpture* The Spirit of Communication *over the entrance.*

ABOVE, LEFT: FIG. 134. *A model for* Factory/Farm Worker, *part of Waylande Gregory's terra-cotta installation* American Imports and Exports, *which was featured in the General Motors Corporation Building at the New York World's Fair in 1939.*

ABOVE, RIGHT: FIG. 135. *This terra-cotta detail, used to decorate a structure in the East River Park, New York City, was manufactured by the Eastern Terra Cotta Company.*

oxblood, green, and black, with areas around the chamfered corner entrance highlighted in silver metallic lusters. Both buildings incorporated contemporary design elements, including flat roofs, smooth wall surfaces, asymmetrical composition, and a minimum of architectural ornament. These two post offices also feature commissioned works of art. Above the entrance of the Forest Hills Station is a sculpted terra-cotta female figure, *The Spirit of Communication*, by Sten Jacobsson (*Figure 133*). The Canal Street Station, which is clad in horizontal bands created from two shades of buff-colored terra cotta, "boasts a beautiful mural [*Indian Bowman*] by Wheeler Williams, sculptor, executed in dull ceramic gold against a dull Spanish leather color background."[213] These artworks were commissioned by the Treasury Department's Section of Fine Arts, which sponsored eighty murals and sculpture projects for New York State Post Offices between 1935 and 1942.[214]

Many other public art works were created as part of the Works Progress Administration's construction programs. Artists, craftsmen, and designers joined forces in efforts to enrich the design of buildings and parks of the late 1930s and early 1940s. One such project was Waylande Gregory's large-scale fountain *Light Dispelling Darkness*, constructed in 1936. Located in Roosevelt Park outside of New Brunswick, New Jersey, it represented man's desire to combat evil with knowledge. Gregory was named the Director of Sculpture and Ceramics in New Jersey and for this project he employed twenty WPA artists. During 1933, Gregory made arrangements with the Atlantic Terra Cotta Company to set up a workspace at the plant in Perth Amboy, New Jersey, where he could use the enormous high-firing kilns to make large sculptures that would be impervious to the elements.[215] It is likely that the Roosevelt Park fountain as well as his later commissions were all made there.

Gregory created two monumental works for the grounds of the New York World's Fair in 1939, *The Fountain of the Atom* and a sculptural group designed for the General Motors Corporation with the title *American Imports and Exports*[216] (*Figure 134*). The year after his success at the World's Fair, Gregory began an eighty-foot ceramic mural for the Municipal Center in Washington, D.C. It was one of two friezes commissioned to illustrate the services provided by the city government. Hildreth Meiere, a gifted artist known for her varied architectural decorations, was chosen to create the second terra-cotta mural. Although it takes some persistence to

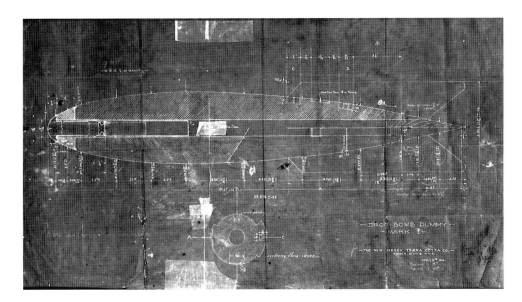

FIG. 136. *A 1918 blueprint for the manufacture of dummy bombs, intended for target practice. (New Jersey Terra Cotta Company)*

find these two murals because they are in a courtyard that is largely unknown to the public, they are well worth visiting.

In New York City, the government-supported projects of Robert Moses helped to provide jobs as well as useful public works on a scale of civic grandeur that the city had not seen since Olmsted and Vaux's design for Central Park in 1858. Many small buildings constructed by the Department of Parks under Moses' expansive programs used terra cotta. Unfailingly, terra cotta could be found in the comfort stations built for these programs, which included glazed "MEN" and "WOMEN" plaques over the appropriate doorways. Terra cotta was also employed for more elaborate structures such as the buildings in East River Park, which were ornamented with metallic and polychrome material manufactured by the Eastern Terra Cotta Company (*Figure 135*). Surviving records from that company indicate that between 1936 and 1938, more than one hundred jobs were completed for the Department of Parks, many of them alterations, additions, or new construction of comfort stations and other small structures.[217]

With drastically curtailed construction activities during both World Wars, the terra cotta industry was forced to find unusual uses for clay—often stretching the imagination to extraordinary lengths. Limited availability of metals during World War I, for example, led the Perth Amboy Terra Cotta Company to play an important role in United States Army aviation. "Experience in the dropping of bombs by our aviators was essential. Harry Gerns (The Seaboard Terra Cotta Company) went to Washington at the request of the War Department. Major Burgardees asked whether practice bombs weighing about 20 pounds could be made. They were made at the Perth Amboy plant from drawings furnished by the Major. An order was immediately placed for 500,000, and three plants were kept busy throughout the war."[218]

A blueprint dated April 11, 1918 for a dummy bomb from the New Jersey Terra Cotta Company provides evidence that other companies were occupied during wartime with this type of unusual production (*Figure 136*). George A. Berry, III, the last owner of the American Terra Cotta Company, explained that these hollow-clay practice bombs, which his company also produced, were filled with flour or powdered plaster, whichever was available. The spot where the bomb "exploded" would thus be covered with a white powder which was easily visible and helped to assess the accuracy of each drop.[219] In a very different vein, the Ludowici-Celadon Company, which specialized in roof tile, turned to consumer products. During World War II they employed more than seventy workers to produce a variety of slip-cast cookie jars, including "Fluffy the Cat" and "Dumbo the Elephant."[220] These creative flashes were too few, however, and as imagination and orders fell, the industry continued to decline.

Not only were materials scarce during wartime, but so were able-bodied factory workers. The difficulties experienced by Federal Seaboard were expressed in a 1944 letter written by their president, Peter Olsen. "As to the factory, we are extremely limited in manpower and for that reason cannot work very efficiently. We have men who are one day working in the pressing shops, and the next day grinding, and perhaps the day following are drawing kilns.... This would all be overcome by having say 12 or 15 of our old skilled men back."[221]

Following World War II, the industry faced another serious issue—that of deteriorating terra cotta. Because a substantial amount of time had passed since many terra-cotta jobs had been completed, problems resulting from improper installation or deferred maintenance began to occur. Although the finger was pointed at the material itself, it really should have been pointing to a number of issues. Successful long-term performance of masonry generally depends upon three factors—adequate support, proper anchoring or bonding, and protection from water infiltration. Although the durability of terra cotta had long been recognized, these three factors, particularly water seepage, caused a variety of material failures. Thus, the material's ability to perform on the exterior of buildings came under scrutiny during the late 1940s.

This unwelcoming environment offered many challenges for the seven struggling companies that remained in operation after 1945. They tried to address the questions of durability, and also sought to adapt terra cotta to the evolving tastes and technology in the building industry. To help achieve these aims, the Architectural Terra Cotta Institute was started in 1947. The member companies were the American Terra Cotta Corporation in Chicago; the Denver Terra Cotta Company in Denver; the Federal Seaboard Terra Cotta Corporation in Perth Amboy; Gladding, McBean & Company in Lincoln; O. W. Ketcham in Philadelphia; the Northwestern Terra Cotta Corporation in Chicago; and the Winkle Terra Cotta Incorporated in St. Louis. The Institute's goals were:

1. To educate building professionals about the uses and properties of terra cotta.
2. To address the shortage of trained terra-cotta craftsmen.
3. To compile statistics on the quantities of terra cotta being bought throughout the United States.
4. To manufacture new products that would be appropriate for the architectural styles of the period.

In an effort to achieve their fourth goal, most of the companies began to produce simplified, extruded forms with large, flat surfaces and very shallow backs.

RICH'S STORE
WASHINGTON, D.C.

FEDERAL SEABOARD TERRA COTTA CORPORATION
10 EAST 40TH STREET
NEW YORK 16, N. Y.

FIG. 137. *These flat terra-cotta blocks, each emblazoned with a large 'R' for Rich's Shoes, are an example of design that is perhaps worthy of the label "terrible cotta."*

Known as wall ashlars, these units suited the bland aesthetics of the period, and could be adhered to plaster, brick, or tile. Extruded units were typically eighteen by forty inches, although in unusual situations, they could be made slightly larger. Each firm had its own brand name, and promotional flyers featured "Atlantic Wall Units" or "American Wall Block" in an astounding rainbow of colors from powder blue to a deep vermilion. The Northwestern Terra Cotta Company produced a line of extruded ashlars called "Art-I-San Blocks," while Gladding, McBean offered "Unit Ceramic Veneer." Being economical and easy to maintain, varied brands of ceramic veneer were frequently used in small buildings such as gas stations, automobile show-rooms, shops, and other commercial structures. Since their introduction in the late 1920s, none of these extruded items gained an enthusiastic following, and machine-made veneer earned the disparaging epithet "terrible cotta"[222] (*Figure 137*).

Daniel Barton, the president of O. W. Ketcham, was the last president of the Architectural Terra Cotta Institute, and according to him, general frustration within the organization led the group to disband in 1959. The larger companies felt that the dues structure, which was based on a percentage of sales, was unfair and that they could better use the money for individual promotional efforts. In a May 1995 letter, Barton explained that another problem existed: the West Coast terminology "Ceramic Veneer" became the focus of the organization's publicity efforts, leaving little room in national publications to feature the hand-molded pieces made by sev-eral companies including O. W. Ketcham. The final split came when Gladding, McBean & Company withdrew from the Institute. As Barton explained, "the reason for the break between the East and the West was because all the West Coast specifica-tions had to include earthquake construction requirements, and we in the East felt that the excessive cost of the structural procedure was a detriment to our sales effort here."[223]

TOP, RIGHT: FIG. 138. *This sculptural panel is just one example of the many varied doorway ornaments found in Parkchester, an enormous apartment complex in the Bronx, New York.*

RIGHT: FIG. 139. *A stark contrast exists between this voluptuous blue-and-white rondel and its background, a yellow terra-cotta veneer used frequently in Parkchester's shopping area.*

ABOVE: FIG. 140 A AND B. *Lively polychrome figures can be found throughout Parkchester. These two terra-cotta women were made from the same plaster molds but have been decorated with different costumes and accessories.*

T HE INDUSTRY'S CONTINUED DETERMINATION TO SURVIVE can be understood best by exploring some of the developments that the Federal Seaboard Terra Cotta Corporation faced from 1940 until it ceased operation in 1968. Archival material has been located that illuminates this struggle and provides insight into the hardy perseverance, yet ultimate failure of this company, the last of the East Coast terra-cotta manufacturers. The company, which formed in 1928, resulted from the merger of three New Jersey firms, the New Jersey Terra Cotta Company in Perth Amboy, the South Amboy Terra Cotta Company in South Amboy and the Federal Terra Cotta Company in Woodbridge.

In 1941, Federal Seaboard completed a large order for Parkchester, a massive residential community in the Bronx, New York. It contained apartment buildings and appropriate amenities intended to serve the needs of more than twelve thousand families. Federal Seaboard manufactured simple terra-cotta units as well as brightly glazed "playful statues (500 accordion players, skiers, girls with umbrellas, etc.) and small plaques (600 dachshunds, ducks, pigs, etc.) above entrances"[224] (*Figure 138*). In addition, elaborately sculpted and glazed ornamentation for storefronts, theaters and other commercial establishments sprinkled throughout the 129-acre project were created in terra cotta (*Figures 139, 140a and b*). Raymond Barger, Chief Sculptor, worked with eight other artists to design models for the desired ornament. These sculptural decorations, which include works by Joseph Kiselewski, who may also have created pieces for Rockefeller Center, continue to be admired by many of Parkchester's forty-two thousand residents today.[225] In the mid-1980s a festive ceremony was held to mark the forty-fifth anniversary of the Parkchester community, with Raymond Barger as the guest of honor.

Although little is known about other jobs in which the company was involved during these years, records show that in the last months of 1943 sales averaged $13,400 per month, while for the first eight months of 1944 the average rose to $35,875.[226] These numbers, from a 1944 report to the directors of Federal Seaboard, may have encouraged shareholder (and future president) Aslag Eskesen to urge the board of directors not to close the company during wartime: "I am not of the opinion that operations of the Federal Seaboard Terra Cotta Corporation should be suspended entirely....My reason for this is that an idle organization disintegrates entirely, and eventual re-opening costs become a speculative risk."[227]

FEDERAL SEABOARD TERRA COTTA CORPORATION

BATTERY PARK UNDERPASS

FIG. 141. *In 1950, the Federal Seaboard Terra Cotta Corporation completed production of wall units for the Brooklyn Battery Tunnel, New York City.*

This same report also recorded the closing of the Eastern Terra Cotta Company's plant in Old Bridge, New Jersey. Federal Seaboard demonstrated optimism by purchasing a variety of materials and equipment from the defunct company for approximately $3,000. These purchases were intended to enable Federal Seaboard to reopen another factory in South Amboy, New Jersey, reducing the work load at their Perth Amboy plant. A firm note of reality was provided by Aslag Eskesen, who warned in a letter that same year, "Despite all the rosy visions of post war business, it is my feeling that such business will be developed only by the most aggressive methods of salesmanship...."[228]

In December, 1948, the *Perth Amboy Evening News* covered the anniversary celebration of sixty years of continuous operation of a terra cotta factory in Perth Amboy, owned at that time by Federal Seaboard.[229] The article stated that the company had doubled in size since 1946, employing more than two hundred workers. It described the demand for terra cotta as on the upswing, with job orders coming from "all over the country and many foreign countries including such distant spots as Australia and Persia."[230] Less exotic destinations, such as twenty-five modern housing projects spread among New York City's five boroughs, also sought terra cotta during this period. Machine-made units were used for entrances and lobbies, and for occasional jobs such as the Lester Patterson Houses in the Bronx, sculptural ornament was manufactured.

Terra cotta was also used in many of the new schools, libraries, and hospitals built between 1946 and 1953, a period that historian Robert A. Caro has called "the seven years of plenty in public construction in the city, seven years marked by the most intensive such construction in its history."[231] Other new projects for Federal Seaboard included the Brooklyn Battery Tunnel, completed in 1950, as well as the lobbies of the three large ventilating plants that furnish fresh air for the tunnel (*Figure 141*). Developers and planners soon began to recognize that New York City was not simply involved in a catching-up process, but was experiencing a major expansion of its business economy comparable to the activities of the 1920s. *Newsweek* reported in 1956 that "since World War II, construction had begun on more than eighty new office buildings with 22,418,000 square feet of rentable space."[232] A rare example of terra cotta being employed in one of these buildings is the thirty-eight-story Dime Savings Bank Building at 111 West 40th Street by Kahn & Jacobs. Completed in 1957, it was a modern skyscraper with six miles of piers faced in material manufactured by Federal Seaboard.[233] The 1950s were a healthy period for the company, and the production and profits caused the years 1957–59 to be lauded as "the good years" in a 1963 report.[234]

The company was eager to impress clients with its advanced technology, and one of its publications claimed: "Far from the early hand labor processes, Federal Seaboard's modern ceramic veneer plant is fully mechanized. Hand pressing is now a very small part of the production, since all but the most intricate shapes are machine

extruded. Large automatic grinding machines, pyrometric control of firing, and other improved techniques insure the precision product made today."[235] Ceramic Veneer Durathin, Ceramic Veneer Solar Grilles, and specialty items such as skid-proof curb copings were being manufactured (*Figure 142*). Remodeling projects aimed at providing the client with an up-to-date image frequently used ceramic veneer. Unfortunately, the way in which terra cotta was used in these refacing jobs resulted in banal and bland street facades. The creation of a "modern appearance" through inappropriate alteration was usually done at the expense of the original building design. The results often appeared to be callously grafted onto the older structure. In some cases, the entire building was covered with a new terra-cotta cladding, which often proved to be less offensive than covering only the lower one or two stories (*see Figure 132*).

Cultivating the perception of being cutting-edge also required Federal Seaboard to explore fresh design ideas, including new color possibilities and a broad range of textures and motifs. The two-story facade of the Hahn Store, designed by E. W. Dreyfuss & Associates in Washington, D. C. is a example of a modernization with the "grafted look" (*Figure 143*). It used a textured ceramic veneer, one of more than twenty new designs available, to help create handsome effects in low-relief sculptured walls. Company literature confidently declared that "in combination with CV Durathin smooth surfaces, the design you select or create will enable you to give the desired architectural expression....In CV Durathin you have the choice of any ceramic color under the sun" [236] (*Figure 144*). One example of this type of modernization in New York City could be found until recently on the Price Building, located at 604–612 Sixth Avenue. Designed by Buchman & Fox, this building dates from 1910–12 and was originally clad in terra cotta. In 1949, when it was converted into the Knickerbocker Motors Showroom, the lower floors were modernized with extruded terra cotta. This ceramic veneer has now been removed and replaced in a historical style matching the rest of the original facade.[237]

Handmade terra cotta was also used during these years, most frequently on religious structures, as well as on a surprising range of other special commissions.[238] One

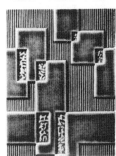

TOP, LEFT: FIG. 142. *Ceramic Veneer Solar Grilles were used on this remodeled YMCA entrance in Buffalo, New York.*

TOP, RIGHT: FIG. 143. *The ceramic veneer used to "modernize" the lower floors of this terra-cotta building has been insensitively superimposed on the original structure.*

ABOVE: FIG. 144. *These four textures are examples of the many patterned CV Durathin designs introduced by the Federal Seaboard Terra Cotta Corporation.*

of the largest of these was the Birdhouse at the Cleveland Zoo, designed by J. Byers Hays and completed in 1952. The terra-cotta ornamentation, including five large (five-by-eight-foot, two-thousand-pound) panels decorating the sixty-foot chimney and twenty-four smaller panels, was designed by the nationally respected artist Viktor Schreckengost. The project required twenty-two different color glazes, and took three years to complete.[239] *The New Brunswick Times* reported that Federal Seaboard was the "only one in the nation able to undertake such highly specialized work."[240] Schreckengost was awarded a special citation at the 16th Ceramic National Exhibition for the best example of ceramic sculpture integrated into an architectural project in recent years (*Figure 145*).

Overwhelming satisfaction with Schrenckengost's Birdhouse led in 1955 to a commission for two large murals for the Pachyderm Building, also at the Cleveland Zoo. Their size was a real challenge—one sculpted relief of a mammoth with its young is 13' x 25' and a second, which portrays a mastodon with its young, is 11' 6" x 24' (*Figure 146*). For this project, along with the Birdhouse, and a 1954 mural for the Lakewood High School Auditorium, Lakewood City, Ohio, Schreckengost was awarded the American Institute of Architects Fine Arts Medal. It recognizes his mastery of ceramic sculpture and states: "Sculpture has long been a powerful ally of architecture, and color has often shown itself a welcome aid, but to you have come the inspiration and the opportunity to combine both of these aids in restoring appeal to an architecture which was beginning to prefer its own nakedness."[241] Even though the Cleveland Zoo has recently expanded, the Pachyderm building "is the most photographed place over at the zoo, kids are always in front of the murals getting their picture taken," according to Schrekengost[242] (*Figure 147*).

One of the most exotic handmade terra-cotta projects of this period was a sphinx for the Scottish Rite Temple in El Paso, Texas. The sphinx was sculpted and fired in one piece, measuring more than ten feet long by three feet wide by five feet high. It was necessary to create the piece from the start inside the kiln because it was too large to move in an unfired state. The finished sphinx was sent on a flatbed truck to its destination (*Figure 148*).

Other unusual projects were carried out by Federal Seaboard using varied methods to embellish stock items. The Hotel Habana Hilton in Cuba commissioned Rene Portocarrero, a well-known Cuban artist, to make a series of enormous panels for its lobby. He tooled the mural designs into wet clay and applied the glaze colors at the plant in Perth Amboy (*Figure 149*). These murals were made up of standard 12" x 12" units. In 1955, Federal Seaboard was asked to execute a mural for the entry of P. S. 41 on West 11th Street in New York City. John M. Barton designed a one-quarter scale cartoon for this 11' 2" x 17' 6" project. From the cartoon a full-size drawing was made so that the brightly colored glazes could be transferred onto standard terra-cotta units. In the early 1960s, the New York architectural firm Chapman, Evans & Delehanty created abstract designs for ten polychrome panels of custom-

PACHYDERM BUILDING
CLEVELAND ZOOLOGICAL PARK

Hayes & Ruth—*Architects*
Viktor Schreckengost—*Sculptor*
H. F. Juergens—*Builders*

Polychrome Architectural Terra Cotta
was specified for two huge figures—
Mammoth (illustrated) 13' x 25';
Mastodon 11'6" x 24'.

Try sculpture for
greater architectural character

ABOVE, LEFT: FIG. 145. *Viktor Schreckengost with models for the Birdhouse at the Cleveland Zoo, circa 1951.*

ABOVE, RIGHT: FIG. 146. *The Federal Seaboard Terra Cotta Corporation factory where Viktor Schreckengost prepared a huge model for one of his murals designed for the Pachyderm Building at the Cleveland Zoo, circa 1955.*

LEFT: FIG. 147. *The size and accessibility of the terra-cotta murals on the Pachyderm Building make them the most-photographed spot in the Cleveland Zoo, more than forty years after their installation.*

made CV Durathin. These were installed in four elevator lobbies of the Brooklyn College Student Center, where they still provide a colorful decor (*Figure 150*).

In 1961, O. E. Mathiasen, president of Federal Seaboard, prepared a promotion and sales plan. This report explored the loss of large jobs to competitive materials such as concrete, enameled metals, marble, unpolished stone, ceramic tile, and glazed brick; customers' dissatisfaction because of terra-cotta failure or trouble; and austerity programs that eliminated terra cotta.[243] Two years later, Aslag Eskesen studied the question of whether to liquidate or continue the company in an exhaustive

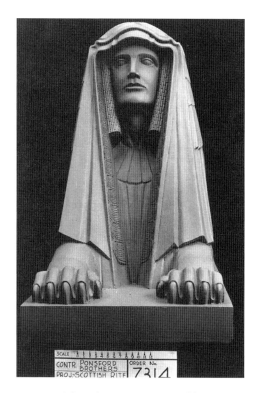

FIG. 148. *This sphinx is very unusual because it was modeled directly in clay and is one enormous piece. Typically, such a sculpture is created in many parts from sections that have been pressed in plaster molds.*

paper titled "Problems, Possibilities, Prospects." He investigated the reasons for a gradually shrinking terra-cotta market in an era of national dynamism within the United States industrial sector. He came to the conclusion that "Basically, it seems not consistent that an enterprise which can create products of imaginative beauty should not reap appropriate rewards for its artful contribution....It is from the conviction that such rewards for efforts and funds committed can be attained, that springs the reasonable confidence in the future enhancement of FSTC to its owners."[244]

Federal Seaboard earnings nearly doubled between 1965 and 1966, and the report to stockholders targeted optimistic earnings for 1967. The company had begun to produce a ceramic air-heater element for use in large boiler installations in collaboration with Foster Wheeler. A positive attitude was expressed: "We are far from a condition of hopeless weakness. In the final analysis, our recovery to strength depends upon our capacity to operate at a profit and in a degree this depends upon obtaining sufficient volume at appropriate price-levels—both objectives being deemed to be within reach at this moment in time."[245]

Fifteen months later, on June 5, 1968, the Board of Directors of Federal Seaboard unanimously approved the possibility of a merger.[246] However, this never occurred and the company ceased operation in 1968. Alice Eskesen Ganzel, sister of the president, reflected on possible reasons for the company's failure. She wrote in 1987 that "he [Aslag Eskesen] tried to renew the dying industry (in the 1960s) by moving away from...hand industry to a new plant in Edison, New Jersey, with the emphasis on a mechanized extruded product called Durathin. The move required enormous amounts of capital, and sadly the venture failed. The factory was closed—bankrupt—possibly just when they were on the verge of creating a successful new building material in conjunction with the steel industry."[247]

Federal Seaboard stopped production as it neared the completion of an order for the Hunter College School of Social Work, at 129–33 East 79th Street in New York City. Evidently, the architects, Wank Adams & Slavin, who specified a gray, speckled glaze that resembled granite, were unhappy with some of the finished units. They rejected a number of pieces, but upon learning that terra-cotta production had ceased, they reviewed the previously rejected terra cotta and proceeded to use it in the project. Nonetheless, there was not enough terra cotta to complete the facade, and ultimately the ground floor and entrance were finished with dark gray three-quarter-inch-square glass mosaics.[248]

Looking back, it is interesting to note Aslag Eskesen's perceptive thoughts in 1963 about the survival of the terra-cotta company: "Possible answers may lie in concentrating upon the uniqueness of the product [terra cotta] as a flexible material due to its plasticity with endless possibilities as to color."[249] Earlier, during the 1950s, Daniel Barton, president of O. W. Ketcham, felt that the terra-cotta industry should not have tried to compete with the capabilities of other newly developed materials.

FIG. 149. *The Cuban artist Rene Portocarrero executed these murals for a hotel in Havana at the Federal Seaboard Terra Cotta Corporation factory in Perth Amboy, New Jersey.*

Rather, it should have continued to emphasize the *strength* of terra cotta as a unique ornamental material.[250] This attitude was always evident in the work produced by Ketcham, the most distinctly recognizable terra cotta manufactured in the United States. The pieces combined very artistic sculpting with an unusual use of colored glazes (*Figure 151*). Frequently a single unit would have large areas of slip-coated clay with only the decorative relief coated in bright glazes. Most of the other companies were larger and produced much more standard ware which served the needs of a larger client base. A paradox resulted from trying to stay in business by manufacturing terra cotta that resembled other materials, because this activity further obscured the identity of terra cotta.

Proof that the distinctive qualities of terra cotta were increasingly overlooked can be found in *New York 1960* by Robert A. M. Stern, Thomas Mellins, and David Fishman, published in 1995. Three unusual "firsts" in New York construction, each using clay products manufactured by the Federal Seaboard Terra Cotta Corporation, are discussed and illustrated. However, terra cotta is either ignored or mistakenly identified as concrete, and in one case, as enamel on metal.[251]

These three "firsts" are the city's first glazed brick apartment building, Manhattan House;[252] the first urban motel in the country, Skyline Motor Inn on 10th Avenue between 49th and 50th Street;[253] and Edward Durell Stone's Gulf Station, the first "architect-designed gas station," located at Idlewild Airport (now JFK Airport).[254] These are worthy of mention—not so much for any aesthetic contribution of the terra cotta, but rather because it is important to realize that the material did manage to survive and become part of the architectural legacy of New York City through the 1960s. Seven additional projects that used terra cotta, most notably the Catholic Seamen's Institute, Barnard College's Lehman Hall in the Wollman Library,

TOP: FIG. 150. *These custom-made ceramic murals are still visible at the Brooklyn College Student Center, which was completed in 1962.*

BELOW: FIG. 151. *Detail of the terra-cotta columns from the 63rd Street YMCA, manufactured by O. W. Ketcham in 1928–30.*

BELOW, RIGHT: 152. *The Catholic Seaman's Institute, 653 Hicks Street, Brooklyn, New York, combines brick, polychrome terra cotta, and glass block to create a very contemporary architectural statement.*

FIG. 154. *Portions of the polychrome terra cotta used on the Mecca Temple (now City Center) by architect H. P. Knowles were replaced in the mid-1980s.*

and the American Airlines Terminal at JFK Airport, were included in *New York 1960*[255] (*Figure 152*).

Unfortunately, the potential of terra cotta to provide lasting color in architecture was never fully exploited. Instead, this unique quality was obscured by the continued demand for a product which mimicked other building materials. One is inclined to place some of the blame for this on the architectural profession. Limited imagination, shortsightedness, and an overwhelming desire to please clients led many architects to work in the latest styles and newest materials. The American Ceramic Society proceedings make it clear that manufacturers had a difficult time with architects (one frustrated member referred to them "hashitects").[256] A true idealist in the Society urged the skeptical companies to trust the architect: "Go to him and show him your productions, bore him, if I may say so, with your wares, annoy him to the point when, in order to get rid of you, he will give you a chance. Then, after he has realized and seen what you can produce, I am confident he will be so pleased as never to stop using your material...."[257] This confidence appears to have been sadly optimistic (*Figure 153*).

Following the demise of the Federal Seaboard Terra Cotta Corporation in 1968, architects did not use terra cotta in New York for nearly fifteen years, with the exception of the Prospect Park Boathouse in 1971.[258] By the mid-1980s, several architects specified terra cotta for restoration purposes. Portions of Carnegie Hall, a light

FIG. 153. *These terra-cotta heads were rejects for a building in San Francisco around the time of the 1906 earthquake. Eventually they were used to shore up a sagging street in Perth Amboy, New Jersey. They serve as a poignant reminder of a once-thriving industry.*

brown, unglazed building designed by William Tuthill in 1891, and City Center, H. P. Knowles's polychrome facade from 1924, used replacement pieces manufactured in the 1980s by Gladding, McBean & Company (*Figure 154*). Ironically, in the last thirty years many terra-cotta buildings have been restored with replacement pieces made out of materials such as concrete or fiberglass. Thus, substitutes were chosen to replace terra cotta, which itself had often been a substitute for stone. Now, a decade later, many New York restoration projects are being supplied with new terra cotta of fine quality and exceptional beauty.

One anticipates the day when terra cotta will also be found in contemporary New York architecture, a phenomenon that has begun to occur in a number of other American cities. Robert Venturi, one architect who has incorporated terra cotta into some of his buildings, has made insightful comments on its role in new designs: "Opportunities abound for using terra-cotta for the sensual enrichment of architecture....Because of its easy repetitiveness and inherent refinement, terra-cotta can be a means of creating small-scale articulation as a counterpoint to the big size of many of our buildings today: it is a way to bring back 'human scale' to our cities, as well as color and ornament."[259] I hope this book will inspire today's craftsmen, owners, designers, and builders by returning architectural terra cotta to its rightful place: front and center in New York's skyline.

1. AMERICAN ENCAUSTIC TILING COMPANY BUILDING *(Figure 155)*
16 East 41st Street
1920 (new facade on existing structure), Rich & Mathesius
Atlantic Terra Cotta Company, American Encaustic Tiling Company
Defaced in 1993

This stucco facade, inset with tile and terra cotta, was a showplace for the American Encaustic Tiling Company, one of the largest and most important American manufacturers of tile. The company was based in Zanesville, Ohio, but this building served as the New York office and was designed in collaboration with Leon Solon, architectural colorist and art director for the company from 1912 to 1928. The lower story of the facade was covered with beautifully colored and patterned tiles.

The building was very severely disfigured in 1993 by the ground-floor tenant, the owner of a pizza parlor that is now defunct. Although the tenant was approached about keeping the existing facade, which had served the previous tenant (also a restaurant) well, he was vehemently opposed. On Sunday, July 11, 1993 the *New York Times* ran an article titled "Going, Going…A Terra Cotta Splash on 41 St." It included a photograph and information about the impending plans for change. The tenant saw the article when the paper was available on Saturday, July 10, 1993. That very day he proceeded to illegally sledgehammer the tiles, even though he was reprimanded by a number of outraged citizens. He continued to destroy the tiles and was photographed in the process. The street-level facade is an embarrassment, but there are remnants of ceramic ornament still visible on the upper stories.

2. BICKFORD'S RESTAURANT *(Figure 156)*
45th Street and Lexington Avenue
1930–32, F. Russell Stuckert
Atlantic Terra Cotta Company
Original facade destroyed, 1993

This three-story commercial structure, originally part of a restaurant chain, was clad in exceptional polychrome deco terra cotta. Pink, yellow, orange, tan, and green glazes were used and the corner of the building had an octagonal clock with a beautiful terra-cotta surround.

On Sunday, July 18, 1993, just one week after the previously mentioned *New York Times* article appeared, Christopher Gray wrote a story titled "The Flaying of a Midtown East Art Deco Oddity," which was also published in the *New York Times*. He described the building as "a memorable midtown sight, a jazzy, polychrome terra-cotta facade." Evidently, the owner had the entire facade removed, down to the steel columns, to allow for reinforcing that was needed for a three-story addition that had been planned. However, the owner changed his mind and the architects, who had considered the original facade to be in pretty good condition and had recommended that it be preserved, ended up covering the existing metal structure with a banal cladding material. Another sad sight!

3. FOLIES-BERGERE THEATER *(Figure 157)*
(Later, the FULTON THEATER and finally, the HELEN HAYES THEATER)
210 West 46th Street
1911, Herts & Tallant
Federal Terra Cotta Company
Demolished 1982

This structure was one of the finest of Broadway's theaters to disappear; the *AIA Guide to New York City* described the diamond designs of its lavish blue and cream terra-cotta facade as "worked by a crochet hook."[260]

LEFT: FIG. 155. *The renowned architectural colorist Leon Solon helped design the superb facade of the American Encaustic Tiling Company Building.*

BELOW: FIG. 156. *A detail of the polychrome Art Deco facade of Bickford's Restaurant.*

BOTTOM, LEFT: FIG. 159. *A view of one corner of the Marine Grill Room in the McAlpin Hotel. The mural on the left shows the* Commonwealth *with its searchlight, leaving New York's harbor. The* Half Moon, *with Henry Hudson discovering the Hudson River, is visible on the right.*

BOTTOM, RIGHT: FIG. 160. *The* Mauretania, *docking in New York, also from the Marine Grill Room. Fred Dana Marsh created the designs and the Atlantic Terra Cotta Company manufactured them.*

ABOVE, LEFT: FIG. 157. *Beautifully articulated terra cotta designed by Herts & Tallant in 1911 for the Folies-Bergere Theater.*

ABOVE, RIGHT: FIG. 158. *This Indian with drawn bow, which ornamented an "Indian Walk" Shoe Store, was an extremely handsome and unusual design.*

Although the plans to destroy this theater were executed in a legal fashion, a provision had been made by the Landmarks Preservation Commission that the facade would be dismantled and saved. This agreement was broken by the owner and the facade was wantonly smashed. Angry New Yorkers helped to pressure the city and the LPC to protect portions of the theater district after this occurred.

4. INDIAN WALK SHOE STORE (*Figure 158*)
   13 West 39th Street
   1930 (facade alteration), Chas. B. Whinston
   Demolished mid-1980s

This small commercial building with terra-cotta cladding had a beautifully detailed plaque depicting an Indian with a drawn bow and arrow. The facade used black and white glazed terra cotta.
   Quietly, with no one taking notice, this building disappeared from New York's terra-cotta legacy.

5. MARINE GRILL ROOM (McAlpin Hotel) (*Figures 159, 160*)
   34th Street and Herald Square
   1915, F. M. Andrews
   Atlantic Terra Cotta Company
   Demolished 1990

Sets of six murals depicting the maritime history of New York lined the walls of this fine room. Designed by Fred Dana Marsh, father of painter Reginald Marsh, they included the following scenes: the *Half Moon* and the discovery of the Hudson River, a British frigate firing upon the New Amsterdam, a scene from the water showing a hanging in the Old Fort, Fulton's *Clermont* on her first voyage up the river, a night scene of the *Commonwealth* leaving its dock with a searchlight illuminating the water, and the docking of the *Mauretania* surrounded by the New York skyline.
   This superb rathskeller, the finest surviving example of its kind in the United States, was legally destroyed by Grenadier Realty Corporation, owners of the building. They had been approached about designating it an Interior Landmark and opposed the idea. Quickly, a Department of Buildings permit was obtained, and demolition of this room, with its completely intact murals, began. The discovery of this action was made when an architectural salvage company called the Friends of Terra Cotta to ask for historic information on a mural they had just removed from the space. Efforts were made to

FIG. 161. *Thomas Lamb's Rivoli Theater, several blocks north of Times Square.*

prevent further destruction, and negotiations with the owners eventually led to the removal of some of the murals which had not yet been hammered to smithereens. These murals are still in storage and plans are underway to install some of these harbor scenes in the Broadway-Nassau Subway Station (8th Avenue Line) in New York City. They belonged in the room they were made for, which now serves as a storage room for The Gap. This is the worst example of the unnecessary, willful destruction of New York's terra-cotta heritage to happen in recent years.

6. RIVOLI THEATER (*Figure 161*)
1614–1622 Broadway
1917, Thomas Lamb
New York Architectural Terra Cotta Company
Demolished in the late 1980s

This white terra-cotta-clad theater included a pediment with beautiful classical ornamentation.

The Rivoli suffered the indignity of being defaced in two stages. Shortly after the Helen Hayes Theater was demolished in 1982, this facade was stripped of most of its ornament. This rendered it ineligible for Landmark designation, an issue that was being considered for sections of the theater district. The entire building was demolished a number of years later. It was one of the early Times Square sites on which a large, inappropriate, and uninspired structure was built.

This material was part of Susan McDaniel Ceccacci's unpublished thesis "Architectural Terra-Cotta in the United States Before 1870" (Master of Arts Thesis, Boston University Graduate School, 1991). Special thanks are due for her careful research and generosity.

Listed below are companies cited in literature on the history of architectural terra cotta. In some cases the original citation was the only source of information on the company available at the time the thesis was written.

Henry Tolman, Jr. (1848–51)
West Sterling, Massachusetts
architectural terra cotta, pottery

Tolman, Luther & Company (1851–53)
Worcester, Massachusetts
architectural terra cotta, garden vases

Tolman, Hathaway & Stone (1853–55)
Worcester, Massachusetts
architectural terra cotta, garden vases

Hathaway & Stone (1855–56)
Worcester, Massachusetts
architectural terra cotta, garden vases, stoneware

William Stone (1857–60)
Worcester, Massachusetts
architectural terra cotta, garden vases

The above-listed companies were all related; they were the "Tolman" companies that made architectural terra cotta for Elbridge Boyden. Tolman, Luther & Company exhibited at the Worcester Country Mechanics Association Exhibition in 1851 (diploma). Tolman, Hathaway & Stone showed their wares at the Massachusetts Charitable Mechanics Association Exhibition in 1853 and at the New York Crystal Palace Exhibition in 1853–1854. Tolman, Hathaway & Stone terra cotta was published in Benjamin Silliman's The World of Science, Art and Industry, *1854. William Stone exhibited at the Worcester County Mechanics Association Exhibition in 1857 (diploma).*

Hudson River Pottery (c. 1851)
(Roche Bros, agents)
12th Street, New York City
architectural terra cotta

Edward Roche (c. 1851–57)
12th & 13th Streets, New York City
architectural terra cotta, drainpipes

The relationship between the previous two companies is not clear. Edward Roche may have been the company that made terra cotta for Richard Upjohn's Trinity Building. (Letters that prove this hypothesis are cited in footnote 5.) Edward Roche exhibited at the New York Crystal Palace Exhibition in 1853–54.

Alexander Young (1851–53)
41st Street, New York City
Sewer pipe c. 1853–c. 1859
architectural terra cotta, etc.
This company manufactured terra cotta for James Renwick. Young showed his wares at the New York Crystal Palace Exhibition. His work was also published in Benjamin Silliman's *The World of Science, Art and Industry,* 1854. From 1853–c. 1859 he manufactured only sewer pipe.

Winter & Company (1852–58)
Prospect & Nicholas Streets, Newark,
    New Jersey
architectural terra cotta, etc.
This company made the terra cotta for Richard Upjohn's Corn Exchange Building. Winter showed their wares at the New York Crystal Palace Exhibition in 1853–54.

Quinn & Hill (1853–54)
87 Nassau Street, New York City
architectural terra cotta, garden vases, etc.
This company exhibited at the New York Crystal Palace Exhibition in 1853–54. No further information has yet been gathered on the life span of the company.

Trenton Terra Cotta Works (1855)
Trenton, New Jersey
architectural terra cotta
Nothing more is currently known about this company.

Patrick Bannon (1855–c. 1869)
Louisville, Kentucky
architectural terra cotta, garden vases
This company made terra cotta for Isaiah Rogers. In 1855–56 the Louisville Directory listed

Richard and Patrick Bannon. In later years only Patrick was listed as a terra-cotta manufacturer. In 1859 the company was known as Falls City Terra Cotta Works, but the directory listing was still as Patrick Bannon without the official name of the company.

Louis Scharf & William Gilinger (est. 1856)
Whitemarsh, Montgomery County, Pennsylvania
architectural terra cotta
Nothing more is currently known about this company.

Long Island Pottery (1856)
possibly located on Long Island, New York
chimney tops
Nothing more is currently known about this company.

Lorenze Staudacher (1858)
Philadelphia, Pennsylvania
chimney tops, vases, and brackets
Nothing more is currently known about this company.

Willard Steam Terra Cotta Works (1860)
Cincinnati, Ohio
architectural terra cotta
Nothing more is currently known about this company.

Charles D. Foote & Company; Queen City Terra Cotta Works (1860)
Cincinnati, Ohio
architectural terra cotta
Nothing more is currently known about this company.

Moorehead's Terra Cotta Works (est. 1866)
Montgomery County, Pennsylvania
possibly made architectural terra cotta
Nothing more is currently known about this company.

Joseph N. Glover (1866–67)
Louisville, Kentucky
architecture terra cotta
Glover has been found to have been listed in Louisville directories as a plasterer, not as a maker of terra cotta.

Joseph N. Glover (1866–68)
Indianapolis, Indiana
architectural terra cotta
Glover is said to have moved his company from Louisville to Indianapolis.

Wright & Elbreg (pre-1868)
Indianapolis, Indiana
firebrick, tile
This may be the company or one of the companies bought by Hovey & Nichols of Chicago and ultimately moved to Chicago to become the Chicago Terra Cotta Company, later the Chicago Terra Cotta Works.

Hovey & Nichols (1868)
Indianapolis, Indiana
architectural terra cotta
This company was a Chicago-based group that bought out one or both of the two Indianapolis companies listed above. In 1869, the company transferred to Chicago and changed its name to the Chicago Terra Cotta Company.

Chicago Terra Cotta Company (1869)
Chicago, Illinois
architectural terra cotta, vases, chimney tops
In 1870 this company was reorganized to become the Chicago Terra Cotta Works.

Chicago Terra Cotta Works (1870–80)
Chicago, Illinois
architectural terra cotta, vases, chimney tops, terra cotta for fireproofing
This company was to become the first major manufacturer of American architectural terra cotta.

Boston Works, Chicago Terra Cotta Works (1878–79)
Boston, Massachusetts
architectural terra cotta
For a brief time, a Boston branch of the company was operated.

The last four companies listed, beginning with Hovey & Nichols, were related to one another.

The Story of Terra Cotta, published in 1920 by Walter Geer, was "printed for subscribers only" and was "limited to one hundred copies." This 303-page book is a unique (if sometimes incorrect) source of information about the American terra-cotta industry. Walter Geer was president of the New York Architectural Terra Cotta Company from 1886 to 1919, when he became chairman of the board (*Figure 162*). Although he was a lawyer, history was his hobby, and he also wrote *Genealogy of the Geer Family in America* (1914).

Because *The Story of Terra Cotta* is very difficult to obtain (although the Library of Congress does have one copy), ideally it should be reprinted in its entirety. Since this is not possible at present, two chapters were chosen to be reprinted in this Appendix. They both provide information on important American terra-cotta companies: Chapter XVI is titled "The Society Members," and Chapter XVII is titled "The Former Manufacturers" (*Figure 163*).

In Chapter XVI, I have updated information on the East Coast companies. This additional material is printed in italics, in brackets, to distinguish it from Geer's original text. Otherwise, the original spelling and punctuation have been retained throughout these two reprinted chapters.

While researching the East Coast companies, I began to understand the important role that they played in the social and economic life of the towns where they were located. Not only did families have fathers and sons (and sometimes grandsons) working together in the same plant, but picnics, parties, strikes, and accidents were all part of their shared experience. In many of these communities, buildings that are richly ornamented in terra cotta made by the local plants still exist. The following anecdote from Walter Kilham, Jr.'s excellent book *Raymond Hood, Architect* illustrates this point with wit and humor:

> One of the members of the League was Howard Greenley, a graduate of the Beaux Arts in Paris, and a great raconteur. One of his stories was about himself as a young man returning from Paris to his home town in Bayonne, New Jersey. At this time the area was the center of the terra cotta industry. Glazed terra cotta, particularly, had developed into a most useful material on the exterior of buildings. Whether for structural or ornamental purpose it was shaped while in the plastic state of clay and then baked into a most durable weather resisting material. The Woolworth Building is a great example of its use.
>
> The ornamental work was limited only by the sculptural talents of the artisan in following out the designs of the architect, and Howard Greenley's father was one of these skillful artisans. His son was to take the next step up the ladder and become an architect, and ways and means were found to send the boy to the École des Beaux-Arts in Paris.
>
> When Greenley returned several years later, he was a polished young man, speaking French beautifully, and an "Architecte Diplômé par le Gouvernement Français." The whole town shared in the family pride, and more than that they wanted to give this distinguished young man a good start. In those horse and buggy days, it was decided a most suitable project would be the design of a great public fountain in the main square, which would include a basin for watering tired and thirsty horses. The fountain itself would be built of terra cotta in recognition of the home industry.
>
> The young man worked hard on his first commission, and the Committee, including the Mayor, was more than pleased with the results. A great celebration was planned for the unveiling, and it seemed appropriate that this unveiling of the fountain be accompanied by a demonstration of its purpose. As part of the parade, it was arranged to obtain from the Anheuser-Busch Company their finest dray, complete with beer barrels and drawn by a magnificent team of Clydesdales.
>
> The multitude assembled, the band played, and speeches followed. Our young hero accepted the accolade to the blare of trumpets as the veil was lifted. The pavement began to tremble as down the main avenue came the great team of horses at a full gallop. High in the seat the driver cracked his long whip. It was a magnificent spectacle as the team neared the fountain that gleamed in the sun, splashing with water. With all the skill of an excellent driver, he reined in his

*And so I penned
It down, until at last it came to be,
For length and breadth, the bigness
which you see.*
—Bunyan, *Apology for his Book,* from the
frontispiece of *The Story of Terra Cotta*

FIG. 162. *Portrait of Walter Geer from his book,*
The Story of Terra Cotta.

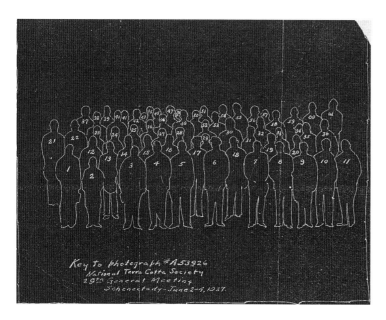

horses at the last possible moment. But he had forgotten one thing. The horses were hitched to the wagon by a long center pole, and as the horses pulled back in the breeching at the very edge of the fountain, the pole, driven by the wagon's momentum, shot forward with all the force of a battering ram.

From dedication to demolition, probably no architectural monument in history ever had a shorter life. The young man's father said, "Well, son," as he kicked aside a few shattered fragments, "I guess that's that."[261]

Greenley, who opened an architectural office in New York in 1903, did not let this incident turn him against terra cotta. His 1925 Cheney Brothers Building, at 181–183 Madison Avenue, which features the exceptional decorative metalwork by the Frenchman Edgar Brandt is also an example of his excellent use of terra cotta.

OPPOSITE: FIG. 163. *Group photograph from the National Terra Cotta Society's 29th General Meeting, Schenectady, New York, June 2–4, 1927.*

ABOVE: KEY TO FIG. 163.

1. *W. J. Stephani, Ceramist,* O. W. Ketcham.
4. *Thomas F. Armstrong, President,* Conkling-Armstrong Terra Cotta Company.
6. *De Forest Grant, President,* Federal Terra Cotta Company.
7. *George P. Fackt, Vice-President,* Northwestern Terra Cotta Company.
8. *F. S. Laurence, Executive Secretary,* National Terra Cotta Society.
11. *Fritz Wagner,* American Terra Cotta and Ceramic Company *(also representing* Indianapolis Terra Cotta Company).
13. *E. C. Hill, Ceramist,* Conkling-Armstrong Terra Cotta Company.
14. *A. D. Groff, Newspaper Publicity Service,* National Terra Cotta Society.
16. *W. F. Heath,* Gladding, McBean & Company.
17. *H. J. Lucas, President,* National Terra Cotta Society *and Vice-President,* Northwestern Terra Cotta Company.
18. *W. H. Powell, President,* Atlantic Terra Cotta Company.
22. *Robert Ketcham,* O. W. Ketcham.
23. *G. M. Tucker, Ceramist,* New York Architectural Terra Cotta Company.
26. *W. A. Hull, Ceramist,* Midland Terra Cotta Company.
27. *Walter Geer, Jr.,* New York Architectural Terra Cotta Company.
28. *Karl Mathiasen,* New Jersey Terra Cotta Company.
29. *S. H. Conkling, Vice-President,* Conkling-Armstrong Terra Cotta Company.
30. *F. A. Scheepers,* American Terra Cotta and Ceramic Company.
31. *Ray Riley,* American Terra Cotta and Ceramic Company.
33. *R. F. Grady, Vice-President,* Northwestern Terra Cotta Company.
34. *Leo Thurlimann, Ceramist,* Midland Terra Cotta Company.
35. *Homer G. Thompson, Ceramist,* Midland Terra Cotta Company.
36. *H. C. Schurecht,* National Terra Cotta Society *(Fellow, National Bureau of Standards).*
37. *O. W. Ketcham,* O. W. Ketcham Terra Cotta Works.
38. *W. L. Howatt, Ceramist,* Atlantic Terra Cotta Company.
42. *H. B. Wey, Vice-President and General Manager,* Atlanta Terra Cotta Company.
45. *George Gregory,* Corning Terra Cotta Company.
46. *B. S. Radcliffe, Ceramist,* Northwestern Terra Cotta Company.
49. *M. C. Gregory, President,* Corning Terra Cotta Company.
50. *P. H. Bates, Chief, Ceramics Division,* National Bureau of Standards.
51. *C. Fidler, Engineer of Standards,* Atlantic Terra Cotta Company.
52. *Oscar Mathiasen, Ceramist,* New Jersey Terra Cotta Company.
53. *R. S. Johnston, Director of Engineering,* National Terra Cotta Society.
54. *R. F. Dalton, President,* New York Architectural Terra Cotta Company.
55. *Peter C. Olsen, Treasurer and General Manager,* South Amboy Terra Cotta Company.
56. *H. L. Clare, Superintendent Ceramist,* Federal Terra Cotta Company.
58. *Adolph Hottinger, Vice-President,* Northwestern Terra Cotta Company.
59. *Jack Curry, Manager,* Terra Cotta Service Bureau, *Chicago.*
60. *E. H. Putnam, Publicity Manager,* Atlantic Terra Cotta Company.
61. *M. H. Gates,* American Terra Cotta and Ceramic Company.

The figures omitted from this list were members of various divisions of the General Electric Company, including the Illuminating Engineering Laboratory, Industrial Department, General Research Laboratory, Lamp Department, Porcelain Works, and Floodlighting Sales Section.

The Story of Terra Cotta *by Walter Geer*

Chapter XVI · The Society Members

Following is a complete list of the Members of the National Terra Cotta Society, arranged according to location in the order of incorporation, with brief Histories of the Companies, the names of present Officers, and lists of prominent Building for which terra cotta has been furnished:

Eastern

1886 NEW YORK ARCHITECTURAL TERRA-COTTA COMPANY, 401 Vernon Avenue, Long Island City, New York. (*Figure 164*)

HISTORY: The New York Company was founded 23 January, 1886, by Orlando Bronson Potter and Asahel Clarke Geer. The Plant occupies a five acre plot on the East River, just south of the Queensborough Bridge, in Long Island City, Borough of Queens, New York City.

OFFICERS: Chairman of the Board, Walter Geer; President, Richard F. Dalton; Vice-President, Ferdinand C. Townsend; Vice-President and Treasurer, Walter Geer, Jr.; Secretary, John P. Geib; and Superintendent, John Clark.

BUILDINGS: Rivoli Theatre, New York City; Ritz-Carlton Hotel, Philadelphia; Statler Hotel, Detroit; Municipal Building, Dallas, Texas;

Valley National Bank, Des Moines, Iowa; and H. Birks and Son Building, Vancouver, British Columbia.

[*Other notable buildings include: Carnegie Hall, New York City (1889–91, William Tuthill); the Montauk Club, Brooklyn, N.Y. (1889–91, Francis H. Kimball); and the Plaza Hotel, New York City (1905–7, Henry Hardenbergh). The company hired Francis Kimball to design an office building for them in 1892. This remarkable building, located next to the factory in Long Island City, was designated a New York City Landmark in 1982. Archives from the company were discovered in the attic crawl space of this building. They were saved, cleaned, and catalogued by the Friends of Terra Cotta (with support from the National Endowment for the Arts and the New York State Council on the Arts).*

This collection contains nearly six thousand files that cover the period from 1911 to 1920. Many of the files contain architectural bid documents, each including architect, building, and location, as well as estimated costs, sketches, and related correspondence. Buildings designed by such notable architects and firms as McKim, Mead, & White; Cass Gilbert; George B. Post; D. H. Burnham & Company; and Furness & Evans are represented.

A small portion of the archives are comprised of correspondence files that range from daily office memos to letters describing the formative years (1911–14) of the National Terra Cotta Society. This collection, which has been entered into a database, was donated to Columbia University's Avery Architecture and Fine

FIG. 164. *Model of one of the deco faces visible on the Webbtree Building, 1887 Webster Avenue, New York City. This detail was sculpted by Isadore Kaplan at the New York Architectural Terra Cotta Company.*

Arts Library. It is available for research purposes. For information contact the Curator of Drawings and Archives, Avery Library, Columbia University, New York, NY 10027, telephone: (212) 280-4110.

In 1932, the New York Architectural Terra Cotta Company went into bankruptcy. Although the employees continued to receive their wages until the very end, the Geer family, who owned a great majority of the company's stock, suffered serious financial consequences. By 1933, a new company, the Eastern Terra Cotta Company, was incorporated and took over the New York Architectural Terra Cotta Company's former plants in both Long Island City and Old Bridge, New Jersey. The president of this new company was Richard Dalton, a former officer (vice-president and, for a period, treasurer) of the New York Architectural Terra Cotta Company from the time it was established in 1886.

The Eastern Terra Cotta Company manufactured material for many of the Robert Moses park projects through the late 1930s. The company closed and its materials and equipment were purchased by the Federal Seaboard Terra Cotta Corporation in 1944. (The factory building was torn down in the early 1970s.)

1889 CELADON TERRA COTTA COMPANY, Alfred, New York
    (Figure 165)

Although Walter Geer did not include this company in The Story of Terra Cotta, *since it was never a member of the National Terra Cotta Society, its history is important, and therefore has been added to this chapter.*

OFFICERS: D. S. Burdick, President (1889–1890; William Clarke, Secretary; and George Babcock, Treasurer; John Merrill, President (1890–1891). Mr. Babcock followed Mr. Merrill as president in 1891 and remained in this position until his death in 1893. The company continued, with support from Mrs. Babcock, under J. A. Hubbard, the new president.

HISTORY: The company's first efforts at manufacture included architectural terra cotta, chimney tops, roof tile, and brick. George Babcock designed and patented twenty-five types of tiles and two pressing machines used for their manufacture. The company's name originated from the clay it first used, which turned a beautiful sea green during firing when coated with salt. This pale green was reminiscent of the classic Chinese ceramic wares known as celadons.

FIG. 165. *Modeler William Kenym, of the Celadon Terra Cotta Company, working on an enormous ornamental roof tile for the Finch Building in Scranton, Pennsylvania.*

In 1892, the Celadon Terra Cotta Company built a beautiful small office building which was so highly praised that a reproduction of it was exhibited at the 1892 Chicago World's Fair.

This building, which has been moved from its original site, has been restored through the great efforts of two local historical societies. The company's impact on the town has always been substantial. "Alfred had blossomed like the rose and its people have lived in a degree of comfort which would have been impossible without the substantial benefits that the terra cotta interests have brought." (Alfred Sun, 6 April, 1898). Although the census of Alfred at that time was less than eight hundred, more than a quarter of the families had men and boys employed at the terra-cotta company.

In 1897 the company expanded and was sold in 1906 to an Ohio ceramics firm, Ludowici Ceramics Company. Production continued at the Alfred plant until it was destroyed by fire in 1909. Following the fire, the company was reorganized as the Ludowici-Celadon Company and operated out of a plant in Ohio. Since that time it has continued to be a major manufacturer of roof tiles in the United States. "The tile roof is especially attractive, it is much handsomer than any stained shingle roof—as constructed is windproof, rainproof, fireproof, and timeproof." (The Clay-Worker [1901]: 682). In the early 1980s, the com-

FIG. 166. *Letterhead from the New Jersey Terra Cotta Company, showing the factory at Perth Amboy, New Jersey.*

pany decided to expand and began to design terra-cotta products for new construction as well as for restoration. By the early 1990s, the company returned to the sole production of roof tile under the name Ludowici Roofing Tile.

BUILDINGS: In 1895 Celadon had offices in New York and Chicago with sales representatives in cities from Boston to Minneapolis. Examples of the firm's many important contracts include: twenty-six buildings for the Army and Navy Hospital, Washington, D.C.; four buildings for the League Island Navy Yard, Philadelphia, Pa.; James Bailey (of Barnum and Bailey Circus) Residence, Mount Vernon, N.Y.; Finch Building, Scranton, Pa.]

1893 NEW JERSEY TERRA COTTA COMPANY, Singer Building,
  New York City. (Figure 166)

HISTORY: The New Jersey Company was incorporated 26 November, 1893, a successor to the firm of Mathiasen and Hansen, which began business in 1888. The works are located at Perth Amboy, New Jersey.

OFFICERS: President, Karl Mathiasen; Vice-President-Treasurer, Eckardt V. Eskesen; and Secretary, Karl Mathiasen, Jr.

BUILDINGS: Hotel Vanderbilt, Montefiore Home, and Uptown Post Office, New York City; Palace Theatre, Cincinnati, Ohio; Miami Hotel, Dayton, Ohio; and Poli's Palace Theatre, Hartford, Connecticut.

[*In 1928, this company became part of the newly formed Federal Seaboard Terra Cotta Corporation along with the Federal Terra Cotta Company and the South Amboy Terra Cotta Company.*]

1895 CONKLING-ARMSTRONG TERRA COTTA COMPANY,
  Wissahickon Avenue and Juanita Street, Philadelphia, Pennsylvania.

HISTORY: The Conkling-Armstrong Company was founded in January, 1895, by Ira L. Conkling and Thomas F. Armstrong, who had been members of the old firm of Stephens, Armstrong and Conkling (1888). Conkling, until his death in 1915, was the President, and Armstrong the Treasurer. The Plant occupies a plot of over three acres.

OFFICERS: President, Thomas F. Armstrong; Vice-President, Albert R. Taylor; Secretary, Joseph J. Frederickson; and Treasurer, Samuel O. Conkling.

BUILDINGS: Broad Street Station, Baptist Publication Building and Bulletin Building, Philadelphia; Wanamaker Store, and Bowling Green Building, New York City; and Filene Building, Boston, Massachusetts.

1895 ATLANTA TERRA COTTA COMPANY, Third National Bank
  Building, Atlanta, Georgia.

HISTORY: The Atlanta Company was organized in 1895 by Victor H. Kriegshaber. It was a successor to the firm of Pelligrini and Castelberry (1875), the second oldest terra cotta plant in the United States. The stock control was acquired by the Atlantic Company in 1908. The Plant occupies a plot of about twenty acres at East Point, about seven miles from Atlanta.

OFFICERS: President, William H. Powell; Vice-President, William C. Hall; Vice-President and General Manager, Harold B. Wey; Secretary-Treasurer, H. D. Hurlbut.

BUILDINGS: Masonic Temple, Augusta, Georgia; Union National Bank, Columbia, South Carolina; City Hall, Tampa, Florida; County Court House, Houston, Texas; Ansley Hotel, and Terminal Station, Atlanta.

1896 BRICK, TERRA COTTA AND TILE COMPANY, Corning,
  New York.

HISTORY: Established in 1893 under the name of the Corning Brick, Terra Cotta and Supply Company, and also known at different periods as the Corning Brick Works and Corning Terra Cotta Works. In 1896, the business was acquired by Morris E. Gregory, who adopted the style of Brick, Terra Cotta and Tile Company, by which the company has since been known.

PROPRIETOR: Morris E. Gregory.

BUILDINGS: War College, Washington, District of Columbia; Hotel Seneca, Rochester, New York; Hotel Utica, New York; Kalura Temple, Binghamton, New York; State Normal College, Albany, New York; and Dormitory, Columbia College, New York City.

1903 SOUTH AMBOY TERRA COTTA COMPANY, 150 Nassau Street,
  New York City.

HISTORY: The South Amboy Company was founded by the present officers 29 April, 1903, and began business at once, having leased the plant known as the Swan Hill Pottery at South Amboy, one of the oldest clay manufacturing plants in the East. The Plant was purchased in 1905, and has since been entirely modernized and enlarged both as to new buildings, and general power equipment. It now covers about three city blocks.

OFFICERS: President, Christian Mathiasen; Vice-President, William Mathiasen; and Treasurer and General Manager, Peter C. Olsen.

BUILDINGS: Vancouver Terminal Station, Vancouver, British Columbia; Bush Terminal Building, and Lotus Club, New York City; Fireman's Insurance Building, Newark, New Jersey; Commercial National Bank, Charlotte, North Carolina; and Fourth Church Christ Scientist, Cleveland, Ohio.

[*In 1928 this company became part of the newly formed Federal Seaboard Terra Cotta Corporation along with the Federal Terra Cotta Company and the New Jersey Terra Cotta Company.*]

FIG. 167. *A truck from O. W. Ketcham decorated for a July 4th parade, circa 1918.*

1906 O. W. KETCHAM TERRA COTTA WORKS, Builder's Exchange, Philadelphia, Pennsylvania. (*Figure 167*)

HISTORY: This business was founded in July, 1906, by O. W. Ketcham, who had been connected with the former Boston Company, and had later been a dealer in building supplies, acting also as local agent at Philadelphia for the Excelsior Company. The Plant is located at Crum Lynne, Pennsylvania, just north of Chester, on the line of the Pennsylvania Railroad.

PROPRIETOR: Orman W. Ketcham.

BUILDINGS: Chestnut Street Opera House, and many Public Schools, Philadelphia, Pennsylvania; Masonic Temple, Wilkesbarre, Pennsylvania; Masonic Temple, Camden, New Jersey, and Masonic Temple, Worcester, Massachusetts.

[*Other notable buildings include The Brady Residence, Roslyn, NY (1917, John Windrim); a residence in Sarasota, Florida, now the Ringling Museum (1926, Dwight James Baum); the First National Bank Building, Philadelphia (1928, Ritter and Shay); and the F. Cossitt Memorial Building for the YMCA, New York City (1928–30, Dwight James Baum).*
According to Daniel Barton, the last president of O. W. Ketcham and grandson-in-law of Orman W. Ketcham, the company was established in 1895. Perhaps its early activity consisted of supplying terra cotta and other building materials. Walter Geer gave the date of Ketcham's establishment as 1906, since that may have been the year when the company started to manufacture its own terra cotta. The company continued to supply building materials for construction and closed in 1995. Archives from the company have been donated to The Athenaeum of Philadelphia.]

1907 ATLANTIC TERRA COTTA COMPANY, 1170 Broadway, New York City.

HISTORY: The Atlantic Company was incorporated in February, 1907, being a consolidation of three former Companies: Perth Amboy (1897), Excelsior (1894), and Atlantic (1897). The Standard Terra Cotta Works was purchased in 1907. The Atlantic Company acquired a controlling interest in the Atlanta Company (1895), in 1908, and now owns all of the stock. The

Plants are located at Tottenville, Staten Island, Perth Amboy and Rocky Hill, New Jersey, and Atlanta (West Point), Georgia. It is the largest manufacturer of architectural terra cotta in the world.

OFFICERS: President, William H. Powell; Vice-Presidents, Frank G. Evart and W. C. Hall; Secretary-Treasurer, George P. Putnam; Assistant Treasurer George Parsons; and Assistant Secretary, Arthur G. Bisdale.

BUILDINGS: Woolworth Building, and McAlpin Hotel (Exterior and Grill Room Interior), New York City; Union Central Fire Insurance Building, Cincinnati, Ohio; Healey Building, Atlanta, Georgia; and Masonic Temple, Brooklyn.

The Woolworth Building, famous for the beauty of its design and its extraordinary height, contains more terra cotta than any other building in America. The Grill Room of the McAlpin is a most elaborate and extensive example of interior glazed polychrome work.

[*The Philadelphia Museum of Art is another spectacular example of glazed polychrome terra cotta. It was designed in 1927 by Trumbauer, Zantzinger, and Borie. An Atlantic Terra Cotta Company publication from February 1927 describes its impact as follows: "Color is a terrific force when introduced into an architectural combination, and is capable of producing an effect upon the observer equaled only by the fascination which firearms possess for small boys."*]

1909 FEDERAL TERRA COTTA COMPANY, 101 Park Avenue, New York City.

HISTORY: The Federal Company was organized in November, 1909, by De Forest Grant. The Plant, located at Woodbridge, New Jersey, was completed 22 May, 1910, and the first delivery of terra cotta was made the latter part of that month.

OFFICERS: President, De Forest Grant; First Vice-President, Edwin Thorne; Second Vice-President, Lewis R. Morris; Treasurer, W. B. Dinsmore; Secretary and Assistant Treasurer, Dwight W. Taylor; Assistant Secretary, Harry Lee King; and Assistant General Manager, Norman Grant.

BUILDINGS: Whitehall Building, Equitable Building, Biltmore Hotel, and Racquet Club, New York City; Traymore Hotel, Atlantic, City, New Jersey; and Real Estate Exchange, Detroit, Michigan.

[*In 1928 this company became part of the newly formed Federal Seaboard Terra Cotta Corporation along with the South Amboy Terra Cotta Company and the New Jersey Terra Cotta Company.*]

1928 *FEDERAL SEABOARD TERRA COTTA CORPORATION, Perth Amboy, New Jersey.*
Two important mergers occurred among the New York area terra-cotta companies after 1900. The first, in 1907, resulted in the reorganization of the Atlantic Terra Cotta Company, and the second, in 1928, led to the creation of the Federal Seaboard Terra Cotta Corporation. This company was formed by the merger of the New Jersey Terra Cotta Company, Perth Amboy, N. J. (established in 1893), the South Amboy Terra Cotta Company, South Amboy, N. J. (established in 1903), and the Federal Terra Cotta Company, Woodbridge, N. J. (established in 1909).

OFFICERS: Eckardt V. Eskesen, President; De Forest Grant, Chairman of the Board; Peter Olsen, Vice-President (These men served from 1928 until 1943.) Peter Olsen, President (1943–50); Karl Mathiasen II, President (1950–60); Oscar E. Mathiasen, President (1961–62); Aslag Eskesen, President (1963–68).

HISTORY: In 1928 the three plants produced more than three thousand tons of terra cotta monthly and employed between eight and nine hundred workers. After the Depression, however, two of the plants closed and only two hundred to two hundred forty men were actively employed. (For additional information see Chapter 13.)]

Central

1888 NORTHWESTERN TERRA COTTA COMPANY, 2525 Clybourn
    Avenue, Chicago, Illinois. (*Figure 168*)

HISTORY: The Northwestern Company was incorporated 9 January, 1888, a successor to True, Hottinger and Company (1886), and True, Brunkhorst and Company (1877), organized by John R. True, John Brunkhorst, Gustav Hottinger and Henry Rohkam, who had been connected with the Chicago Terra Cotta Works (1870), the oldest manufacturers of architectural terra cotta in the United States. The Plant at Clybourn Avenue covers twenty-four acres, and is the largest in the country.
OFFICERS: President, Gustav Hottinger; First Vice-President, Sherman Taylor; Vice-President and General Manager, Harry J. Lucas; Secretary-Treasurer, Adolph F. Hottinger; Assistant Sales Manager, George W. Van Cleave; and City Sales Manager, John G. Crowe.

BUILDINGS: Railway Exchange Building, Insurance Exchange Building, and Blackstone Hotel, Chicago, Illinois; Frick Arcade, and McCreary Stores, Pittsburgh, Pennsylvania; and Dime Bank Building, Detroit, Mich.

1888 AMERICAN TERRA COTTA AND CERAMIC COMPANY,
    Peoples Gas Building, Chicago, Illinois.

HISTORY: The American Company was founded by William D. Gates in June, 1888. The Plant is located at Terra Cotta, Illinois, about 45 miles northwest of Chicago on the line of the Chicago and North-Western Railway. The Company also manufactures the well-known Teco ware.

OFFICERS: President, William D. Gates; Secretary-Treasurer, Niel [*Neil*] H. Gates; and Assistant General Manager, Major E. Gates.

BUILDINGS: Chicago and North-Western Terminal, and Great Lakes Naval Station, Chicago, Illinois, and many Banks, Schools and Office Buildings, Chicago, St. Paul and Minneapolis.

1889 WINKLE TERRA COTTA COMPANY, Century Building,
    St. Louis, Missouri.

HISTORY: The Winkle Company was founded 15 October, 1889, by Joseph Winkle, a successor to the Winkle Terra Cotta Works which he started in

FIG. 168. *Photograph from The Northwest Terra Cotta Company of a partially completed clay model for the Medical and Surgical Clinic, Sioux Falls, South Dakota. The building was designed in 1919 by Perkins & McWayne.*

1883. The Plant occupies about four acres at 5739 Manchester Avenue, within the city limits.

OFFICERS: President, Andrew Winkle; Vice-President, Andrew J. Hewitt; and Secretary-Treasurer, John G. Hewitt.

BUILDINGS: Fort Dearborn Building, Chicago, Illinois; Railway Exchange, St. Louis, Missouri; Hillman Building, Los Angeles, California; Alaska Building, Seattle, Washington; Dayton Building, Minneapolis, Minnesota; and Rialto Building, Kansas City, Missouri.

1893 INDIANAPOLIS TERRA COTTA COMPANY, Indianapolis,
    Indiana.

HISTORY: The Indianapolis Company was incorporated in April, 1893, a successor to Stilz, Joiner and Company. Reincorporated July, 1899, and May, 1904. The President of the Company, Benjamin D. Walcott, died 21 February, 1916. The Company is now controlled by William D. Gates and leased to the American Company of Chicago. The Plant is located at Brightwood, a few miles east of the city.

OFFICERS: President, William D. Gates; Vice-President, Major E. Gates; Secretary-Treasurer, Niel [*Neil*] H. Gates; and Manager, George H. Lacey.

BUILDINGS: Van Camp Packing Company, Lyric Theatre, Hampton Court Apartments, Hotel Lincoln, and Masonic Building, Indianapolis, Indiana; and Y.M.C.A. Building, Anderson, Indiana.

1898 ST. LOUIS TERRA COTTA COMPANY, Security Building, St. Louis, Missouri.

HISTORY: The St. Louis Company was incorporated 8 August, 1898. Succeeded a company of same name started four years before but never operated successfully. The organizers of the present Company were R. J. Macdonald (President) and Robert F. Grady (Vice-President and Manager). David N. Burruss was elected President in 1904, and W. A. Maguire Second Vice-President in 1916. The Plant is located at 58th Street and Manchester Avenue, St. Louis.

OFFICERS: President, David N. Burruss; Vice-President-Treasurer, Robert F. Grady; Second Vice-President, W. A. Maguire; and Secretary, Edward E. Wall.

BUILDINGS: Union Electric Light and Power Station, Temple Israel, Jane Arcade, King Brindsmede Building, and Franklin Bank, St. Louis, Missouri; and The Temple, Dallas, Texas.

1905 WESTERN TERRA COTTA COMPANY, First and Franklin Avenue, Kansas City, Kansas.

HISTORY: The Western Company was founded in October, 1905, by William Timmerman and Paul C. Baltz, who had previously been employed by St. Louis companies. It began business with one kiln, which has since been increased to four.

OFFICERS: President, William Timmerman; Vice-President, Walter T. Timmerman; and Secretary and Treasurer, Paul C. Baltz.

BUILDINGS: Temple Building and Church, Kansas City, Missouri; Empress Theatre, Grand Rapids, Michigan; Majestic Theatre, San Antonio, Texas; Holy Cross Hospital, Salt Lake City, Utah; St. John's Hospital, Salina, Kansas; and Farmers Barn, Geneseo, Illinois.

1910 MIDLAND TERRA COTTA COMPANY, Lumber Exchange Building, Chicago, Illinois.

HISTORY: The Midland Company was incorporated 10 December, 1910. The first President, who retired in April, 1918, was William G. Krieg, at one time City Architect. The Vice-President, R. S. Ryan, died July 1918. The Plant occupies a twenty acre plot at West 16th Street and South 54th Avenue (Cicero, Illinois).

OFFICERS: President, Hans Mendius; Vice-President, August W. Miller; and Secretary-Treasurer, Walter S. Primley.

BUILDINGS: Municipal Pier, Medinah Temple, Sisson Hotel, and Elks Club, Chicago, Illinois; Central Trust Company, San Antonio, Texas; and Circle Theater, Indianapolis, Indiana.

1911 DENVER TERRA COTTA COMPANY, West First Avenue and Umatilla Street, Denver, Colorado.

HISTORY: The Denver Company was founded 22 September, 1911, by John Fackt, George P. Fackt, and Carl Philip Schwalb. Began operations in March, 1912. The capacity of the Plant was tripled two years later.

OFFICERS: President, John Fackt; Vice-President, George P. Fackt; and Secretary-Treasurer, C. P. Schwalb.

BUILDINGS: Kistler Building, and Union Depot, Denver, Colorado; Stratton Building, Colorado Springs, Colorado; League Building, Galveston, Texas; New Martin Building, El Paso, Texas; and Rialto Theatre, Omaha, Nebraska.

1912 KANSAS CITY TERRA COTTA AND FAIENCE COMPANY, 19th Street and Manchester Avenue, Kansas City, Missouri.

HISTORY: The Kansas City Company was chartered 4 December, 1912. Successor to Southwestern Terra Cotta Company (1910), which bought present site of about five acres, but never operated. Reorganized September, 1911, under above name, and for the third time in 1912. Has been inactive since Spring of 1915. The stock is controlled by interests connected with the New Jersey and South Amboy Companies.

OFFICERS: President, Eckardt V. Eskesen; Vice-President, Marshall S. Neal; Secretary, J. J. Parsons; and Treasurer, Ferdinand P. Neal.

Pacific

1886 GLADDING-MCBEAN AND COMPANY, Crocker Building, San Francisco, California.

HISTORY: The Gladding-McBean Company was incorporated 22 March, 1886, as a successor to a firm of the same name founded at Chicago, 1 May, 1875, by Charles Gladding, George Chambers and Peter McGill McBean. The Plant is located at Lincoln, with a branch at Oakland, California.

OFFICERS: President, Peter McGill McBean; Vice-President, Albert J. Gladding; Vice-President, George R. Chambers; Secretary-Treasurer, Atholl McBean; and Assistant Secretary-Treasurer, Theodore F. Tracy.

BUILDINGS: Hearst Building, Southern Pacific Building, and Insurance Exchange Building, San Francisco, California; Hamburger Building, Los Angeles, California; Meier and Frank Building, Portland, Oregon; and L. C. Smith Building, Seattle, Washington.

1889 N. CLARK AND SONS, 116 Natoma Street, San Francisco, California.

HISTORY: The N. Clark Company was incorporated 11 January, 1889, succeeding a business started in 1864 by Nehemiah Clark, one of the California Pioneers. The business was conducted at Sacramento until 1887 when a large plant was built at West Alameda. Shortly afterwards, the Sacramento plant was destroyed by fire and never rebuilt. The Alameda works were also burned in July, 1917, and not rebuilt, owing to war conditions, until 1919.

OFFICERS: President and Superintendent, Albert V. Clark; and Secretary-Treasurer and General Manager, George D. Clark.

BUILDINGS: Islam Temple, and First Church Christ Scientist, San Francisco, California; Federal Realty Building, Oakland, California; Boyle Heights Library, Los Angeles, California; County Court House, Sacramento, California; and Morgan Building, Portland, Oregon.

1903 LOS ANGELES PRESSED BRICK COMPANY, Frost Building, Los Angeles, California.

HISTORY: The Los Angeles Company was incorporated in March, 1903, being a successor to the Los Angeles Pressed Brick and Terra Cotta Company of Santa Monica, founded by the late Charles H. Frost in 1887. The Company owns and operates four large plants, manufacturing all kinds of clay products.

OFFICERS: President, Howard Frost; Vice-President, H. West Hughes; and Secretary-Treasurer, Harlow B. Potter.

BUILDINGS: Scottish Rite Cathedral, Joplin, Missouri; Ellanay Theatre, El Paso, Texas; Terry Apartments, Long Beach, California; First National Bank, King City, California; Bullocks Department Store, Los Angeles, California; and Mittry Theatre, Idaho Falls, Idaho.

1905 DENNY-RENTON CLAY AND COAL COMPANY, Hoge Building, Seattle, Washington.

HISTORY: The Denny-Renton Clay and Coal Company was organized in June, 1905, taking over the business of the Denny Clay Company, which had succeeded a business started in 1882 under the name of the Puget Sound Fire Clay Company. In 1912 the new Company bought out the business of the Western Clay Company and the Diamond Brick Company, of Portland. The plants, all of which are operated under the one management, are located at Van Asselt, Taylor, Renton, and Portland. The paving brick plant at Renton is the largest single unit plant in the world. At the Van Asselt plant, which is located inside the city limits of Seattle, is manufactured architectural terra cotta, silica brick and magnesite brick. The silica and magnesite plant capacity was increased in 1919 and is now in shape to supply the rapid and growing demand for these products.

OFFICERS: President, E. J. Mathews; Vice-President, Moritz Thomsen; Secretary and General Manager, John F. Keenan.

BUILDINGS: Kings County Court House, Times Building, Artic Club Building, Home Economics Building, University of Washington, University State Bank Building, and Franklin High School.

1908 NORTHERN CLAY COMPANY, Auburn, Washington.

HISTORY: The Northern Clay Company was incorporated in October,

1908, successor to the Northern Clay Products Company, which had purchased a business started by Arthur H. Meade in May, 1903, and known as the Auburn Pottery.

OFFICERS: President, Paul S. MacMichael; Vice-President, John Wooding; Secretary, I. B. Knickerbocker; and Treasurer, K. R. Ehle.

BUILDINGS: Joshua Green Building, Securities Building, Pantages Theatre, Frederick and Nelson Building, and Home Economics Building (University of Washington), Seattle, Washington.

1909 WASHINGTON BRICK, LIME AND SEWER PIPE COMPANY, Spokane, Washington.

HISTORY: The Washington Company was incorporated in 1909, a successor to the Washington Brick and Lime Company. The name was changed when the latter company was consolidated with the Spokane Sewer Pipe Company. The Plants are located at Clayton, Spear and Freeman, Washington, and Bayview, Idaho. Mr. J. H. Spear the founder of the Company (1886) sold his interests and retired in May, 1919.

OFFICERS: President, A. B. Fosseen; Vice-President, Victor E. Piollet; Secretary, C. P. Lund; and Treasurer, E. C. Van Brundt.

BUILDINGS: Paulsen Building, and Crescent Store, Spokane, Washington; Montana Building, Lewistown, Montana; Wilcox Building, Portland, Oregon; Rialto Building, Butte, Montana; and First National Bank, Wallace, Idaho.

Chapter XVII · Former Manufacturers

In addition to the twenty-four Companies now active in the business, during the past fifty years at least twenty-eight other plants have been at different periods engaged in the manufacture of architectural terra cotta in the United States. Most of these Companies were the out-growth of old brick or pottery works, and began operations prior to the year 1900. Nearly all of these works were located in the East. All are now out of the business, five having failed, ten having been merged in other companies, and the balance having discontinued operations.

1875 B. KREISCHER AND SONS, Kreischerville, Staten Island.
Were pioneers in the manufacture of fire brick in the United States. Balthaser Kreischer, the founder, was born in Germany. In 1836 he came to New York. In 1845 he began the manufacture of fire bricks, which before that time were all imported from England. He bought a supply of clay in New Jersey, and built a small plant on leased ground in Goerck Street, New York City. Having outgrown his works in the city, in 1852 he purchased extensive clay deposits at Charleston (now Kreischerville), Staten Island, built new works, and then abandoned the New York plant. Later he admitted his three sons to partnership, and finally the business was incorporated under the old firm name. The products included fire brick, face brick, and terra cotta. Mr. Kreischer died in 1886. Company failed in 1899.

1875 SOUTHERN TERRA COTTA WORKS, Atlanta, Georgia.
About 1872, P. Pelligrini and another Italian named Georgi began operating a small plant for the manufacture of flower pots, chimney tops and architectural terra cotta. In 1875 Jack Castelberry bought an interest in the business, and they organized the firm of Pelligrini and Castelberry, which was sometimes called the Southern Terra Cotta Company. About 1893, some of the workmen started a little plant which later became known as the Atlanta Terra Cotta Company.

1879 PERTH AMBOY TERRA COTTA COMPANY, Perth Amboy,
    New Jersey.
Succeeded A. Hall and Sons Fire Brick Works in 1879. Officers from 1881 to 1907, Edward J. Hall, President; William C. Hall, Vice-President; George P. Putnam, Treasurer; Harry A. Lewis and Oswald Speir, Directors. For nearly thirty years leading manufacturers of terra cotta in the East. Merged in the Atlantic Company in 1907.

1879 H. A. LEWIS ARCHITECTURAL TERRA COTTA WORKS,
    Boston, Massachusetts.
Began in 1879 as Lewis and Wood. Later, Lewis and Lane. After July, 1883, under above style. Business sold to Perth Amboy Company in 1887.

1879 LONG ISLAND TERRA COTTA COMPANY, Ravenswood,
    Long Island.
Established by Rudolph Franke in 1879. The plant was located on the East River opposite 53rd Street, New York City. Discontinued in 1880.

1880 BOSTON TERRA COTTA COMPANY, Boston, Massachusetts.
Organized 19 October, 1880. Successor to Boston Fire Brick Company. Officers: R. G. F. Candage, President; George M. Fiske, Treasurer; James Taylor, Superintendent. Sold to the Perth Amboy and New York Companies December, 1893, and the business liquidated.

1883 A. HALL TERRA COTTA COMPANY, Perth Amboy, New Jersey.
Founded in 1883 by Alfred Hall, two years after his retirement from the Perth Amboy Company. The officers were: Alfred Hall, President; his son Eber H. Hall, Vice-President; Fred C. Greenley, Treasurer; and Robert W. Taylor, Superintendent. Eber H. Hall died in January, 1886, and Alfred Hall in April, 1887. The plant was then shut down. Two years later the works were leased jointly by the Perth Amboy and New York Companies and finally closed.

1883 LAKE VIEW TERRA COTTA AND BRICK COMPANY, Chicago,
    Illinois.
Failed in 1884, and did not resume business, the plant being leased by the Northwestern Company.

1885 BURNS-RUSSELL COMPANY, Baltimore, Maryland.
Large manufacturers of face brick. Early in the eighties they began to make terra cotta under style of the Baltimore Terra Cotta Company. In 1905 they sold their terra cotta business the Maryland Company.

1886 WALNUT HILLS BRICK AND TERRA COTTA COMPANY,
    Cincinnati, Ohio.
Incorporated as a Stock Company in 1886. Succeeded the firm of Wilson and Gould. No further reports.

1886 GLENS FALLS TERRA COTTA AND BRICK COMPANY,
    Glens Falls, New York.
Succeeded Clark Colored Brick and Terra Cotta Company, which failed in 1884. J. M. Coolidge was President, and Charles Scales, Treasurer. Discontinued manufacture of terra cotta early in the nineties.

1886 WILLIAM GALLAWAY [Galloway], Philadelphia, Pennsylvania.
An old well-established pottery business which has made a little terra cotta from time to time, but none of late years.

1888 STEPHENS, ARMSTRONG AND CONKLING, Philadelphia,
    Pennsylvania.
Began in 1886 as Stephens and Leach; changed in 1887 to Stephens, Leach and Conkling, and in 1888 to above style. In 1893 became a branch of the New York Company. In 1894, Armstrong and Conkling withdrew and founded the Conkling-Armstrong Company. The two Stephens brothers retired from the terra cotta business in 1896.

1890 CALVIN PARDEE TERRA COTTA WORKS, Perth Amboy,
    New Jersey.
In January, 1890, Calvin Pardee, a wealthy coal miner of Philadelphia, purchased about 166 acres on the Raritan River and erected a plant for the manufacture of front, fire and paving bricks, sewer pipe and floor and glazed tiling. But little, if any, architectural terra cotta was made. Robert W. Taylor, of the old A. Hall Terra Cotta Company, was the first Superintendent.

1890 STANDARD TERRA COTTA WORKS, Perth Amboy, New Jersey.
Began as Architectural Terra Cotta Works in 1890, and in 1892 was incorporated as Standard Terra Cotta Company. Failed in 1898 and was taken over by Henry Doscher, who continued the business under above name. Merged in the Atlantic Company in 1907.

1892 WHITE BRICK AND TERRA COTTA COMPANY, Clayton,
    Massachusetts.
Was first known as the White Brick and Art Tile Company, the title being later changed to the above when the Company was incorporated in 1892. The leading spirit in the organization was Charles Siedler, who had made a fortune in the tobacco business. The Company discontinued operations in the early twentieth century.

1892 NEW BRITAIN ARCHITECTURAL TERRA COTTA
    COMPANY, New Britain, Connecticut.
Was incorporated in 1892 with Philip Corbin as President; C. E. Wetmore, Treasurer; George B. Post, Secretary; and G. S. Barkentin, Manager. They purchased three acres of land at Berlin Junction and established their works there. Had two kilns.

1893 STATEN ISLAND LUMBER COMPANY, Staten Island, New York. Manufactured terra cotta from the Spring of 1895 to 1898 inclusive. Officers: J. Edward Addicks, President; George Kelly, Treasurer; Robert W. Lyle, Secretary and General Manager; James B. Toomey, Superintendent. This Company failed in 1895. Was reorganized in 1898 under the name of Staten Island Clay Company, after which it did not make any terra cotta.

1894 EXCELSIOR TERRA COTTA COMPANY, Rocky Hill, New Jersey. Incorporated in January, 1894, as successor to the Partridge, Powell and Storer Company, manufacturers of face brick. Merged in Atlantic Company, 1907.

1897 ATLANTIC TERRA COTTA COMPANY, Tottenville, Staten Island. In the Spring of 1897, a meeting was held at one of the Good Government Clubs in New York, at which were present De Forest Grant, William D. Frerichs, S. S. Whitehurst and Charles U. Thrall. At this meeting it was decided to form a terra cotta company to be located at Tottenville, Staten Island. Later in the same year the Atlantic Terra Cotta Company was organized. De Forest Grant became its President and General Manager; S. S. Whitehurst, Sales Manager; William D. Frerichs, Superintendent; and Charles U. Thrall, Assistant Superintendent. Grant had formerly been Manager of the New York Office of the Staten Island Lumber Company, and Frerichs, Whitehurst and Thrall had all been connected with the Perth Amboy Terra Cotta Company, where they had received their technical training. The Company turned out its first material September, 1897. In January, 1907, the Company entered the combination of the Atlantic, Perth Amboy, Excelsior, and Standard Companies.

1898 STEIGER TERRA COTTA AND POTTERY WORKS, San Francisco, California.
Was organized 28 November, 1898, by members of the City Street Improvement Company, the largest contracting concern on the Pacific Coast. Walter E. Dennison was made President and continued as such up to the end. It developed from a three to an eleven kiln plant and produced a general line of clay wares. It was the first on the Pacific Coast to engage in the manufacture of a general line of acid earthenware. It also developed "thru-an-thru" terra cotta, invented by its President, and first employed in the San Francisco Hospital in 1916. The plant was totally destroyed by fire 8 March, 1917, and it was decided to liquidate. The Company made the terra cotta for the Grant, Monadnock, and Rialto Buildings, the Humboldt Savings Bank Building, the first terra cotta structure erected in San Francisco after the fire of 1906, and for many other buildings. The Company was a member of the National Terra Cotta Society.

1901 ROGERS TERRA COTTA COMPANY, Stanwick, New Jersey.
Organized in April 1901. A closed corporation, all the stock being held by the Rogers family. Name changed in 1913 to Central Terra Cotta Company. Has made a little terra cotta from time to time.

1902 AMERICAN CLAY PRODUCTS COMPANY, Forty Fort, Pennsylvania.
Began business on a small scale in October, 1902, but had little success, and discontinued some years later. The plant was dismantled and the contents sold at auction in the Spring of 1916.

1905 NORTH EASTERN TERRA COTTA COMPANY, Bradford, Pennsylvania.
This Company was organized by several practical men who had been employed at New York and elsewhere. It never had much success and after a short existence suspended operations for lack of sufficient capital.

1905 MARYLAND TERRA COTTA COMPANY, Baltimore, Maryland.
This Company acquired the terra cotta business of the Burns-Russell Company in September, 1905, and was incorporated under the above name. The principal officers, John J. Kelly and Harry P. Boyd, were connected with the National Building Supply Company. The Company did a very small business and was discontinued in 1915. It was a member of the National Terra Cotta Society.

1908 CHICAGO TERRA COTTA COMPANY, Chicago, Illinois.
In March, 1908, the name of the Hahne-Brunkhorst Company, owning a plant at Blodgett, about one mile west of Highland Park, Illinois, was changed to Chicago Terra Cotta Company. Alfred Brunkhorst, who was formerly connected with the Northwestern Terra Cotta Company, was Vice-President. It is not known how much terra cotta business this Company did. They were formerly in the brick business, and when Brunkhorst came with them changed their name and apparently engaged in the manufacture of terra cotta. This Company was purchased by Northwestern Terra Cotta Company about 1 January, 1910.

1911 KANSAS CITY TERRA COTTA COMPANY, Kansas City, Missouri.
This Company was started in December, 1910, by A. F. Brooker, a lawyer originally from Columbia, South Carolina, and a man by the name of Slater, who was at one time with the Conkling-Armstrong Terra Cotta Company. The plant began business in March, 1911. Brooker withdrew from the Company in September, 1912, and started the National Terra Cotta Company immediately thereafter. This Company went into bankruptcy in January, 1916, having been in difficulties for some time. Harvey Striver, a builder and general contractor of Kansas City, became interested in the property in 1914.

1915 UNITED STATES TERRA COTTA COMPANY, Chicago, Illinois.
This Company was incorporated 1 November, 1915, with John G. Crowe as President. Mr. Crowe had formerly been President and Treasurer of the American Terra Cotta and Ceramic Company. Fred F. Ellersdorfer was Secretary and Treasurer. He had been with the Northwestern Company for years and lost his position with the Company at the time of the change in management. They started to erect a plant at Harvey, Illinois, a suburb of Chicago. The concern never made any headway and it is not known whether or not they ever actually manufactured any material. Mr. Crowe is now the City Sales Manager of the Northwestern Terra Cotta Company.

Appendix D • Two Hundred Significant Terra-Cotta

Buildings in New York City

*Denotes a New York City Landmark (This includes buildings within a historic district, as well as interior and exterior individual designations.)

PART I: Manhattan (1–106, listed south to north)

South of Houston Street

1. BEAVER BUILDING*
82–92 Beaver Street
1903–4, Clinton & Russell
Brick with brightly glazed terra-cotta ornament
Office building

2. CORBIN BUILDING
11 John Street
1888–89, Francis H. Kimball
New York Architectural Terra Cotta Company
Brick with brightly glazed terra-cotta ornament
Office building

3. LIBERTY TOWER*
55 Liberty Street
1909–10, Henry Ives Cobb
Atlantic Terra Cotta Company
White terra-cotta cladding
Office building converted to apartments

4. NEW YORK EVENING POST BUILDING
110 Washington Street
1925–26, Horace Trumbauer
Atlantic Terra Cotta Company
Brightly glazed terra-cotta ornament
Office building

5. WEST STREET BUILDING
90 West Street
1905–7, Cass Gilbert
Perth Amboy Terra Cotta Company
White terra-cotta cladding with glazed, colored terra-cotta ornament
Office building

6. 19 RECTOR STREET
1929–30, Lafayette A. Goldstone
New York Architectural Terra Cotta Company
Brick with brightly glazed terra-cotta ornament
Office building

7. POTTER BUILDING*
38 Park Row
1883–84, Norris G. Starkweather
Boston Terra Cotta Company
Brick with terra-cotta ornament
Office building converted to apartments

8. WOOLWORTH BUILDING*
233 Broadway
1910–13, Cass Gilbert
Atlantic Terra Cotta Company
White terra-cotta cladding with glazed, colored terra-cotta ornament
Office building

9. BROADWAY-CHAMBERS BUILDING*
277 Broadway
1899–1900, Cass Gilbert
Perth Amboy Terra Cotta Company
Brick with brightly glazed terra-cotta ornament
Office building

10. DEPARTMENT OF WATER SUPPLY, GAS & ELECTRICITY, HIGH PRESSURE SERVICE HEADQUARTERS
226 West Broadway
1912–18, Augustus Shepard
White terra-cotta cladding
Office building converted to apartments

11. CANAL STREET STATION POST OFFICE
350 Canal Street
1937–39, Alan B. Mills
Federal Seaboard Terra Cotta Corporation
Extruded terra cotta on the facade and interior
Lobby has a ceramic mural, *Indian Bowman*, by Wheeler Williams, 1938.
Post Office

12. LITTLE SINGER BUILDING*
561–63 Broadway
1902–4, Ernest Flagg
Terra-cotta units set within a framework of steel
Industrial converted to commercial and residential

13. 560–66 BROADWAY*
1883–84, Thomas Stent
Boston Terra Cotta Company
Brick with terra-cotta ornament
Industrial converted to commercial

Houston Street to 14th Street

14. BAYARD-CONDICT BUILDING*
65 Bleecker Street
1897–99, Louis Sullivan
Perth Amboy Terra Cotta Company
Buff-colored terra-cotta cladding and ornamentation
Industrial converted to offices

15. AGELOFF TOWERS
141 East 3rd Street
1928–29, Shampan & Shampan
Brick with terra-cotta ornament
Apartments

16. 376–80 LAFAYETTE STREET*
1888–89, Henry J. Hardenbergh
New York Architectural Terra Cotta Company
Brick and stone with terra-cotta ornament
Commercial

17. DE VINNE PRESS BUILDING*
393–399 Lafayette Street
1885–86, Babb, Cook & Willard
Brick with terra-cotta ornament
Commercial

18. JUDSON MEMORIAL CHURCH*
54–57 Washington Square South
1888–93, Church; 1895–96 Tower; Both by McKim, Mead & White
Perth Amboy Terra Cotta Company
Brick with terra-cotta ornament
Church

19. 37 WASHINGTON SQUARE WEST*
1928–29, Gronenberg & Leuchtag
New York Architectural Terra Cotta Company
Brick with brightly glazed terra-cotta ornament
Apartments

20. 73–75 CHRISTOPHER STREET*
1932–33, Phelps Barnum
New York Architectural Terra Cotta Company
Brick with glazed and lustered terra-cotta ornament
Commercial

21. 716 BROADWAY
1890–91, Alfred Zucker
New York Architectural Terra Cotta Company
Brick with terra-cotta ornament
Industrial converted to commercial and residential

22. NEW YORK FREE CIRCULATING LIBRARY* (now New York Public Library, Ottendorfer Branch)
135 Second Avenue
1883–84, William Schickel
Brick with terra-cotta ornament
Library

23. GERMAN DISPENSARY*
(now Stuyvesant Polyclinic)
137 Second Avenue
1883–84, William Schickel
Brick with terra-cotta ornament
Clinic

24. 136 WAVERLY PLACE*
1928, Walter S. Schneider
Brick with glazed, colored terra-cotta ornament
Apartments

25. 746–750 BROADWAY
1881–83, Starkweather & Gibbs
Boston Terra Cotta Company
Brick with terra-cotta ornament
Commercial

26. FIFTH AVENUE HOTEL*
24 Fifth Avenue
1925–26, Emery Roth
Brick with glazed, colored terra-cotta ornament
Hotel converted to apartments

27. THE GROSVENOR*
39 Fifth Avenue
1922, Emery Roth
New York Architectural Terra Cotta Company
Brick with brightly glazed terra-cotta ornament
Apartments

28. 808 BROADWAY
1887–88, Renwick, Aspinwall & Russell
New York Architectural Terra Cotta Company
Brick and stone with terra-cotta ornament
Industrial converted to residential

29. CHURCH HOUSE OF THE FIRST
PRESBYTERIAN CHURCH OF NEW
YORK CITY*
12 West 12th Street
1960, Edgar Tafel
Gladding, McBean & Company
Green glazed, extruded terra cotta in
    combination with cast stone
Church House

30. INTERNATIONAL TAILORING
COMPANY
111 Fourth Avenue
1919–21, Starrett & Van Vleck
New York Architectural Terra Cotta Company
White terra-cotta cladding and ornament
Industrial converted to commercial and residential

31. 817 BROADWAY
1895–97, George B. Post
Brick with terra-cotta ornament
Commercial

32. ROOSEVELT BUILDING
841 Broadway
1893, Stephen Decatur Hatch
Brick with terra-cotta ornament
Commercial

14th Street to 19th Street

33. 154–60 WEST 14th STREET
1912–13, Herman Lee Meader
New York Architectural Terra Cotta Company
White terra-cotta cladding with brightly
    glazed ornament
Mixed commercial use

34. DECKER BUILDING*
(now Union Building)
33 Union Square West
1893, Alfred Zucker
Brick with textured terra-cotta ornament
Office building

35. JUDGE BUILDING*
2 West 16th Street
1888–89, McKim, Mead & White
Perth Amboy Terra Cotta Company
Brick with terra-cotta ornament
Commercial

36. 91 FIFTH AVENUE
1894–96, Louis Korn
Brick with terra-cotta ornament
Commercial

37. CENTURY BUILDING*
33–37 East 17th Street
1880–81, William Schickel
Brick with terra-cotta ornament
Office building converted to commercial

38. EVERETT BUILDING*
39–45 East 17th Street
1908, Starrett & Van Vleck
New York Architectural Terra Cotta Company
Brick with glazed, colored terra-cotta ornament
Office building

39. ST. ANN BUILDING
3–5 West 18th Street
1895–96, Cleverdon & Putzel
Brick with textured terra-cotta ornament
Commercial

40. SIEGEL-COOPER BUILDING*
616–632 Sixth Avenue
1895–97, Delemos & Cordes
Brick with terra-cotta ornament
Department store converted to mixed
    commercial use

41. 81 IRVING PLACE
1929–30, George F. Pelham
New York Architectural Terra Cotta Company
Brick with terra-cotta ornament
Apartments

20th Street to 29th Street

42. THE GRAMERCY APARTMENTS*
34 Gramercy Park East
1882–83, George DaCunha
Brick with terra-cotta ornament
Apartments

43. 36 GRAMERCY PARK EAST*
1908–10, James Reily Gordon
Atlantic Terra Cotta Company
White terra-cotta cladding
Apartments

44. SEAMAN'S HOUSE YMCA
(now Bayview Correctional Facility)
550 West 20th Street
1930–31, Shreve, Lamb & Harmon
Brick with brightly glazed terra-cotta ornament
YMCA hotel converted to correctional facility

45. EAGLE BUILDING
257 Park Avenue South
1912–13, Warren & Wetmore
Federal Terra Cotta Company
Brick with terra-cotta ornament
Office building

46. GRAMERCY HOUSE
235 East 22nd Street
1929–30, George & Edward Blum
Brick with brightly glazed terra-cotta ornament
Apartments

47. GRAMERCY COURT
152–56 East 22nd Street
1907–8, Bernstein & Bernstein
Brick with terra-cotta ornament
Apartments

48. MANHATTAN TRADE SCHOOL FOR
GIRLS (later Mabel Dean Bacon Vocational High
School; now New Manhattan High School
Collaborative)
127 East 22nd Street
1915–19, C. B. J. Snyder
Atlantic Terra Cotta Company
White terra-cotta cladding
School

49. GEORGE WASHINGTON HOTEL
135–147 East 23rd Street
1928–30, Frank M. Andrews
Brick and cast stone with glazed, colored
    terra-cotta ornament
Hotel

50. CHELSEA APARTMENTS*
222 West 23rd Street
1883–85, Hubert, Pirsson & Company
Boston Terra Cotta Company
Brick and brownstone with terra-cotta ornament
Hotel and apartments

51. NEW YORK SOCIETY FOR THE
PREVENTION OF CRUELTY TO
CHILDREN
295 Park Avenue South
1892, Renwick, Aspinwall & Renwick
Perth Amboy Terra Cotta Company
Brick with terra-cotta ornament
Commercial

52. FLATIRON BUILDING*
175 Fifth Avenue
1901–3, D. H. Burnham
Atlantic Terra Cotta Company
Brick with terra-cotta ornament
Office building

53. 245 SEVENTH AVENUE
1910–12, Squires & Wynkoop
Brick with terra-cotta ornament and an unusual
    terra-cotta cornice
Commercial

54. FOLTIS-FISCHER BUILDING
411–13 Park Avenue South
1929–30, Erhard Djorup
Terra-cotta cladding with Deco motifs and
    gold luster
Restaurant converted to mixed commercial use

55. BOWKER BUILDING
419 Park Avenue South
1926–27, Walter Haefeli
Brick with brightly glazed terra-cotta ornament
Commercial

56. GREEN CENTRAL BUILDING
425 Park Avenue South
1927, Shampan & Shampan
New York Architectural Terra Cotta Company
Brick with terra-cotta ornament on the facade
and in the lobby
Office building converted to apartments

57. HUDNUT BUILDING
115–117 East 29th Street
1905–6, Henry Ives Cobb
Standard Terra Cotta Company
Brick with terra-cotta ornament
Commercial

58. 261 FIFTH AVENUE
1928–29, Buchman & Kahn
Federal Seaboard Terra Cotta Corporation
Brick with brightly colored terra-cotta ornament
and gold luster
Office building

59. THE EMMET BUILDING
95 Madison Avenue
1911–13, J. Stewart Barney
Federal Terra Cotta Company
White terra-cotta cladding and ornament
Office building

60. 838 SIXTH AVENUE
1911, Gillespie & Carrel
White terra-cotta cladding
Commercial

61. 1220 BROADWAY
1931, Levy & Berger
Brick with brightly glazed terra-cotta ornament
Office building

30th Street to 39th Street

62. "SMJ" BUILDING
130 West 30th Street
1927–29, Cass Gilbert
Atlantic Terra Cotta Company
Brick with glazed, colored terra-cotta ornament
Commercial

63. 460 PARK AVENUE SOUTH
1911–12, Herts & Tallant
Federal Terra Cotta Company
White terra-cotta cladding
Office building

64. GROLIER CLUB*
29 East 32nd Street
1889–90, C. W. Romeyn & Company
New York Architectural Terra Cotta Company
Brick and brownstone with terra-cotta ornament
Club converted to offices

65. FURNITURE EXCHANGE
200 Lexington Avenue
1925–26, Kahn & Buchman, York & Sawyer
Brick with terra-cotta ornament
Office building

66. 2 PARK AVENUE
1926–27, Ely Jacques Kahn
Federal Seaboard Terra Cotta Corporation

Brick with brightly colored terra-cotta ornament
Office building

67. VANDERBILT HOTEL
4 Park Avenue
1910–13, Warren & Wetmore
New Jersey Terra Cotta Company
Brick with terra-cotta ornament
Interior Landmark: the Della Robbia Bar
(currently Fiori's restaurant)*
Guastavino Company tiles and polychrome terra
cotta from the Rookwood Pottery are used on
the vaulted ceiling.
Hotel converted to commercial and residential

68. ARSENAL BUILDING
463 Seventh Avenue
1924–25, Buchman & Kahn
Brick with terra-cotta ornament
Office building

69. 402–04 FIFTH AVENUE
1914, Warren & Wetmore
New York Architectural Terra Cotta Company
Glazed, colored terra-cotta cladding
Commercial

70. THE TOWN HOUSE
108 East 38th Street
1929–30, Bowden & Russell
Brick with brightly glazed terra-cotta ornament
Apartments

71. 300 WEST 38th STREET
1902–3, Stein, Cohen & Emery Roth
Brick with terra-cotta ornament
Commercial

72. LEFCOURT NORMANDIE BUILDING
1384–88 Broadway
1926–28, Bark & Djorup
Gold lustered terra-cotta finials ornament the
roofline.
Office building

73. 42 WEST 39th STREET
1927, Buchman & Kahn
Brick with brightly glazed terra-cotta ornament
Office building

40th Street to 49th Street

74. TUDOR CITY
40th to 43rd Street between First and
Second Avenues
1925–28, H. Douglas Ives
Atlantic Terra Cotta Company
Brick with terra-cotta ornament
Apartment complex

75. 10 EAST 40th STREET
1928–29, Ludlow & Peabody
Federal Seaboard Terra Cotta Corporation
Brick with brightly glazed terra-cotta ornament
Office building

76. 110 WEST 40th STREET
1912–14, Buchman & Fox
Federal Terra Cotta Company

White terra-cotta cladding
Office building

77. 295 MADISON AVENUE
1928–30, Bark & Djorup
Brick with glazed, colored terra-cotta ornament
Office building

78. 18 EAST 41st STREET
1912–14, George & Edward Blum
White terra-cotta cladding with glazed, colored
ornament
Office building

79. CHANIN BUILDING*
122 East 42nd Street
1927–29, Sloan & Robertson
Atlantic Terra Cotta Company
Brick with terra-cotta ornament
Commercial

80. PERSHING SQUARE BUILDING
100 East 42nd Street
1921–23, John Sloan, York & Sawyer
Atlantic Terra Cotta Company
Brick with glazed, colored terra-cotta ornament
Office building

81. 500 FIFTH AVENUE
1930–31, Shreve, Lamb & Harmon
Brick with terra-cotta window spandrels
Office building

82. NEW AMSTERDAM THEATER*
214 West 42nd Street
1901–3, Herts & Tallant
Interior Landmark: Terra-cotta banister and newel
posts designed by architect Thorbjorn Bassoe
and executed by *Perth Amboy Terra Cotta
Company.*
Terra-cotta cladding and ornament
Theater

83. LYRIC THEATER
213 West 42nd Street (main entrance on
43rd Street)
1902–3, V. Hugo Koehler
Attributed to *Conkling-Armstrong Terra Cotta
Company*
Terra-cotta cladding and ornament
Theater

84. McGRAW-HILL BUILDING*
330 West 42nd Street
1930–31, Hood, Godley & Fouilhoux
Federal Seaboard Terra Cotta Corporation
Blue-green terra-cotta cladding
Office building

85. CENTURY ASSOCIATION
7 West 43rd Street
1889–91, McKim, Mead & White
Perth Amboy Terra Cotta Company
Brick with terra-cotta ornament
Clubhouse

86. STATE AND TRUST BANK BUILDING
681 Eighth Avenue
1927–28, Dennison & Hirons
Atlantic Terra Cotta Company

Brick with brightly glazed terra-cotta ornament
Bank converted to mixed commercial use

87. BEAUX-ARTS INSTITUTE OF
DESIGN*
304 East 44th Street
1928, Frederick C. Hirons
Atlantic Terra Cotta Company
Brick with brightly glazed terra-cotta ornament
and murals
School converted to commercial use

88. FILM CENTER BUILDING*
630 Ninth Avenue
1928–29, Buchman & Kahn
Atlantic Terra Cotta Company
Brick with terra-cotta ornament
Office building

89. DAILY MIRROR BUILDING
235 East 45th Street
1928–29, Emery Roth
Brick with brightly glazed terra-cotta ornament
Office building

90. NEW YORK CENTRAL BUILDING*
(now Helmsley Building)
230 Park Avenue
1927–29, Warren & Wetmore
Atlantic Terra Cotta Company
Brick with terra-cotta ornament
Viaducts and office building

91. THE FRED F. FRENCH BUILDING*
551 Fifth Avenue
1926–27, H. Douglas Ives; Sloan & Robertson
Atlantic Terra Cotta Company
Brick with brightly glazed terra-cotta ornament;
large murals at the top of the building
Office building

92. LYCEUM THEATER*
149–157 West 45th Street
1901–3, Herts & Tallant
White terra-cotta cladding and ornament
Theater

93. 21–27 WEST 46th STREET
1928–29, William C. Sommerfeld
Brick with brightly glazed terra-cotta ornament
Office building

94. HOTEL BELVEDERE
319 West 48th Street
1925–26, Bertram N. Marcus
Brick with polychrome terra-cotta ornament
Hotel

50th Street to 59th Street

95. RCA VICTOR BUILDING*
(now General Electric Building)
570 Lexington Avenue
1929–31, Cross & Cross
Federal Seaboard Terra Cotta Corporation
Brick with terra-cotta ornament
Office building

96. MECCA TEMPLE* (now City Center)
131 West 55th Street

1922–24, H. P. Knowles
New York Architectural Terra Cotta Company
Brick and brightly glazed terra-cotta
Theater

97. 340 EAST 57th STREET
1929–30, Rosario Candela
Atlantic Terra Cotta Company
Brick with glazed terra-cotta ornament
Apartments

98. 320 EAST 57th STREET
1925–26, George & Edward Blum
Brick with terra-cotta ornament
Apartments

99. FULLER BUILDING*
41 East 57th Street
1928–29, Walker & Gillette
Atlantic Terra Cotta Company
Brick with terra-cotta ornament
Office building

100. CHALIF STUDIOS (now CAMI Hall)
165 West 57th Street
1915–16, G. A. and H. Boehm
Brick with glazed colored terra-cotta ornament
Dance studio converted to concert hall and
office building

101. CARNEGIE HALL*
West 57th Street and Seventh Avenue
1889–91, William B. Tuthill
New York Architectural Terra Cotta Company
Brick with terra-cotta ornament
Concert Hall

102. SQUIBB BUILDING
745 Fifth Avenue
1929–31, Office of Ely Jacques Kahn
Glazed brick with terra-cotta ornament
Office building

103. ALWYN COURT APARTMENTS*
180 West 58th Street
1907–9, Harde & Short
White terra-cotta cladding
Apartments

104. PLAZA HOTEL*
58–59th Street and Fifth Avenue at
Central Park South
1905–7, Henry J. Hardenbergh
Atlantic Terra Cotta Company
Brick with white terra-cotta cladding
Hotel

105. GAINSBOROUGH STUDIOS*
222 Central Park South
1907–8, Charles W. Buckham
Conkling-Armstrong Terra Cotta Company
Brick with terra-cotta and tile ornament
Apartments

106. 240 CENTRAL PARK SOUTH
1939–41, Mayer & Whittlesey
Brick with extruded terra-cotta panels at street level
Apartments

East Side, 60th Street to 110th
Street

107. LOUIS SHERRY*
691 Madison Avenue
1928, McKim, Mead & White
New York Architectural Terra Cotta Company
Brightly glazed terra-cotta ornament
Stores

108. HOTEL LOWELL*
28 East 63rd Street
1925–26, Henry S. Churchill
New York Architectural Terra Cotta Company
Brick with brightly glazed terra-cotta ornament
Hotel and apartments

109. 45 EAST 66th STREET*
1906–8, Harde & Short
Atlantic Terra Cotta Company
Brick with terra-cotta ornament
Apartments

110. PARK EAST SYNAGOGUE*
163 East 67th Street
1889–90, Schneider & Herter
Brick with terra-cotta ornament
Synagogue

111. 210 EAST 68th STREET
1928–29, George & Edward Blum
Brick with brightly glazed terra-cotta ornament
Apartments

112. CARLYLE HOTEL*
35 East 76th Street
1929–30, Sylvan Bien
Brick with terra-cotta ornament
Hotel

113. ARDSLEY GARAGE
165 East 77th Street
1913–14, George F. Pelham
New York Architectural Terra Cotta Company
White terra-cotta cladding
Garage

114. 898 PARK AVENUE*
1923–24, John Sloan
Atlantic Terra Cotta Company
Brick with glazed, colored terra-cotta ornament
Apartments

115. HUNTER COLLEGE SCHOOL OF
SOCIAL WORK
127–135 East 79th Street
1967–68, Enlarged 1988; Both by Wank, Adams,
Slavin Associates
Federal Seaboard Terra Cotta Corporation
Extruded terra-cotta cladding
School

116. 240 EAST 79th STREET
1928–29, Godwin, Thompson & Patterson
Brick with brightly glazed terra-cotta ornament
Apartments

117. 935 PARK AVENUE
1923–24, Sugarman & Berger and Hess
Brick with glazed, colored terra-cotta ornament
Apartments

118. 940 PARK AVENUE
1925–26, George & Edward Blum
Brick with glazed, colored terra-cotta ornament
Apartments

119. 944 PARK AVENUE
1929–30, George F. Pelham
New York Architectural Terra Cotta Company
Brick with glazed terra-cotta ornament
Apartments

120. 1491–93 THIRD AVENUE
1930, George Dress
Glazed, colored terra-cotta ornament
Commercial

121. 157–161 EAST 86th STREET
1903–4, George Keister
Brick with terra-cotta ornament
Commercial

122. CAPITOL*
12 East 87th Street
1910–11, George & Edward Blum
Brick with white terra-cotta cladding
Apartments

123. ALAN GARAGE
154 East 87th Street
1929–30, J. H. Galloway
Brick, white terra cotta, and glazed, colored
   ornament
Garage

124. CHURCH OF THE HOLY TRINITY*
316 East 88th Street
1897–99, Barney & Chapman
Perth Amboy Terra Cotta Company
Brick with terra-cotta ornament and sculpture;
   portions of the interior use terra cotta.
Church

125. 1082 PARK AVENUE
1925 (new facade on existing structure),
   Augustus N. Allen
Federal Terra Cotta Company
Brightly glazed terra-cotta ornament
Rowhouse converted to stores and apartments

126. WEBER BUILDING
1377–79 Lexington Avenue
1889–90, Weber & Drosser
Brick with terra-cotta ornament
Apartments

127. ST. NICHOLAS RUSSIAN
ORTHODOX CATHEDRAL*
15 East 97th Street
1901–2, John Bergesen
Attributed to *Grueby Faience*
Brick with brightly glazed terra-cotta ornament
Church

128. ALL SAINTS R. C. CHURCH
AND RECTORY
47 East 129th Street
1889, Renwick, Aspinwall & Russell
New York Architectural Terra Cotta Company
Brick with terra-cotta ornament
Church

West Side, 60th Street to 110th
Street

129. SOFIA BROTHERS WAREHOUSE*
(now Sofia Apartments)
47 Columbus Avenue
1929–30, Jardine, Hill & Murdock
Brick with glazed, colored terra-cotta ornament
Warehouse converted to apartments

130. YMCA—THE F. COSSITT MEMORIAL
BUILDING*
5 West 63rd Street
1928–30, Dwight James Baum
O. W. Ketcham
Brick with brightly glazed terra-cotta ornament
YMCA

131. PYTHIAN TEMPLE
135 West 70th Street
1926–27, Thomas Lamb
Brick with brightly glazed terra-cotta ornament
Masonic temple converted to apartments

132. DAKOTA APARTMENTS*
1 West 72nd Street
1880–84, Henry Hardenbergh
Lewis & Lane Architectural Terra Cotta Works
Brick and brownstone with terra-cotta ornament
Apartments

133. ANSONIA HOTEL*
2109 Broadway
1899–1904, Paul E. M. Duboy
New York Architectural Terra Cotta Company
Brick with terra-cotta ornament
Apartments

134. STUDIO BUILDING*
44 West 77th Street
1907–9, Harde & Short
Atlantic Terra Cotta Company
Brick with terra-cotta ornament
Apartments

135. WEST END COLLEGIATE CHURCH
and SCHOOL*
77th Street and West End Avenue
1892–93, Robert W. Gibson
New York Architectural Terra Cotta Company
Brick with terra-cotta ornament
Church and school

136. THE EVELYN*
101 West 78th Street
1882–86, Emile Gruwé
Brick with terra-cotta ornament
Apartments

137. 121–131 WEST 78th STREET*
1885–86, Rafael Guastavino

Brick with terra-cotta ornament
Rowhouses

138. HOTEL LUCERNE*
201 West 79th Street
1903–4, Harry B. Mulliken
New York Architectural Terra Cotta Company
Brick with terra-cotta ornament
Hotel and apartments

139. BROADWAY FASHION BUILDING
2315 Broadway
1930–31, Sugarman & Berger
Terra-cotta window spandrels on the facade
Commercial

140. RED HOUSE*
350 West 85th Street
1903–4, Harde & Short
Brick with terra-cotta ornament
Apartments

141. 40 WEST 86th STREET*
1930–31, J. M. Felson
New York Architectural Terra Cotta Company
Brick with brightly glazed terra-cotta ornament
Apartments

142. ST. PAUL'S METHODIST EPISCOPAL
CHURCH and PARISH HOUSE*
(now Church of St. Paul and St. Andrew, United
Methodist)
540 West End Avenue
1895–97, R. H. Robertson
Brick with terra-cotta ornament; circular windows
surrounded by terra-cotta figures
Church

143. 201 WEST 89th STREET
1924–25, Emery Roth
Brick with brightly glazed terra-cotta ornament
Apartments

144. CLIFF DWELLER'S APARTMENTS
243 Riverside Drive
1914–17, Herman Lee Meader
New York Architectural Terra Cotta Company
Brick and terra-cotta ornament
Apartments

145. MIDTOWN THEATER*
(now Metro Theater)
2624–2626 Broadway
1932–33, Boak & Paris
Brightly glazed terra-cotta cladding with terra-cotta
   rondel of Comedy and Tragedy
Movie theater

146. DALLIEU
838 West End Avenue
1912–13, George & Edward Blum
Brick with terra-cotta ornament
Apartments

147. HORN AND HARDART AUTOMAT
2710 Broadway
1930, F. P. Platt Brothers
Stone facade with brightly glazed terra-cotta
   ornament
Restaurant converted to mixed commercial use

West Side, North of 110th Street
(148-162, listed south to north)

148. REGENT THEATER*
(now First Corinthian Baptist Church)
1910 Seventh Avenue
1912–13, Thomas Lamb
South Amboy Terra Cotta Company
Brightly glazed terra-cotta ornament
Movie theater converted to a church

149. BARNARD COLLEGE (MILBANK,
BRINCKERHOFF, AND FISKE HALLS)
606 West 120th Street
1896–97, Charles Rich (Lamb & Rich)
B. Kreischer's Sons
Brick with terra-cotta ornament
School

150. 133–142 WEST 122nd STREET
1885–87, Francis H. Kimball
Brick with terra-cotta ornament
Rowhouses

151. HARLEM CLUB*
(now Bethelite Community Baptist Church)
36 West 123rd Street
1888–89, Lamb & Rich
New York Architectural Terra Cotta Company
Brick with terra-cotta ornament
Club converted to a church

152. 45 TIEMANN PLACE
1909, Emery Roth
Brick with brightly colored terra-cotta ornament
Apartments

153. HOTEL THERESA*
2090 Adam Clayton Powell, Jr. Boulevard
(Seventh Avenue)
1912–13, George & Edward Blum
New Jersey Terra Cotta Company
White brick and terra-cotta ornament
Hotel converted to mixed commercial use

154. ST. ALOYSIUS R. C. CHURCH
209–19 West 132nd Street
1902–4, William W. Renwick
New York Architectural Terra Cotta Company;
Grueby Faience Company
Brick with terra-cotta ornament
Church

155. COLLEGE HEIGHTS
500 West 140th Street
1915–16, George & Edward Blum
New Jersey Terra Cotta Company
Brick with terra-cotta ornament
Apartments

156. ANDREW JACKSON
730 Riverside Drive
1911–12, George & Edward Blum
Federal Terra Cotta Company
Brick with terra-cotta ornament
Apartments

157. THE HISPANIC SOCIETY OF
AMERICA*
613 West 155th Street

1904–8, Charles Pratt Huntington
Interiors constructed of ornate terra cotta
Hispanic Society of America (open to the public)

158. AUDUBON BALLROOM
3940–60 Broadway
1912, Thomas Lamb
White terra-cotta cladding with brightly
glazed ornament
Theater largely replaced by biomedical research
facility

159. LOEW'S 175th STREET THEATER
(now Reverend Ike's United Church)
175th Street and Broadway
1930, Thomas Lamb
White and buff terra-cotta cladding and ornament
Movie theater converted to a church

160. YESHIVA UNIVERSITY (MAIN
BUILDING)
2540 Amsterdam Avenue
1928, Charles Meyers
Brick with brightly glazed and lustered
terra-cotta ornament
School

161. 501 WEST 187th STREET
1913, George F. Pelham
New York Architectural Terra Cotta Company
Brick with brightly glazed terra-cotta ornament
Apartments

162. 145 WADSWORTH TERRACE
1929, H. I. Feldman
New York Architectural Terra Cotta Company
Brick with brightly glazed terra-cotta ornament
Apartments

PART II: BROOKLYN (163-182, listed
alphabetically)

163. HERMAN BEHR RESIDENCE*
84 Pierrepont Street
1890, Frank Freeman
Brick, brownstone, and terra-cotta ornament
House converted to apartments

164. BERKELEY and GROSVENOR
APARTMENTS*
111 and 115 Montague Street
1885, Parfitt Brothers
Brick, brownstone, and terra-cotta ornament
Apartments

165. BROOKLYN ACADEMY OF MUSIC*
30 Lafayette Avenue
1907–8, Herts & Tallant
Atlantic Terra Cotta Company
Brick with brightly colored terra-cotta ornament
BAM

166. BROOKLYN MASONIC TEMPLE*
317 Clermont Avenue
1908–9, Lord & Hewlett with Pell & Corbett
Atlantic Terra Cotta Company
Brick with brightly colored terra-cotta ornament
Masonic temple converted to community facility

167. CATHOLIC SEAMAN'S INSTITUTE
653 Hicks Street
1941–43, Henry V. Murphy
Brick and polychrome terra-cotta ornament in a
streamline style
Institutional Service Center, Roman Catholic
Diocese of Brooklyn

168. CHILD'S RESTAURANT
21st Street and the Boardwalk
1923, Dennison & Hirons (Sculptor,
Maxfield H. Keck)
Atlantic Terra Cotta Company
Brightly glazed terra-cotta ornament
Restaurant converted to mixed commercial use

169. PRUDENTIAL SAVINGS BANK
(now Emigrant Savings Bank)
1954 Flatbush Avenue at Kings Highway
1946–48, Kenneth B. Norton
Stone facade with terra-cotta mural over
the entrance
Bank

170. GRACE UNITED METHODIST
CHURCH*
29–35 Seventh Avenue
1887, Parfitt Brothers
Boston Terra Cotta Company
Stone with terra-cotta ornament
Church

171. THE GRIFFIN
101 Lafayette Avenue
1931–32, Fred Klie
Atlantic Terra Cotta Company
Brick with polychrome terra-cotta ornament on
the facade and in the lobby
Apartments

172. IMPERIAL APARTMENTS*
1198 Pacific Street; 1327–1339 Bedford Avenue
1892, Montrose Morris
New York Architectural Terra Cotta Company
Brick and terra-cotta ornament
Apartments

173. 474–476 LAFAYETTE AVENUE
1881, Parfitt Brothers
Brick and terra-cotta ornament
Apartments

174. LONG ISLAND HISTORICAL
SOCIETY*
(now Brooklyn Historical Society)
128 Pierrepont Street
1878–81, George B. Post
Perth Amboy Terra Cotta Company
Brick with terra-cotta ornament
Museum and library

175. THE MONTAGUE*
105 Montague Street
1885, Parfitt Brothers
Brick and brownstone with terra-cotta ornament
Apartments

176. MONTAUK CLUB*
    25 Eighth Avenue
    1889–91, Francis H. Kimball
    New York Architectural Terra Cotta Company
    Brick with terra-cotta frieze and ornament
    Clubhouse

177. PROSPECT PARK BOATHOUSE*
    1904, Helmle & Huberty
    White terra-cotta cladding
    Boathouse

178. PUBLIC BATH NO. 7*
    227–231 Fourth Avenue
    1906–10, Raymond F. Almirall
    Brick and brightly glazed terra-cotta ornament
    Vacant

179. ST. AMBROSE R. C. CHURCH
    (now Mount Pisgah Baptist Church)
    222 Tomkins Avenue
    1905–6, George H. Streeton
    Excelsior Terra Cotta Company
    Brick and polychrome terra-cotta ornament
    Church

180. ST. BARBARA'S R. C. CHURCH
    Central Avenue and Bleecker Street
    1907–10, Helmle & Huberty
    Brick with white and cream terra-cotta ornament
    Church

181. ST. MICHAEL'S R. C. CHURCH
    4200 Fourth Avenue
    1905, Raymond F. Almirall
    Grueby Faience
    Brick and brightly glazed terra-cotta ornament
        and tile
    Church

182. THOMPSON METER COMPANY
    BUILDING
    Bridge Street between York & Tillman Streets
    1909–10, Louis Jallade (Henry J. Hardenbergh,
        designer)
    Concrete with polychrome terra-cotta ornament
    Vacant

PART III: BRONX (183-188, listed
        alphabetically)

183. BRONX ZOO
    Bronx Park, south of East Fordham Road
    1901, Primate House; 1903, Lion House; 1905, Bird
        House, Heins & La Farge
    Brick with sculpted terra-cotta animals
    Zoo

184. FIFTY-SECOND POLICE PRECINCT
    STATION HOUSE* (now the Forty-First
    Police Precinct Station House)
    3016 Webster Avenue
    1904–6, Stoughton & Stoughton
    Patterned brick with polychrome terra-cotta
        ornament and tile roof
    Police Station

185. MORRIS HIGH SCHOOL*
    East 166th Street at Boston Road

1900–1904, C. B. J. Snyder
    New York Architectural Terra Cotta Company
    Brick with terra-cotta ornament
    School

186. PARKCHESTER
    East Tremont Avenue, Purdy Street, McGraw
        Avenue, Hugh Grant Circle, White Plains Road
    1938–42, Richmond H. Shreve (Chair of the Board
        of Design)
    Federal Seaboard Terra Cotta Corporation
    Brick with many polychrome terra-cotta
        sculptures, reliefs, and murals
    Apartment complex

187. PARK PLAZA APARTMENTS*
    1005 Jerome Avenue
    1929–31, Horace Ginsberg and Marvin Fine
    Brick with polychrome terra-cotta ornament
    Apartments

188. WEBBTREE BUILDING
    1887 Webster Avenue
    1928, Lucian Pisciotta
    New York Architectural Terra Cotta Company
    White terra-cotta cladding and ornament
    Commercial

PART IV: QUEENS (189-196, listed
        alphabetically)

189. BOWERY BAY SEWAGE TREATMENT
    WORKS (PUMP & BLOWER
    BUILDING)
    Steinway and Bowery Bay, Nineteenth Avenue at
        the foot of 45th Street
    1938–39, Murals by Cesare Steat and Joseph Konzal
    Entrance flanked by large terra-cotta murals
        portraying the construction of the building
    Sewage treatment plant

190. FLUSHING HIGH SCHOOL*
    35–01 Union Street
    1912–15, C. B. J. Snyder
    Brick with terra-cotta ornament
    School

191. FOREST HILLS STATION POST
    OFFICE
    106–28 Queens Boulevard
    1937–38, Lorimer A. Rich
    Atlantic Terra Cotta Company
    Extruded terra-cotta units and *Spirit of
        Communication*, a terra-cotta relief by
        Sten Jacobsson
    Post Office

192. HILLCREST COURT
    70–35 Broadway, Jackson Heights
    1927, S. L. Malkind
    Brick with terra-cotta ornament
    Apartments

193. MARINE AIR TERMINAL*
    La Guardia Airport
    1939–40, Delano & Aldrich
    Brick with brightly colored terra-cotta
        "flying dolphins"
    Airline terminal

194. ROMAN CATHOLIC CHURCH OF
    THE MOST PRECIOUS BLOOD
    (Interior)
    32–33 36th Street, Long Island City
    1931–32, Henry J. McGill
    *Atlantic Terra Cotta Company; Mosaic
        Tile Company*
    Church interior covered with tile and extruded
        terra cotta
    Church

195. NEW YORK ARCHITECTURAL
    TERRA COTTA COMPANY OFFICE*
    42–10 Vernon Boulevard, Long Island City
    1892, Francis H. Kimball
    New York Architectural Terra Cotta Company
    Brick with elaborate terra-cotta ornament
        including signage plaques and chimney pots
    Vacant

196. SUFFOLK TITLE & GUARANTEE
    BUILDING
    90–04 161st Street, Jamaica
    1929, Dennison & Hirons
    Limestone facade with polychrome terra-cotta
        ornament
    Commercial

PART V: STATEN ISLAND (197-200,
        listed alphabetically)

197. AMBASSADOR APARTMENTS
    30 Daniel Low Terrace
    1932, Lucian Pisciotta
    Brick and brightly colored terra-cotta ornament
        with Deco motifs
    Apartments

198. ATLANTIC TERRA COTTA
    COMPANY BUILDING
    101 Ellis Street, Tottenville
    Remaining factory building with large terra-cotta
        rondel and several small plaques
    Factory converted to mixed commercial use

199. PARAMOUNT THEATER
    560 Bay Street
    1935, Rapp & Rapp
    Orange brick with polychrome terra-cotta
        ornament
    Vacant

200. SEAVIEW HOSPITAL*
    Manor Road and Rockland Avenue
    1905, Raymond F. Almirall
    Ceramic details by *Joost Thooft and Labouchere of
        the De Porceleyne Fles Company*, Holland
    Brick with terra-cotta mosaic panels and sculpted
        ornament
    Vacant

*The formation of this list began in 1981 with a grant
from the Educational Facilities Laboratory, a division
of the Academy for Educational Development.*

Organizations

Friends of Terra Cotta
c/o Tunick
771 West End Avenue, 10E
New York, NY 10025
(212) 932-1750

Historic Districts Council
45 West 67th Street
New York, NY 10023
(212) 799-5837

Municipal Art Society
457 Madison Avenue
New York, NY 10022
(212) 935-3960

New York City Landmarks Preservation
Commission
100 Old Slip
New York, NY 10005
(212) 487-6800

New York Landmarks Conservancy
141 Fifth Avenue
New York, NY 10010
(212) 995-5260

Tile Heritage Foundation
2340 North Fitch Mt. Road
Healdsburg, CA 95448
(707) 433-8022

Tiles & Architectural Ceramics Society
c/o K. Huggins, Reabrook Lodge,
8 Sutton Road, Shrewsbury SY2 6DD
England
0743-236127

Terra-Cotta Manufacturers

Boston Valley Terra Cotta
6860 South Abbott Road
Orchard Park, NY 14127
(716) 649-7490

Gladding, McBean & Company
P. O. Box 97
Lincoln, CA 95648
(916) 645-3341

Ibstock Hathernware, Ltd.
Station Works, Rempstone Road
Normanton on Soar
Loughborough, Leicestershire
LE12 5EW
England
1509-842273

Shaws of Darwen, Ltd.
Waterside, Darwen
Lancashire BB3 3NX
England
0254-775111

Notes

Preface

1. Margaret Henderson Floyd, "A Terra Cotta Cornerstone for Copley Square: An Assessment of the Museum of Fine Arts, Boston, by Sturgis and Brigham (1870–1876), in the Context of Its Technological and Stylistic Origins" (Ph. D. dissertation, Boston University, 1974); Theodore Prudon, "Architectural Terra Cotta and Ceramic Veneer in the United States Prior to World War II: A History of Its Development and An Analysis of Its Deterioration Problems and Possible Repair Methodologies" (Doctor of Philosophy in the Graduate School of Arts and Sciences, Columbia University, 1981); Dale H. Ferns, "A Conservation Analysis of the Terra Cotta Cladding of Liberty Tower" (Master's thesis, Columbia University, 1980).

2. "Architectural Terra Cotta A Big Factor In New Building," *New York Times*, 14 May 1911, sec. 8, 1.

3. Anatole Broyard, "Reading and Writing: New York, New York," *New York Times*, 13 September 1981, sec. 7, 59.

4. Carol Willis, *Form Follows Finance* (New York: Princeton Architectural Press, 1995), 30–33. There is clear evidence in this publication that a powerful architectural presence could result in the rapid rental of office space.

5. Charles Fergus Binns, *Transactions of the American Ceramic Society* 7 (1905): 48.

6. Rose Slivka and Karen Tsujimoto, *The Art of Peter Voulkos* (Japan: Kodansha International, 1995), 52. "In New York, the craft world welcomed him as their hero…but the larger segment of the art world remained aloof in the traditional posture of disdain for "craft" connections." This comment refers to the 1960 New York solo exhibition of Peter Voulkos's work at the Museum of Modern Art as part of the "New Talent" series organized by Peter Selz.

7. Ibid., 60.

8. Paul Goldberger, *The City Observed: New York* (New York: Vintage Books, 1979), 219–20.

9. "Adoption of Victorian Gothic," *Real Estate Record and Builders Guide* (3 April 1909): 646.

PART ONE

Chapter 1

10. Susan McDaniel Ceccacci, "Architectural Terra-Cotta in the United States Before 1870" (Master of Arts thesis, Boston University Graduate School, 1991), 23–24.

11. Ibid., 24.

12. Benjamin Silliman, *The World of Science, Art & Industry Illustrated from Examples in the New York Exhibition, 1853–54* (New York: G. P. Putnam & Co.; London: Low, Son & Co., 1854). By 1853, when it exhibited wares in the Crystal Palace Exhibition, the company was called Tolman, Hathaway, & Stone.

13. The company name changes that followed were: Hathaway & Stone (1855–56) and then William Stone (1857–1860).

14. Letter to Messrs. Upjohn & Co. from Edward Roche (1 September 1852), Box 6, Upjohn Papers, New York Public Library, emphasis in original. Many thanks to Sarah Bradford Landau, who sent me a copy of this letter since the original can no longer be found in the Upjohn Papers. The letter states: "I received ordering 48 additional imitation brown stone key stones in terra cotta to be delivered at the Trinity Buildings. Broadway for the sum of $82.80 dollars." Also, Ceccacci, "Architectural Terra-Cotta in the United States Before 1870," 31.

15. New Jersey State Museum, *New Jersey Pottery and Porcelain Prior to 1876* (Newark, N. J.: The Museum, 1915), 19–20. The company ceased operation in 1858. The four partners were Paul Huber, an architect; Anton Winter, a civil engineer; Frederick Schrag; and Franz Haefeli, a practical potter.

16. Edward H. Putnam, "New York City's First Terra Cotta," *American Architect* (20 November 1925): 429–30.

17. Walter Geer, *The Story of Terra Cotta* (New York: Tobias A. Wright, 1920), 35.

18. Thomas Cusack, "Architectural Terra-Cotta," *The Brickbuilder* 5 (December 1896): 227.

19. Ceccacci, "Architectural Terra-cotta in the United States Before 1870," 91–95.

Chapter 2

20. Michael Stratton, *The Terracotta Revival* (London: Victor Gollancz, 1993), 22.

21. Sarah Bradford Landau and Carl W. Condit, *Rise of the New York Skyscraper 1865–1913* (New Haven: Yale University Press, 1996), 46. It is not known what architect spoke these words, although the quote from page 46 provides possible names. "Upjohn moved his office into the [Trinity] building when it was completed and also took other rooms, which he then leased out. In 1857 Upjohn was one of the founders of the American Institute of Architects, which was established in the Trinity Building. The first office of Henry Hobson Richardson was in this building, and other well-known architects shared the address…."

22. *A History of Real Estate Building and Architecture in New York During the Last Quarter of a Century* (New York: Record and Guide, 1898; reprinted New York: Arno Press, Inc., 1967), 509–10.

23. P. B. Wight, "Fireproof Construction—And the Practice of American Architects," *American Architect and Building News* (19 August 1893): 114. A paper read to the 27th Annual Convention of the A. I. A.

24. Stratton, *The Terracotta Revival*, 148.

25. *The Clay-Worker* 8 (1887): 113, quoted in Stratton, *The Terracotta Revival*, 148. Taylor's influence extended beyond his vision for the future of terra cotta. He not only reconfigured the manufacturing process of terra cotta but also helped to place employees. One of these, his brother Robert, worked as the foreman for the Chicago Terra Cotta Company and later was the superintendent of A. Hall and Sons Terra Cotta Works in Perth Amboy, N. J.

26. Sharon S. Darling, *Chicago Ceramics & Glass* (Chicago: Chicago Historical Society, 1979), 164. Also see James Taylor, "The Manufacture of Terra Cotta in Chicago," *American Architect and Building News* (30 December 1876): 420–21.

27. Taylor, "The Manufacture of Terra Cotta in Chicago," 420–21.

28. Stratton, *The Terracotta Revival*, 155. Marcus Spring, the wealthy dry-goods merchant who befriended James Taylor when he first arrived in New York in 1870, was the father of Edward Spring. This was confirmed in a telephone conversation with Ila G. Miller, who was doing research on Eagleswood Art Pottery, Sept. 1995.

29. Charles Binns, "Education in Clay," *Craftsman* 4 (July 1903): 160–68.

30. Edwin Atlee Barber, *The Pottery and Porcelain of the United States* (3rd Edition, Revised and Enlarged, New York: Feingold & Lewis, 1976), 304.

31. Susan R. Strong, *History of American Ceramics: An Annotated Bibliography* (Metuchen, N. J.: The Scarecrow Press, Inc., 1983), 46.

32. Ibid.

33. *The Clay-Worker* 27 (1897): 529–30, *The Clay-Worker* 25 (1896): 40–42.

34. See Part IV, Chapter 12, page 105 for information on the two earliest schools.

35. Geer, *The Story of Terra Cotta*, 61. The City of Boston architect for the school was George Clough.

36. Lewis and Wood closed in 1880, and the following year a new partnership, Lewis and Lane, was formed. In July 1883, H. A. Lewis Architectural Terra Cotta Works was established, remaining in operation until 1887. For more information, see Appendix C, page 142.

37. Geer, *The Story of Terra Cotta*, 69.

38. Geer, *The Story of Terra Cotta*, 70. Also relevant is a quote from the article "A Tribute to the Memory of James Taylor," *13th Annual Convention, National Brick Manufacturer's Association*, 31: "There [at the Boston Terra Cotta Company] he remained until Dec. 31, 1885, when he left, going to New York at the earnest solicitation of O. B. Potter, Esq., who had been brought in contact with him in the course of construction by the former of several large buildings in which a large amount of terra cotta had been used, and who had become attracted to him." Also see Stratton, *The Terracotta Revival*, 160. In this reference the claim is made that O. B. Potter induced Taylor to become the superintendent of the New York Company.

39. Jack Finney, *Time and Again* (New York: Simon & Schuster, 1970).

40. "New Potter Building," *Special Illustrated Edition of Building* 3 (October 1884–December 1885): 89. "The old building made itself notorious the country over for burning up in the shortest time on record. The new structure will be famous as the result of much thought and many experiments in order to put up an ideal fireproof building and it will endure for ages."

41. Stratton, *The Terracotta Revival*, 42.

42. Geer, *The Story of Terra Cotta*, 70. The New York Architectural Terra Cotta Company Office (1892), a New York City landmark, is located at 42–10 Vernon Boulevard, Long Island City, N. Y. The fireplace plaque mentioned is inside the building but another identical one is on the north side of the building.

43. Letter to the author (17 January 1985) from grandson David Taylor states that James Taylor is buried in Fair View Cemetery, Red Bank, N. J. Arthur Taylor and his family have plots in another section of the Fair View Cemetery. The author obtained the following information by visiting James Taylor's grave on April 1, 1996: Taylor's wife was Elizabeth Hamnell (1840–1931) and his children included Mrs. Chas. H. Walling of Port Monmouth, Mrs. A. G. Waldecker of Long Island City (Minnie Taylor, 1867–1945), Miss Edith H. Taylor (who married E. A. Wheller sometime after 1898) and Arthur Taylor. Frank Taylor (1874–1888), son of James and Elizabeth, predeceased his parents.

44. Terra-cotta headstones were made by many of the terra-cotta manufacturers. See Richard Veit, "'A Piece of Granite That's Been Made in Two Weeks': Terra-Cotta Gravemarkers from New Jersey and New York, 1875–1930," *Markers: Journal of the Association for Gravestone Studies* XII (1995): 1–29.

45. A piece of terra cotta with this mark is in the possession of the current owner of the house (which is located at 108 Wilson Avenue, Port Monmouth, N. J.), Steven Hofmann. This piece was photographed on April 1, 1996.

46. Randall Gabrielan, *Images of America, Middletown Township* (New Hampshire: Arcadia Publishing, 1994), 84–85. *The Clay-Worker* 31 (1899): 15. (This obituary, titled "James Taylor, a Pioneer Terra Cotta Manufacturer and Writer," states that he bought his farm from a Reverend W. V. Wilson in 1870.)

47. "A Tribute to the Memory of James Taylor," *13th Annual Convention, National Brick Manufacturer's Association*, 30–32. For additional information about James Taylor, see Stratton, *The Terracotta Revival* and Geer, *The Story of Terra Cotta*.

48. "A Tribute to the Memory of James Taylor," program for the

13th Annual Convention, National Brick Manufacturer's Association, 30–32.

49. These letters are in the archives of Gladding, McBean & Company, Lincoln, California. This material, which is twenty-seven pages in length, covers many aspects of manufacturing, including appropriate clays, clay mixtures and color, preparation and application of slip, kiln stacking, and methods of firing. In one letter Taylor referred to their financial arrangement and requested an additional $150 in payment for continued assistance.

50. Advice Letter #5 (12 October 1888) from James Taylor to Gladding, McBean & Company.

51. Geer, *The Story of Terra Cotta*, 92.

52. James Taylor, "Front Brick, Their Relation To Architectural Design," Proceeding of the 7th Annual National Brick Manufacturers Association (1893): 165.

53. Geer, *The Story of Terra Cotta*, 137–38. "After all other resources had failed, Mathiasen went and saw his friend James Taylor, who at that time [1896] was living in retirement on his farm at [Port] Monmouth, New Jersey.... Taylor went and saw the inspector and the contractor, and in his usual persuasive...way soon convinced the inspector that the terra cotta was up to specifications and the best ever made."

54. *Long Island City Star*, 5 February 1886, sec. 2, 4.

55. *A History of Real Estate Building and Architecture in New York During the Last Quarter of a Century*, 509–31. Taylor included the following East Coast manufacturers: Celadon Terra-Cotta Company, Limited, Alfred, New York; Excelsior Terra-Cotta Company, Rocky Hill, New Jersey; Standard Terra-Cotta Company, Perth Amboy, New Jersey; New Jersey Terra-Cotta Company, Perth Amboy, New Jersey; Perth Amboy Terra-Cotta Company, Perth Amboy, New Jersey. His list omitted these East Coast manufacturers who were active at the time: New York Architectural Terra Cotta Company, Long Island City, New York; Conkling-Armstrong Company, Philadelphia, Pennsylvania; Atlantic Terra Cotta Company, Tottenville, New York; Brick, Terra Cotta & Tile, Corning, New York.

56. *The Clay-Worker*, Vol. 6 (July 1886): 241–42.

Chapter 3

57. Taylor, "Terra Cotta—Some of Its Characteristics," 65.

58. Ibid., 154.

59. "About Terra Cotta," *Record Estate Record and Builders Guide* 40 (22 October 1887): 1319.

60. Herbert Croly, "The Proper Use of Terra Cotta," *Architectural Record* 19 (January. 1906): 73–80.

61. "Terra Cotta in Architecture," *Carpentry and Building* 1 (December 1879): 226.

62. "Terra Cotta–Ancient and Modern," *The Clay-Worker* 32 (1899): 192.

Chapter 4

63. *Atlantic Terra Cotta Company 1879–1881* 8 (April 1926), n. p.

64. Stratton, *The Terracotta Revival*, 151.

65. For more on George B. Post, see *Atlantic Terra Cotta Company 1879–1881* 8 (April 1926). Also see *SITES* 18 (1986): 12.

66. *A History of Real Estate Building and Architecture During the Last Quarter of a Century*, 516. Also see Taylor, "The Manufacture of Terra Cotta in Chicago," 420–21.

67. Geer, *The Story of Terra Cotta*, 80.

68. The Morse Building has been altered and added to over the years and only some small, square terra-cotta plaques remain on the building. Illustrations of the original structure can be found in "Artistic Brickwork, The Morse Building,"

Carpentry and Building 1 (June 1879): 101–3; and (July 1879): 121–23.

69. *A History of Real Estate Building and Architecture During the Last Quarter of a Century*, 516.

70. Stratton, *The Terracotta Revival*, 156. Stratton states that the job was started by the Boston branch of the Chicago Terra Cotta Company and that they actually supplied some of the material before the architects changed manufacturers and employed the Perth Amboy Terra Cotta Company.

71. Geer, *The Story of Terra Cotta*, 51. Written statement sent to Walter Geer by George P. Putnam, treasurer of the Perth Amboy Terra Cotta Company.

72. *Atlantic Terra Cotta Company 1879–1881* 8 (April 1926).

73. *Real Estate Record and Builders Guide* 33 (16 February 1884): 135.

74. Geer, *The Story of Terra Cotta*, 81. The Long Island Terra Cotta Works was established in 1879 in Ravenswood, Long Island City, very near the site of the New York Architectural Terra Cotta Company. The former remained in operation for only eighteen months.

Chapter 5

75. Carl W. Condit, *The Rise of the Skyscraper* (Chicago: University of Chicago Press, 1952), 15.

76. Donald Friedman, *Historical Building Construction, Design, Materials & Technology* (New York and London: W. W. Norton & Company, 1995). Chapter 4, "The Emergence of the Steel Skeleton Frame: 1870–1904," contains much detailed information about construction techniques.

77. Landau and Condit, *Rise of the New York Skyscraper 1865–1913*, 140. My thanks to Jay Shockley for his patient discussion of this building and the entire issue of skyscraper construction.

78. *Boston Terra Cotta Company Catalogue* (Boston: P.H. Foster & Co., 1885), n. p.

79. *New York Architectural Terra Cotta Company Catalogue* (New York: Lowe & Company, 1888): 17–18.

80. Sheldon Cheney, *The New World Architecture* (New York: 1920), 20.

81. *A History of Real Estate Building and Architecture During the Last Quarter of a Century*, 527. Eidlitz used this surface treatment on his Cortland Street Telephone Building and the Racquet Clubhouse, both in New York City. Both have been demolished.

82. "Terra Cotta in Architecture," *Real Estate Record and Builders Guide* 33, 154.

83. Wright, "In the Cause of Architecture," 556.

84. Robert A. M. Stern, Gregory Gilmartin, and John Montague Massengale, *New York 1900* (New York: Rizzoli, 1983), 153.

85. John Randall moved to Buffalo in the early 1980s with the express intention of helping to save the Guaranty Building. After he achieved his aim he moved to California; no additional information about him is known. An excellent restoration of the Guaranty Building, completed in 1983, used new terra-cotta replacement pieces made by Boston Valley Terra Cotta in nearby Orchard Park, New York.

PART TWO

Chapter 6

86. Frank Lloyd Wright, quotation on the inside cover of the publication of the *Atlantic Terra Cotta Company* 11 (June 1932).

87. Edward Roche to Messrs. Upjohn & Co., 1 September 1852, Box 6, Upjohn Papers, New York Public Library.

88. An excellent idea of the interaction between the architect,

contractor, and terra-cotta manufacturer can be obtained by reading the "Specifications for Architectural Terra Cotta" for the Brooklyn Masonic Temple (February 1906), 27–30, in the collection of Livingston Masonic Library, New York, New York.

89. Darling, *Chicago Ceramics & Glass*, 198. In the early 1980s, more than fifty thousand ink-on-linen drawings from this company were donated to the National Building Museum in Washington, D.C. They are a valuable archive, particularly for those involved in the field of historic restoration.

90. "American High Art Terra Cotta," *Brick* 1 (September 1894): 162.

91. *The Clay-Worker* 40 (July 1903): 34.

92. *Common Clay*, (October 1920): 13.

93. Ibid.

94. Willard Connely, *Louis Sullivan As He Lived* (New York: Horizon Press, 1960), 284.

95. Taylor, "The Manufacture of Terra Cotta in Chicago," 421.

96. "History of Statue," *Perth Amboy Evening News*, 22 June 1959, sec. A, 6.

97. Darling, *Chicago Ceramics & Glass*, 200.

98. *Atlantic Terra Cotta Company, A 52-Story Facade*, brochure published by the Atlantic Terra Cotta Company about the Woolworth Building (1913), 11.

99. Linda Brody Lyons, *A Handbook to the Pension Building, Home of the National Building Museum* (Washington, D.C.: National Building Museum, 1989), 26. Meigs was not satisfied with the models prepared by the Boston Terra Cotta Company and hired Caspar Buberl (1834–99) to create the twenty-eight individual panels from 2 to 4 feet in length representing 69 1/2 linear feet of original designs.

100. "McKim, Mead & White, Early Work in Atlantic Terra Cotta Atlantic," *Atlantic Terra Cotta Company* 9 (June 1927).

101. Binns, "Education in Clay," 166.

102. Edward H. Putnam, "Architectural Terra Cotta Its Physical and Structural Properties," *The Brickbuilder* (February 1911): 33.

103. Ibid., 32.

104. *Common Clay* (July 1920): 13.

105. Hildegard J. Safford, "The Terra Cotta Industry and the Atlantic Terra Cotta Company," *The Staten Island Historian* 31 (April–June 1974). Quarterly publication by the Staten Island Historical Society.

106. *Common Clay* (November 1920): 15.

107. "Keyport Feels Loss of Noted Manufacturer," *Keyport Weekly*, 6 August 1920, 1.

108. "Midsummer Meeting of American Ceramic Society," *The Clay-Worker* 60 (August 1913): 163–64.

109. Ibid.

110. Brochure written by Ken McGee, "The Tile Man, Inc.": "Fried mud—that's what my Dad called clay tile, he was the Chief Operating Officer of the Ludowici-Celadon Company in the 1950s."

PART THREE

Chapter 7

111. Taylor, "Front Bricks, Their Relation to Architectural Design," 165.

112. Sam Howe, "Polychrome Terra Cotta," *American Architect* 101 (28 February 1912): 105.

113. The Charlesgate is now owned and used by Emerson College.

114. Susan J. Montgomery, *The Ceramics of William H. Grueby* (Arts & Crafts Quarterly Press, 1993), 13. "Atwood and Grueby became the third subsidiary of Fiske, Homes and Company, a

Boston management company specializing in brick, terra cotta, and other masonry products. They managed the Boston Terra Cotta Company and thus, from a business standpoint, the alliance of Atwood and Grueby with a larger company was a wise decision. In exchange for their glaze expertise and tile manufacturing experience, Atwood and Grueby avoided the expense of building a factory and establishing an independent clientele." Thanks to Susan Montgomery for the many discussions she had with me concerning the early use of colored glazes on architectural terra cotta.

115. "On Use of Colored Terra Cotta," *The Brickbuilder* (January 1892): 12.

116. Taylor, "The Manufacture of Terra Cotta in Chicago," 421. "Some attempts have been made at producing wall-tiles with carved patterns colored with opaque glazes." No information indicates that these experiments were actually used in buildings.

117. "Glazed Terra Cotta," *Brick* 3 (December 1895): 380.

118. Ibid.: 381.

119. Geer, *The Story of Terra Cotta*, 208.

120. J. Monroe Hewlett, "Polychrome Terra Cotta in Exterior Architecture," *The Brickbuilder* 20 (April 1911): 71.

121. Geer, *The Story of Terra Cotta*, 209.

122. Ibid., 209–10. Also "The Brooklyn Academy of Music," *The American Architect and Building News* 94 (7 October 1908): 114. "The greater portion of the exterior finish has already been sandblasted, but in many cases the glaze has been left undisturbed to afford an opportunity to study the 'weathering' effect on the more brilliant tones." Starting around the time of the construction of the Dun Building, glazes were often sandblasted. Eventually it became clear that this was not a good practice because the slightly roughened surface attracted dirt and was difficult to clean.

123. "Polychromatic Terra Cotta Effects on the Broadway-Chambers, NY," *Brick* 13 (August 1900): 91.

124. Edward H. Putnam, "Polychrome Terra-Cotta," *Architecture* 45 (January 1922): 22. Also Geer, *The Story of Terra Cotta*, 209–10.

125. "McKim, Mead & White, Early Work in Atlantic Terra Cotta (Stanford White Designed *for* Terra Cotta)," *Atlantic Terra Cotta Company* 9 (June 1927).

126. "League and T Square Club Exhibition," *The Brickbuilder* 1 (January 1899): 26.

127. Herman A. Plusch, "The Ceramic Chemical Development of Architectural Terra Cotta," *The Brickbuilder* 20 (April 1911): 84–85.

128. Madison Square Presbyterian Church was destroyed in 1925 to make way for the Metropolitan Life Insurance Company Building. The importance of the church was recognized, and according to the publication *Atlantic Terra Cotta Company* 7 (1925), three portions were saved. The forty-four-foot-long pediment, designed by H. Siddens Mowbray and modeled by Adolph A. Weinman, was given to the Metropolitan Museum of Art. It was installed in the Library Wing of the Museum, but according to correspondence with Decorative Arts Curator Alice C. Frelinghuysen, its whereabouts are unknown. The Brooklyn Museum received a terra-cotta doorway surround from the front of the church which, according to discussions with Curator Barbara Millstein, has also disappeared. Six granite columns and numerous pieces of terra cotta were salvaged from the church and used in the Hartford Times Building (1920, Donn Barber) which still stands in Hartford, Connecticut. The terra cotta is in good condition. See also Suzannah Lessard, "Stanford White's Ruins," *The New Yorker* (8 July 1996): 54–55. This article comments on the fact that Stanford White's son Lawrence White (the author's grandfather) salvaged terra-cotta fragments from Madison Square Presbyterian Church as it was being torn down. The

fragments remain on the grounds of Box Hill, White's estate on Long Island, which still is owned by his descendants.

129. Hewlett, "Polychrome Terra Cotta in Exterior Architecture," 71.

130. Herbert D. Croly, "Glazed and Colored Terra-Cotta," *Architectural Record* 19 (April 1906): 322.

131. "The Beaver Building," *Architects' and Builders' Magazine* 2 (August 1904): 520.

132. See "Beaver Building," New York City Landmarks Designation Report prepared by Jay Shockley, 13 February 1996, Designation List 271, LP-1942.

133. Croly, "Glazed and Colored Terra-Cotta," 316.

134. Fine examples from the earliest New York City subway lines still survive, including work from Grueby Faience Company, Boston, Massachusetts; Rookwood Pottery, Cincinnati, Ohio; and Atlantic Terra Cotta Company, Perth Amboy, New Jersey. Other important companies making ceramic material for the early subway system include Hartford Faience Company, Hartford, Connecticut and American Encaustic Tiling Company, Zanesville, Ohio. For additional information on the ceramics in the New York City subway system, see Philip A. Coppola, *Silver Connections* Vol. I, Books 1 & 2 (Maplewood, N. J.: Four Oceans Press, 1984). Also see Lee Stookey, *Subway Ceramics* (Brooklyn, New York: 1992).

135. "Color Spreads Glories on City's Architecture," *New York Times*, 12 January 1907, sec. 3, 3.

136. Atlantic Terra Cotta Company Advertisement, *Architecture* 21 (January 1910): xxxvvii.

137. Hewlett, "Polychrome Terra Cotta in Exterior Architecture," 72.

Chapter 8

138. "Terra Cotta—Ancient & Modern," *The Clay-Worker* 32 (1899): 191–92. "In this department can be seen all the colors of native clay, besides those of the different stones which the trade demands in at least 75% of cases."

139. New York Architectural Terra Cotta Company Archive, Avery Library, Columbia University, New York. Letter (18 February 1916) with a carbon copy answer. Correspondence file, no job number.

140. Federal Terra Cotta Company advertisement in *Architectural Record* 42 (November 1917): 9.

141. "Federal Plant Was Organized 60 Years Ago," *Perth Amboy Evening News*, 4 December 1948, 23.

142. Croly, "The Proper Use of Terra Cotta," 80.

143. Herman C. Mueller, "The Independence of Burned Clay as a Decorative Building Material," *Brick* 7 (1900): 274.

144. M. Stapley, "Architectural Terra Cotta—Its Rational Development," *The Brickbuilder* 22 (March Supplement 1913): 25.

145. Gabriel Ferrand, "Ceramic Art and Architecture," *Journal of the American Ceramic Society* 5 (November 1922): 748. Professor Ferrand taught at Washington University School of Architecture, St. Louis.

146. "The Croisic Building—Browne & Almiroty," *The Brickbuilder* 22 (May 1913): 116.

147. Ferrand, "Ceramic Art and Architecture," 751.

148. Ibid.: 754.

149. Ibid.: 756.

150. L. M. Munshaw, "Pulsichrometer vs. Old Method of Applying Glaze," *Journal of the American Ceramic Society* 5 (November 1922): 830.

Chapter 9

151. William H. Powell, "The Rise of Terra Cotta," *Real Estate Record and Builders Guide* (3 April 1909): 636.

152. The existing records mentioned are job-estimating files from the New York Architectural Terra Cotta Company located in Avery Library, Columbia University, New York City.

153. It is interesting to note that the model that was photographed for 30 Beekman Place differs slightly from the ornament that is actually on the building. The cherub's face was reworked into a sphere or globe-like object. (George Pelham was the architect for both 944 Park Avenue, 1928–29, and 30 Beekman Place, 1928–29.)

154. Two noteworthy examples are Liberty Tower, designed in 1909 by Henry Ives Cobb, only several blocks from the site of the Woolworth and George & Edward Blum's 1912 structure at 16 East 41st Street.

155. Ely Jacques Kahn, "Our Skyscrapers Take Simple Forms," *New York Times*, 2 May 1926, 22.

156. "Americans Should Seek Harmony in Architecture," *Mantel, Tile and Grate Monthly* (May 1912): 24–25.

157. Kahn, "Our Skyscrapers Take Simple Forms," 11.

158. A. B. Carson, "Clothing Modern Skyscrapers," *Buildings and Building Management* (24 February 1930): 39.

159. Kahn, "Our Skyscrapers Take Simple Forms," 11.

160. "56 Stories of Modern Architecture," *Atlantic Terra Cotta Company* 9 (February 1929). The Chanin Building had 212 projector lights located at the fifty-fourth story.

161. F. S. Laurence, "Terra Cotta in Architectural Design," *Journal of the American Ceramic Society* 8 (1925): 83.

Chapter 10

162. Leon Solon, "2 Park Avenue," *Architectural Record* 163 (April 1928): 296.

163. "Recent Development in Architectural Ceramics," *Bulletin of the American Ceramic Society* 12 (September 1933): 282.

164. A major source of information on Kahn's career is an unpublished autobiography in Avery Library, Columbia University, New York City. The manuscript, parts of which are dated 1970, was never completed; some chapters exist in several revised versions, and each is paginated separately. Kahn Manuscript II: 4.

165. Ibid.

166. Lewis Mumford, "American Architecture Today," *Architecture* 57 (April 1928): 53–54.

167. Kahn Manuscript II: 14.

168. Ely Jacques Kahn, Terra Cotta Futurities No. 2 (brochure published by the Federal Seaboard Terra Cotta Corporation, 1930).

169. Mumford, "American Architecture Today," 53–54.

170. Atlantic Terra Cotta Bulletin (January 1928): n. p.

171. "Predict New York as City of Color," *New York Times*, 20 February 1927, Real Estate section, 14.

172. Ibid.

173. Ibid.

174. Regina Blaszcyk, "'This Extraordinary Demand for Color': Leon Victor Solon and Architectural Polychromy, 1909–1939," paper presented at the 1993 Tile Heritage Foundation Conference: 5–6.

175. Walter H. Kilham, Jr., *Raymond Hood, Architect* (New York: Architectural Book Publishing Company, 1973): 175–77.

176. Ibid., 174.

177. Ibid., 88.

178. McGraw Hill Building," *The New Yorker* (25 July 1931): 38.

179. *Federal Seaboard Wall Ashlar*, 2nd Edition (1933): 18.

180. J. Burns Helme, "Recent Developments in Architectural Ceramics," *Bulletin of the American Ceramic Society American* 12 (September 1933): 282.

181. Thomas Tallmadge, "The Development of the Office Building Since 1924," *Architectural Forum* 102 (May 1930): 780. According to the publication *Atlantic Terra Cotta*

Company 9 (March 1928), this building was also a resting place for nearly-extinct animals, as evidenced by the seventy-three terra cotta buffalo heads placed on the fifteenth story. Also see *The Clay-Worker* 93 (June 1930): 475–76. According to this journal, trophies that hang from the buffalo heads display various symbols of business and transportation, including a winged helmet of Mercury, the God of Commerce, and wheels of Progress.

182. *Yearbook of the Architecture League of New York and Catalogue of the 45th Annual Exhibition* (1930): 292.

183. A record book from the Eastern Terra Cotta Company lists a job bid (#41036) for "Two heads for Gate Post, Rockefeller Centre, Fifth Ave, NY City, Joseph Kiselewski," dated 18 May 1937. No written information about Rockefeller Center includes Kiselewski among the artists who actually produced work for this project. Terra cotta was used for constructive purposes in some of the Rockefeller Center buildings, but none is visible on the facades.

184. Hildreth Meiere's rondels *Dance, Song,* and *Drama* were made of enameled metal and Barry Faulkner's mosaic mural *Intelligence Awakening Mankind* used colored-glass tessera.

185. Letter to Karl Mathiasen II from Aslag Eskesen (22 June 1944), 2. Karl Mathiasen II was President from 1950–60. (Donated to the Friends of Terra Cotta by the Eskesen Family)

186. Sturgis Laurence, "Faience in Architecture, A Wide Field Under Modern Conditions for Adapting Faience Along the Lines Pursued by the Orientals—Brick Building Gives It Many Opportunities," *Real Estate Record and Builders Guide* 84 (3 April 1909): 639.

Chapter 11

187. The exteriors of twenty-seven theaters in this area have been designated New York City Landmarks. One of the most important of these landmarks, the New Amsterdam Theater is being restored by the Disney Development Company.

188. Donald M. Reynolds, *The Architecture of New York City* (New York: Macmillan, 1984), 176.

189. F. S. Laurence, *Color in Architecture* (National Terra Cotta Society, 1924).

PART FOUR

Chapter 12

190. The origin of the association's name is unknown, but one could speculate that it had something to do with the color of terra cotta!

191. Geer, *The Story of Terra Cotta*, 103–04. The A. Hall Terra Cotta Company practically shut down in 1887, but since the plant remained, concerns that a new company might take it over existed. Therefore it was leased in 1889 by the companies who were planning to create the Second Brown Association for three years, and the lease was twice renewed. The Boston Terra Cotta Company was bought out in 1893 and closed. The New York company merged "for the business of selling terra cotta" with Stephens, Conkling and Armstrong, although the orders were executed at the two plants and manufacturing and financial departments of the companies remained entirely separate.

192. Ibid., 99.

193. Ibid., 145.

194. Ibid., 233.

195. George A. Berry III, "The Business of Terra Cotta," unpublished material sent to the author, 1 November 1995: 2. (Berry's father owned the American Terra Cotta Corporation,

now a company called TC Industries, Crystal Lake, Illinois.)

196. Ibid.: 3.

197. "Terra Cotta Market Study," National Terra Cotta Society (12 August 1930): 5. (Mimeographed mailing sent to members, donated to Friends of Terra Cotta by O. W. Ketcham Company.)

198. *Terra Cotta News-Letter* (22 March 1930): 2. (Mimeographed mailing sent to members, donated to Friends of Terra Cotta by O. W. Ketcham Company.)

199. Ibid.: 6.

200. W. F. Lockhardt, "What The National Terra Cotta Society is Doing," *Terra Cotta News-Letter* (5 February 1930): 3.

201. The eighteen members are listed in *Sweet's Catalogue* (1929): A364. The thirteen members are listed in *TERRA COTTA Information and Service,* National Terra Cotta Society (1930): n. p.

202. W. F. Lockhardt, "Terra Cotta Market Study," National Terra Cotta Society, (11 August 1930): 5. (Mimeographed mailing sent to members, donated to Friends of Terra Cotta by O. W. Ketcham Company.)

203. Eckardt V. Eskesen, "Presidential Address for the Thirty-Fourth Annual Meeting of the American Ceramic Society," *Journal of the American Ceramic Society* 15 (April 1932): 81.

204. "Architectural Terra Cotta Lesson for Thousands," *Ceramic Age* 1 (November 1932): 178.

205. "Clay Trade News from Eastern District," *The Clay-Worker* 97 (June 1932): 311.

206. William F. Lockhardt, "Architectural Terra Cotta," *General Building Contractor* (January 1931): 5.

207. Gary F. Kurutz, *Architectural Terra Cotta of Gladding, McBean* (California: Wingate Press, 1989), 126.

208. Ibid.

209. H. G. Schurecht, "Some Products Which Might Be Made in Terra Cotta Plants as Now Built or With Slight Changes in Present Equipment," (22 January 1935). Donated to Friends of Terra Cotta by Clem Baldwin, former employee of Atlantic Terra Cotta Company.

210. Questionnaire filled out by the Federal Seaboard Terra Cotta Corporation at the request of the Perth Amboy Public Library (30 June 1937).

211. Two other terra-cotta-clad post offices were the Woodhaven Station (1937–38, Louis A. Simon) and the New Rochelle Station (1937–38, Frost, Hart & Sharpe), which has had its terra-cotta cladding removed. Special thanks to Andrew S. Dolkart for bringing these post offices to my attention.

212. *The Federal Architect* 9 (October 1938): 78–79.

213. *The Federal Architect* 9 (October 1939). This quote is from a Federal Seaboard Terra Cotta Corporation ad on the inside back cover and features two exterior photos.

214. The Woodhaven Station has a painted mural by Ben Shahn titled *The First Amendment.*

215. Ross Anderson and Barbara Perry, *The Diversions of Kermos* (Syracuse University: Everson Museum of Art, 1983), 7.

216. Ibid., 11. *The Federal Architect* 9 (April 1939). The inside back cover has an ad that claims: "As Modern As the World's Fair…an architect's description of the *NEW* Federal Seaboard Architectural Terra Cotta." This material was used on the Permanent Field House at the World's Fair. Atlantic Terra Cotta Company provided terra cotta for the New York State Building at the fair.

217. Eastern Terra Cotta Company Record Book, 1936–38, Friends of Terra Cotta Collection.

218. William C. McGinnis, *History of Perth Amboy New Jersey 1651–1960,* vol. 4 (Perth Amboy, New Jersey: American Publishing Company, 1960), 11.

219. Telephone conversation with George A. Berry III, 1995. In a 1996 conversation with Richard Veit, he commented that he had seen references to bombs for target practice produced by

the Atlantic Terra Cotta Company.

220. Lois Lehner, "American Dinnerware and Commercial Pottery," *Antique Trader Weekly* (8 August 1984): 72. Lois Lehner, "A Cookie Jar Update," *Antique Trader Weekly* (29 February 1984): 72.

221. Peter Olsen, "A Memo Sent To The Directors Of The Corporation" (9 October 1944). Olsen was then president of Federal Seaboard Terra Cotta Corporation. Donated to the Friends of Terra Cotta by the Eskesen Family.

222. W. D. Richardson, "Face Brick and Terra Cotta—Today & Tomorrow," *The Clay-Worker* 100 (November 1933): 164.

223. Letter to the author from Daniel Barton (1986).

Chapter 13

224. "Parkchester, A Residential Community, Metropolitan Life Insurance Company," Reprint from *Architectural Forum* (December 1939).

225. Eastern Terra Cotta Company Record Book, 1936–38. Friends of Terra Cotta Collection.

226. Olsen, "A Memo Sent To The Directors Of The Corporation."

227. Letter to E. V. Eskesen from Aslag Eskesen (12 July 1943), 3. Donated to the Friends of Terra Cotta by the Eskesen Family.

228. Olsen, "A Memo Sent To The Directors Of The Corporation."

229. Founded in 1888 as the firm of Mathiasen and Hansen, in 1893 it became the New Jersey Terra Cotta Company (one of the three companies that merged in 1928 to form Federal Seaboard Terra Cotta Corporation).

230. "Federal Plant Was Organized 60 Years Ago," 23.

231. Robert A. Caro, *The Power Broker: Robert Moses and the Fall of New York* (New York: Vintage Books, 1975), 7.

232. "New New York," *Newsweek* 48 (9 July 1956): 87–92.

233. At some point, all the terra cotta was removed from the facade and replaced with a gray, speckled glazed brick. It is assumed that failure of the terra cotta must have led to such an expensive alteration.

234. Aslag Eskesen, "Problems—Possibilities—Prospects" (30 June 1963): 10. Unpublished document for the directors of the Federal Seaboard Terra Cotta Corporation. Donated to the Friends of Terra Cotta by the Eskesen family.

235. "CV Durathin," (13d/Fe) AIA File No. 9A, Federal Seaboard Terra Cotta Corporation Printed Information Sheet. Friends of Terra Cotta Collection.

236. Ibid.

237. This building is part of the Ladies Mile Historic District, but unfortunately a substitute material was used for replacement rather than newly manufactured terra cotta.

238. One of the projects during this period that required handmade units was the restoration of the Woolworth Building.

239. Each of the large panels was made in a traditional manner. The model was cut to create a number of plaster molds so that if any section was damaged, it could be remade easily. This method was also used for Schrekengost's other two terra-cotta projects.

240. "Citation Won By Ceramics Panels Made in Plant in Perth Amboy," *New Brunswick Times,* 27 April 1952, 18.

241. AIA award, in possession of Viktor Schreckengost.

242. Viktor S. Schrenckengost, interviewed by Nancy McCroskey, 21 September 1996; printed in the Friends of Terra Cotta members' mailing, December 1996.

243. O. E. Mathiasen, "Projected Promotion and Sales Plan," (1961). Mathiasen was president of Federal Seaboard Terra Cotta Corporation and this plan, an unpublished document, was intended for the directors of the Federal Seaboard Terra Cotta Corporation. Donated to the Friends of Terra Cotta by the Eskesen family.

244. Eskesen, "Problems—Possibilities—Prospects," 10.

245. A. H. Eskesen, "Report to Stockholders of Federal Seaboard Terra Cotta Corporation" (31 March 1967): 8. A. H. Eskesen was President of the company at this time. Unpublished document for the directors of the Federal Seaboard Terra Cotta Corporation. Donated to the Friends of Terra Cotta by the Eskesen family.

246. O. E. Mathiasen, "Minutes of 290th Meeting of the Board of Directors of Federal Seaboard Terra Cotta Corporation" (5 June 1968). Unpublished document. Donated to the Friends of Terra Cotta by the Eskesen family.

247. Letter to the author from Alice Eskesen Ganzel (1987).

248. Letter to the author from David Wilkenson, President of Wilkenson & Co., Inc., Paterson, N.J., 1995. Also, letter to the author from Bruce Popkin, *WASA/Wank Adams Slavin Associates*, 1995. Cites correspondence from 30 October 1968 that confirms the inability to obtain the remaining ceramic veneer needed for the job.

249. Eskesen, "Problems—Possibilities—Prospects," 10.

250. Barton, letter, 1986.

251. Robert A. M. Stern, Thomas Mellins, and David Fishman, *New York 1960* (New York: The Monacelli Press, 1995), 740.

252. Ibid., 840. Ceramic veneer that matched the light gray glazed brick was manufactured by Federal Seaboard Terra Cotta Corporation and faced portions of the ground floor where shops and parking garage entrances were located.

253. Ibid., 439. Leo Stillman used terra-cotta solar grilles at the entrances. Completed in 1959, it was the first urban motel, not only in New York City, but in the entire country.

254. Ibid., 1019. Again, Federal Seaboard's solar grilles were used in this station, which "was a miniaturization—and a trivialization—of Stone's notable United States Embassy Building (1954) in New Delhi, India." Ada Louise Huxtable dismissed it as "an unpardonable *reductio ad absurdum*" of Stone's earlier triumph.

255. The Catholic Seamen's Institute, designed by Henry Murphy, was constructed in 1941–43. According to Elliot Willensky and Norval White's *American Institute of Architects AIA Guide to New York City* (New York: Harcourt Brace, Jovanovich, 1988): 609, "The faux Art Moderne lighthouse was intended as a moral beacon: 'A challenge of the church to the barrooms of the riverfront.'" Barnard College's Adele Lehman Hall was designed by O'Conner & Kilham in 1959; the American Airlines Terminal was designed by Kahn & Jacobs in 1960. Four additional projects mentioned were the Stephen Foster Houses (William Hohauser, 1946); the James Weldon Johnson Houses (Whittlesey, Prince & Reiley, 1947); the Farragut Houses (Felheimer, Wagner & Vollmer, 1952); and the Children's Zoo in Central Park (Edward Embury, 1961; demolished, 1996). No mention of their glazed terra-cotta surfaces is made in *New York 1960*.

256. Ferrand, "Ceramic Art and Architecture," 749.

257. Ibid.

258. Christopher Gray, "After a 1971 Restoration Fails, It's Time to Re-Restore," *New York Times*, 30 June 1996, Real Estate, 7. Architects Brown, Lawford & Forbes ordered replacement terra cotta from Gladding, McBean & Company in 1971. This material began to fail shortly after completion in 1974 and was partially restored again by The Ehrenkrantz Group in 1980. Another series of facade repairs are planned to begin in 1998.

259. Robert Venturi, "Introduction," in *Impressions of Imagination: Terra-Cotta Seattle* (Allied Arts of Seattle, Inc., 1986), vi. The Seattle Art Museum in Seattle Washington is a well-known building designed by Venturi, Scott Brown and Associates. Completed in 1991, it combines glazed terra cotta with limestone, granite, tile, brownstone, and bluestone.

Appendix A

260. Elliot Willensky and Norval White, *American Institute of Architects AIA Guide to New York City* (New York: Harcourt Brace, Jovanovich, 1988), 870.

Appendix C

261. Kilham, Jr., *Raymond Hood, Architect*, 84–85.

Illustration Credits

All photographs ©Peter Mauss/ESTO unless noted below.

Friends of Terra Cotta Collection: Figures 1, 4-7, 9, 11, 17, 18, 21–25, 32, 34, 36, 40–42, 44–46, 49–51, 54, 57, 60, 63, 66, 70, 73, 76, 78, 79, 81, 82, 87, 95, 112, 115, 116, 124, 125, 129, 134, 145, 148, 160–162, 165, 166, and opening spreads for Parts Two and Three

FIGURE	
2	Collection of the Worcester Historical Museum
3	Collection of The New-York Historical Society
8	Avery Architectural and Fine Arts Library, Columbia University. *Boston Terra Cotta Company Catalogue*, 1885
10	Avery Architectural and Fine Arts Library, Columbia University. *Fiske and Colman Catalogue*, 1878
13	Photograph by Mary Swisher
15	Courtesy of Richard Simpson
16	New York Public Library. *Carpentry & Building*, 1879 (102)
26	Collection Centre Canadien d'Architecture/Canadian Center for Architecture, Montréal
35	Courtesy of Boston Valley Terra Cotta Company
38	Avery Architectural and Fine Arts Library, Columbia University (Guastavino Company Archives, Vanderbilt Hotel files)
58	Photograph by Cleota Reed
59	Courtesy of Emily L. Moore
62	Avery Architectural and Fine Arts Library, Columbia University. *The Brickbuilder* (January 1899)
75, 163	Courtesy of Marilyn Horowitz
127	Courtesy of Gladding, McBean & Company
131	Avery Architectural and Fine Arts Library, Columbia University. *The Federal Architect* 9 (October 1938): 78–79
132	Photograph by Courtney Frisse, courtesy of Charles Blitman
130, 135, 136, 140–42	Courtesy of Bruce Richmond
133	Photograph by Paul A. Tunick
143, 144	Courtesy of Viktor Schreckengost
151	Photograph by Rose Mary Mazzco, 1976, courtesy of John Burns
164	Courtesy of Mrs. Virginia Bassett
167	Courtesy of the National Building Museum, gift of Edward J. Mertes

The objects in Figures 55 and 74 are in the collection of O. Alden James, New York City, and belonged to his grandfather John T. Lowe. (Photograph by Peter Mauss)

The object in Figure 56 was in the collection of Bob Feingold, Lincort, New Jersey before it became part of the Friends of Terra Cotta Collection. (Photograph by Peter Mauss)

The objects in Figure 47 were from the collection of Urban Archaeology, New York City. (Photograph by Peter Mauss)

The photograph on the binding case is ©Peter Mauss/ESTO.

The following three bibliographies contain some useful
entries not listed in this publication:

Prudon, Theodore H. M. "Terra Cotta as a Building
Material." The Association for Preservation Technology,
Inc., *Communiqué* 5 (June 1976).

Tindall, Susan, and James Hamrick. *American Architectural
Terra Cotta: A Bibliography*. Monticello, Ill.: Vance
Bibliographies, 1981.

Wilson, Hewitt. "Monograph and Bibliography on Terra
Cotta." *American Ceramic Society Journal (Bulletin)* 9
(February 1926), 94–136.

Books

*A History of Real Estate Building and Architecture in New York
During the Last Quarter of a Century*. New York: Record
and Guide, 1898; reprinted New York: Arno Press, Inc.,
1967.

Anderson, Ross, and Barbara Perry. *The Diversions of Kermos*.
Syracuse University: Everson Museum of Art, 1983.

Barber, Edwin Atlee. *The Pottery and Porcelain of the United
States*. 3rd Edition, Revised and Enlarged. New York:
Feingold & Lewis, 1976.

Berryman, Nancy D., and Susan M. Tindall. *Terra Cotta:
Preservation and Maintenance of an Historic Building
Material*. Chicago: Landmarks Preservation Council of
Illinois, 1984.

Boston Terra Cotta Company Catalogue. Boston: P. H. Foster
& Co., 1885.

Caro, Robert A. *The Power Broker, Robert Moses and the Fall
of New York*. New York: Knopf, 1974.

Cheney, Sheldon. *The New World Architecture*. New York,
1920.

Condit, Carl W. *The Rise of the Skyscraper*. Chicago:
University of Chicago Press, 1952.

Connely, Willard. *Louis Sullivan As He Lived*. New York:
Horizon Press, 1960.

Coppola, Philip A. *Silver Connections*. Vol. I, Books 1 & 2.
Maplewood, N. J.: Four Oceans Press, 1984.

Darling, Sharon S. *Chicago Ceramics & Glass*. Chicago:
Chicago Historical Society, 1979.

Dolkart, Andrew S. *Guide to New York City Landmarks*.
Washington: The Preservation Press, 1992.

Dolkart, Andrew S., and Susan Tunick. *George and Edward
Blum: Texture and Design in New York Apartment House
Architecture*. New York: Friends of Terra Cotta Press, 1993.

Ferriday, Virginia Guest. *Last of the Handmade Buildings*.
Portland, Oreg.: Mark Publishing Company, 1984.

Finney, Jack. *Time and Again*. New York: Simon & Schuster,
1970.

Friedman, Donald. *Historical Building Construction, Design,
Materials & Technology*. New York and London: W.W.
Norton & Company, 1995.

Gabrielan, Randall. *Images of America, Middletown Township*.
New Hampshire: Arcadia Publishing, 1994.

Geer, Walter. *The Story of Terra Cotta*. New York: Tobias A.
Wright, 1920.

Goldberger, Paul. *The City Observed: New York*. New York:
Vintage Books, 1979.

Impressions of Imagination: Terra-Cotta Seattle. Seattle: Allied
Arts of Seattle, Inc., 1986.

Kilham, Walter H., Jr. *Raymond Hood, Architect*. New York:
Architectural Book Publishing Company, 1973.

Kurutz, Gary F., and Mary Swisher. *Architectural Terra Cotta
of Gladding, McBean*. Sausalito, Calif.: Windgate Press,
1989.

Landau, Sarah Bradford, and Carl W. Condit. *Rise of the New
York Skyscraper 1865–1913*. New Haven: Yale University
Press, 1996.

Laurence, F. S. *Color in Architecture*. National Terra Cotta
Society, 1924.

Lyons, Linda Brody. *A Handbook to the Pension Building,
Home of the National Building Museum*. Washington,
D. C.: National Building Museum, 1989.

McGinnis, William C. *History of Perth Amboy New Jersey
1651–1960*. Perth Amboy, N. J.: American Publishing
Company, 30 November, 1960.

Montgomery, Susan J. *The Ceramics of William H. Grueby*.
Arts & Crafts Quarterly Press, 1993.

National Terra Cotta Society. *Architectural Terra Cotta,
Standard Construction*. New York, 1914.

———. *Architectural Terra Cotta, Standard Construction*.
New York, 1927.

New Jersey Pottery and Porcelain Prior to 1876. Newark, N. J.:
New Jersey State Museum, 1915.

New York Architectural Terra Cotta Company Catalogue. New
York: Lowe & Company, 1888.

Reynolds, Donald M. *The Architecture of New York City*. New
York: Macmillan, 1984.

Silliman, Benjamin. *The World of Science, Art & Industry
Illustrated from Examples in the New York Exhibition,
1853–54*. New York: G. P. Putnam & Co.; London: Low,
Son & Co., 1854.

Slivka, Rose and Karen Tsujimoto. *The Art of Peter Voulkos*.
Japan: Kodansha International, 1995.

Stern, Robert A. M., Gregory Gilmartin, and John Montague
Massengale. *New York 1900*. New York: Rizzoli, 1983.

Stern, Robert A. M., Thomas Mellins, and David Fishman.
New York 1960. New York: The Monacelli Press, 1995.

Stookey, Lee. *Subway Ceramics*. Brooklyn, N. Y.: 1992.

Stratton, Michael. *The Terracotta Revival*. London: Victor
Gollancz, 1993.

Strong, Susan R. *History of American Ceramics: An Annotated
Bibliography*. Metuchen, N. J.: The Scarecrow Press, Inc.,
1983.

Terra Cotta Artful Deceivers. Ontario, Canada: Toronto
Region Architectural Conservancy, 1990.

Tunick, Susan. *Field Guide to Apartment Building
Architecture*. New York: Friends of Terra Cotta Press, 1986.

———. *Terra Cotta: Don't Take It For Granite. Three Walks in
New York Neighborhoods*. New York: Friends of Terra
Cotta Press, 1995.

Willensky, Elliot, and Norval White. *American Institute of
Architects AIA Guide to New York City*. New York:
Harcourt Brace, Jovanovich, 1988.

Willis, Carol. *Form Follows Finance*. New York: Princeton
Architectural Press, 1995.

Periodicals

"About Terra Cotta." *Record Estate Record and Builders Guide*
40 (22 October 1887): 1319.

"Adoption of Victorian Gothic." *Real Estate Record and
Builders Guide* (3 April 1909): 646.

"American High Art Terra Cotta." *Brick* 1 (September 1894):
162.

"Americans Should Seek Harmony in Architecture." *Mantel,
Tile and Grate Monthly* (May 1912): 24–25.

"Architectural Terra Cotta Lesson for Thousands." *Ceramic
Age* 1 (November 1932): 178.

"Artistic Brickwork, The Morse Building." *Carpentry and
Building* 1 (June 1879): 101–3; (July 1879): 121–23.

Atlantic Terra Cotta Company 9 (March 1928).

Atlantic Terra Cotta Company 1879–1881 8 (April 1926).

Atlantic Terra Cotta Company Advertisement in *Architecture*
21 (January 1910): xxxvvii.

"A Tribute to the Memory of James Taylor." *13th Annual
Convention, National Brick Manufacturer's Association*: 31.

Binns, Charles Fergus. *Transactions of the American Ceramic
Society* 7 (1905): 48.

———. "Education in Clay," *Craftsman* 4 (July 1903):
160–68.

Carson, A. B. "Clothing Modern Skyscrapers." *Buildings and
Building Management* (24 February 1930): 39.

"Clay Trade New from Eastern District." *The Clay-Worker* 97
(June 1932): 311.

Common Clay (July 1920): 13.

Common Clay (November 1920): 15.

Common Clay (October 1920): 13.

Croly, Herbert D. "Glazed and Colored Terra-Cotta."
Architectural Record 19 (April 1906): 322.

———. "The Proper Use of Terra Cotta." *Architectural
Record* 19 (Jan. 1906): 73–80.

Cusack, Thomas. "Architectural Terra-Cotta." *Brickbuilder* 5
(December 1896): 227.

Eskesen, Eckardt V. "Presidential Address for the Thirty-
Fourth Annual Meeting of the American Ceramic
Society." *Journal of the American Ceramic Society* 15 (April
1932): 81.

Federal Terra Cotta Company Advertisement in *Architectural
Record* 42 (November 1917): 9

Ferrand, Gabriel. "Ceramic Art and Architecture." *Journal of
the American Ceramic Society* 5 (November 1922): 748.

"56 Stories of Modern Architecture." *Atlantic Terra Cotta
Company* 9 (February 1929).

"Glazed Terra Cotta." *Brick* 3 (December 1895): 380.

Helme, J. Burns. "Recent Developments in Architectural
Ceramics." *Bulletin of the American Ceramic Society
American* 12 (September 1933): 282.

Herman C. Mueller. "The Independence of Burned Clay as a
Decorative Building Material." *Brick* 7 (1900): 274.

Hewlett, J. Monroe. "Polychrome Terra Cotta in Exterior
Architecture." *The Brickbuilder* 20 (April 1911): 71.

Howe, Sam. "Polychrome Terra Cotta." *American Architect*
101 (28 February 1912): 105.

"James Taylor, a Pioneer Terra Cotta Manufacturer and
Writer." *The Clay-Worker* 31 (1899): 15.

Laurence, F. Sturgis. "Terra Cotta in Architectural Design,"
Journal of the American Ceramic Society 8 (1925): 83.

———. "Faience in Architecture, A Wide Field Under
Modern Conditions for Adapting Faience Along the Lines
Pursued by the Orientals—Brick Building Gives It Many
Opportunities." *Real Estate Record and Builders Guide* 84
(3 April 1909): 639.

"League and T Square Club Exhibition." *The Brickbuilder* 1
(January 1899): 26.

Lessard, Suzannah. "Stanford White's Ruins." *The New
Yorker* (8 July 1996): 54–55.

Lockhardt, William F. "Architectural Terra Cotta." *General
Building Contractor* (January 1931): 5.

"McGraw Hill Building." *The New Yorker* (25 July 1931): 38.

"McKim, Mead & White, Early Work in Atlantic Terra
Cotta. (Stanford White Designed *for* Terra Cotta),"
Atlantic Terra Cotta Company 9 (June 1927).

"Midsummer Meeting of American Ceramic Society." *The
Clay-Worker* 60 (August 1913): 163–64.

Mumford, Lewis. "American Architecture Today."
Architecture 57 (April 1928): 53–54.

Munshaw, L. M. "Pulsichrometer vs. Old Method of

Applying Glaze." *Journal of the American Ceramic Society* 5 (November 1922): 830.

"New New York." *Newsweek* 48 (9 July 1956): 87–92.

"New Potter Building." *Special Illustrated Edition of Building* 3 (October 1884–December 1885): 89.

"On Use of Colored Terra Cotta." *The Brickbuilder* (January 1892): 12.

"Parkchester, A Residential Community, Metropolitan Life Insurance Company." *Architectural Forum* (December 1939).

Plusch, Herman A. "The Ceramic Chemical Development of Architectural Terra Cotta." *The Brickbuilder* 20 (April 1911): 84–85.

"Polychromatic Terra Cotta Effects on the Broadway-Chambers, NY." *Brick* 13 (August 1900): 91.

Powell, William H. "The Rise of Terra Cotta." *Real Estate Record and Builders Guide* (3 April 1909): 636.

Putnam, Edward H. "New York City's First Terra Cotta." *American Architect* (20 November 1925): 429–30.

———. "Polychrome Terra-Cotta." *Architecture* 45 (January 1922): 22.

———. "Architectural Terra Cotta: Its Physical and Structural Properties." *The Brickbuilder* (February 1911): 29–33.

Real Estate Record and Builders Guide 33 (16 February 1884): 135.

"Recent Development in Architectural Ceramics." *Bulletin of the American Ceramic Society* 12 (September 1933): 282.

Richardson, W. D. "Face Brick and Terra Cotta—Today & Tomorrow" *The Clay-Worker* 100 (November 1933): 164.

Safford, Hildegard J. "The Terra Cotta Industry and the Atlantic Terra Cotta Company." *The Staten Island Historian* 31 (April–June 1974).

Solon, Leon. "2 Park Avenue." *Architectural Record* 163 (April 1928): 296.

Stapley, M. "Architectural Terra Cotta—Its Rational Development." *The Brickbuilder* 22 (March Supplement 1913): 25.

Sweet's Catalogue (1929): A364.

Tallmadge, Thomas. "The Development of the Office Building Since 1924." *Architectural Forum* 102 (May 1930): 780.

Taylor, James. "Front Brick, Their Relation To Architectural Design." *Proceeding of the 7th Annual National Brick Manufacturers Association* (1893): 165.

———. "The Manufacture of Terra Cotta in Chicago." *American Architect and Building News* (30 December 1876): 420–21.

"Terra Cotta—Ancient and Modern." *The Clay-Worker* 32 (1899): 191–92.

"Terra Cotta in Architecture." *Carpentry and Building* 1 (December 1879): 226.

"Terra Cotta in Architecture." *Real Estate Record and Builders Guide* 33 (16 February 1884): 154.

"The Beaver Building." *Architects' and Builders' Magazine* 2 (August 1904): 520.

"The Brooklyn Academy of Music." *The American Architect and Building News* 94 (7 October 1908): 114.

The Clay-Worker 6 (July 1886): 241–42.

The Clay-Worker 8 (1887): 113.

The Clay-Worker 25 (1896): 40–42.

The Clay-Worker 27 (1897): 529–30.

The Clay-Worker 40 (1903): 34.

The Clay-Worker 93 (1930): 475–76.

"The Croisic Building—Browne & Almiroty." *The Brickbuilder* 22 (May 1913): 116.

The Federal Architect 9 (October 1938): 78–79.

The Federal Architect 9 (April 1939): back cover.

The Federal Architect 9 (October 1939): back cover.

Tiller, de Teel Patterson. "The Preservation of Historic Glazed Architectural Terra-Cotta." *Preservation Brief* No.7, Heritage Conservation and Recreation Service (1979).

Tunick, Susan. "Architectural Terra Cotta: Its Impact on New York." *SITES* 18 (1986): 4–38.

Veit, Richard. "A Piece of Granite That's Been Made in Two Weeks': Terra-Cotta Gravemarkers from New Jersey and New York, 1875–1930." *Markers XII* (Journal of the Association for Gravestone Studies) (1995): 1–29.

Wight, P. B. "Fireproof Construction—And the Practice of American Architects." *American Architect and Building News* (19 August 1893): 114.

Yearbook of the Architecture League of New York and Catalogue of the 45th Annual Exhibition (1930): 292.

Newspapers

"Architectural Terra Cotta A Big Factor In New Building." *New York Times,* 14 May 1911, 8 : 1.

Broyard, Anatole. "Reading and Writing: New York, New York." *New York Times,* 13 September 1981, 7 : 59.

"Citation Won By Ceramics Panels Made in Plant in Perth Amboy." *New Brunswick Times,* 27 April 1952, 18.

"Color Spreads Glories on City's Architecture." *New York Times,* 12 January 1907, 3 : 3.

"Federal Plant Was Organized 60 Years Ago." *Perth Amboy Evening News,* 4 December 1948, 23.

Gray, Christopher. "After a 1971 Restoration Fails, It's Time to Re-Restore." *New York Times,* 30 June 1996, Real Estate: 7.

"History of Statue." *Perth Amboy Evening News,* 22 June 1959, A : 6.

Kahn, Ely Jacques. "Our Skyscrapers Take Simple Forms." *New York Times,* 2 May 1926, 22.

"Keyport Feels Loss of Noted Manufacturer." *Keyport Weekly,* 6 August 1920, 1.

Lehner, Lois. "A Cookie Jar Update." *Antique Trader Weekly,* 29 February 1984, 72.

———."American Dinnerware and Commercial Pottery." *Antique Trader Weekly,* 8 August 1984, 72.

Long Island City Star, 5 February 1886, 2 : 4.

"Predict New York as City of Color." *New York Times,* 20 February 1927, Real Estate: 14.

Unpublished

Blaszcyk, Regina."'This Extraordinary Demand for Color': Leon Victor Solon and Architectural Polychromy, 1909–1939." Paper presented at the 1993 Tile Heritage Foundation Conference: 5–6.

Ceccacci, Susan McDaniel. "Architectural Terra-Cotta in the United States Before 1870." Master of Arts thesis, Boston University Graduate School, 1991.

"CV Durathin." (13d/ Fe) AIA File No. 9A, Federal Seaboard Terra Cotta Corporation Printed Information Sheet. Donated to the Friends of Terra Cotta by Bruce Richmond.

Eastern Terra Cotta Company Record Book. (1936–38) Friends of Terra Cotta Collection.

Eskesen, Aslag. "Report to Stockholders of Federal Seaboard Terra Cotta Corporation." (31 March 1967): 8. Donated to the Friends of Terra Cotta by the Eskesen family.

———. Letter to Karl Mathiasen II (22 June 1944): 2. Donated to the Friends of Terra Cotta by the Eskesen family.

———. "Problems—Possibilities—Prospects." (30 June 1963): 10. Donated to the Friends of Terra Cotta by the Eskesen family.

Ferns, Dale H. "A Conservation Analysis of the Terra Cotta Cladding of Liberty Tower." Master of Science in Historic Preservation thesis, Columbia University, 1980.

Floyd, Margaret Henderson. "A Terra Cotta Cornerstone for Copley Square: An Assessment of the Museum of Fine Arts, Boston, by Sturgis and Brigham (1870–1876), in the Context of Its Technological and Stylistic Origins." Ph. D. dissertation, Boston University, 1974.

Kahn, Ely Jacques. Autobiography manuscript, in Avery Library, Columbia University, New York City.

Knecht, Gary. "Early Uses of Architectural Terra Cotta in the San Francisco Bay Area." unpublished student paper, University of California, Berkeley, 1980.

Lockhardt, W. F. "Terra Cotta Market Study." National Terra Cotta Society.

———. "What The National Terra Cotta Society is Doing." *Terra Cotta News-Letter* (5 February 1930): 3. Donated to the Friends of Terra Cotta by O. W. Ketcham Company.

Mathiasen, O. E. "Minutes of 290th Meeting of the Board of Directors of Federal Seaboard Terra Cotta Corporation." (5 June 1968). Donated to the Friends of Terra Cotta by the Eskesen family.

New York Architectural Terra Cotta Company Archive, Avery Library, Columbia University, New York.

Olsen, Peter. "A Memo Sent To The Directors Of The Corporation." (9 October 1944). Donated to the Friends of Terra Cotta by the Eskesen family.

Prudon, Theodore. "Architectural Terra Cotta and Ceramic Veneer in the United States Prior to World War II: A History of Its Development and An Analysis of Its Deterioration Problems and Possible Repair Methodologies." Doctor of Philosophy in the Graduate School of Arts and Sciences dissertation, Columbia University, 1981.

Roche, Edward, letter to Messrs. Upjohn & Co. (1 September 1852) A copy of the original was placed in Box 6, Upjohn Papers, New York Public Library. Emphasis in original.

Schurecht, H. G. "Some Products Which Might Be Made in Terra Cotta Plants as Now Built or With Slight Changes in Present Equipment." (22 January 1935). Donated to the Friends of Terra Cotta by Clem Baldwin.

Shockley, Jay. "Beaver Building." New York City Landmarks Designation Report. 13 February 1996, Designation List 271, LP-1942.

"Terra Cotta Market Study." National Terra Cotta Society (12 August 1930): 5. Donated to the Friends of Terra Cotta by O. W. Ketcham Company.

Terra Cotta News-Letter (22 March 1930): 2. Donated to the Friends of Terra Cotta by O. W. Ketcham Company.

Miscellaneous

Atlantic Terra Cotta Company, A 52-Story Facade. Brochure published by the Atlantic Terra Cotta Company about the Woolworth Building (1913), 11.

Kahn, Ely Jacques. "Terra Cotta Futurities" No. 2. Brochure published by *Federal Seaboard Terra Cotta Corporation* (1930).

Index